Aho-Girl

\'ahô͵gərl\ *Japanese, noun.*
A clueless girl.

10 | Hiroyuki

D0886082

CHARACTER PROFILES

AHO-GIRL's Cast of Characters

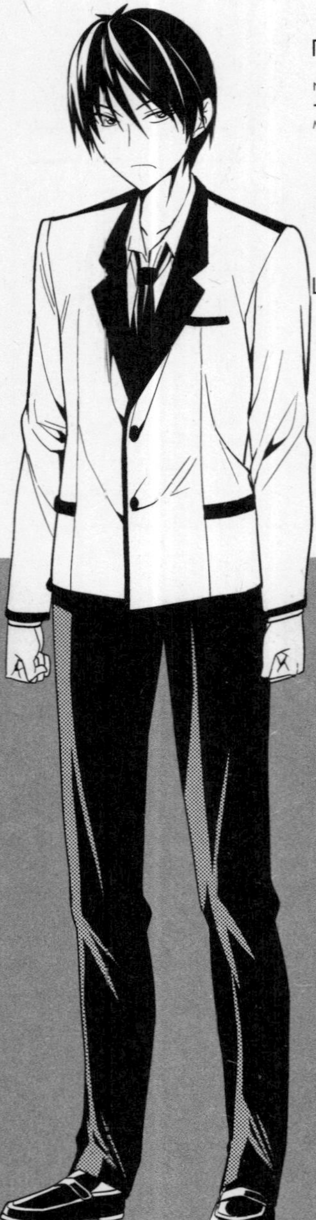

Name **Akuru Akutsu (Akkun)**

Memo

Childhood friend of Yoshiko, who lives next door. Plays the aggravated straight man to Yoshiko's absurdity. Tries to cure Yoshiko of her stupidity, but despite all his effort, it's not going very well.

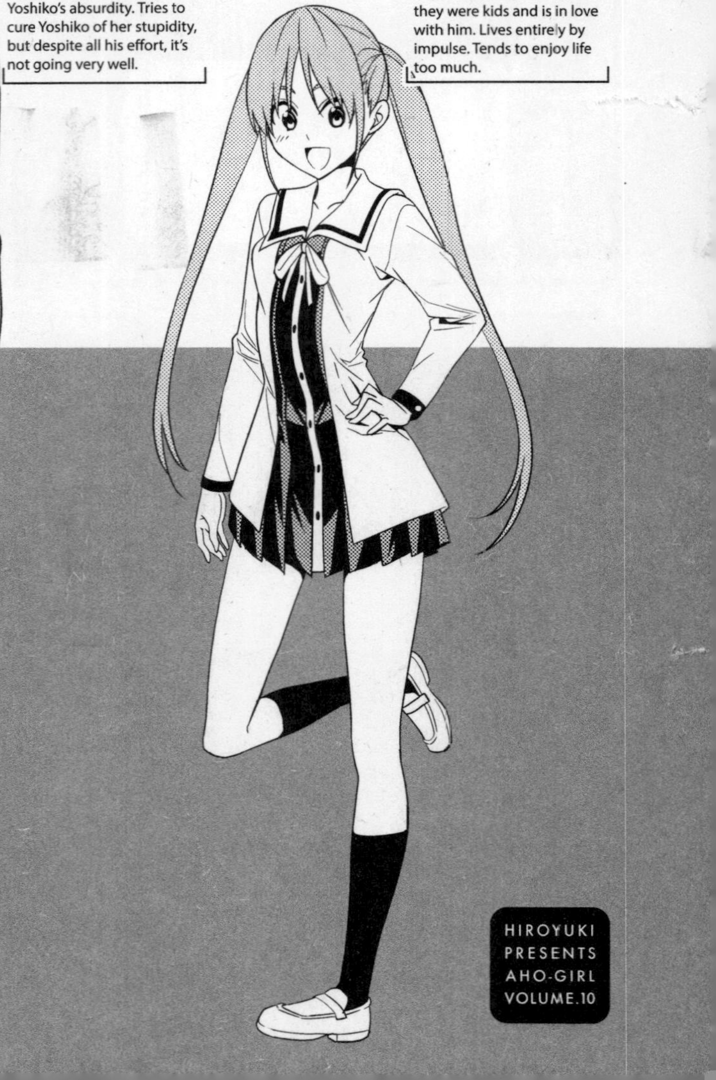

Name **Yoshiko Hanabatake**

Memo

An inexpressibly clueless high school girl. Favorite food: bananas. Has been friends with Akkun since they were kids and is in love with him. Lives entirely by impulse. Tends to enjoy life too much.

HIROYUKI PRESENTS AHO-GIRL VOLUME.10

Name **Sayaka Sumino**

Memo

Yoshiko's friend. She's a very kind girl. She knows her kindness lands her in all sorts of trouble, yet she remains kind. Worries about being boring.

Name **Head Monitor**

Memo

An upperclassman at Yoshiko's school. Has fallen head over heels for Akkun and begun to stray from the moral path, but she doesn't realize it. G cup.

Name **Dog**

Memo

A ridiculously big dog Yoshiko found at the park. Started out vicious, but once vanquished by Yoshiko, has become docile. Is quite clever and tries to stop Yoshiko from her wilder impulses.

Name **Atsuko Oshieda**

Memo

Homeroom teacher for Yoshiko and Akkun's class. A passionate and devoted educator. She has always attended all-girls schools, and so has no romantic experience. Her feelings are running amok over a mysterious young man named "Yoshio."

Name **Kuroko Shiina**

Memo

Akane's friend. A gal who looks very grown-up at first glance. Has a very pure, ongoing relationship with her boyfriend, who she's known since they were little. She's actually very private and sucks at talking about romance.

Name **Akane Eimura**

Memo

A gal in Yoshiko's class. An impulsive person, she is easy to get on board with just about anything. She'd like to have a boyfriend, but then her friend Kii asked her out and now she's panicking over that. She's a pretty lonely person, actually.

Name **Kii Hiiragi**

Memo

Akane's friend. It's hard to tell what this gal is thinking. Of the three, she's the most sedate. Her relationship status isn't very clear…

10 CONTENTS

AHO-GIRL

+ + =

AHO-GIRL

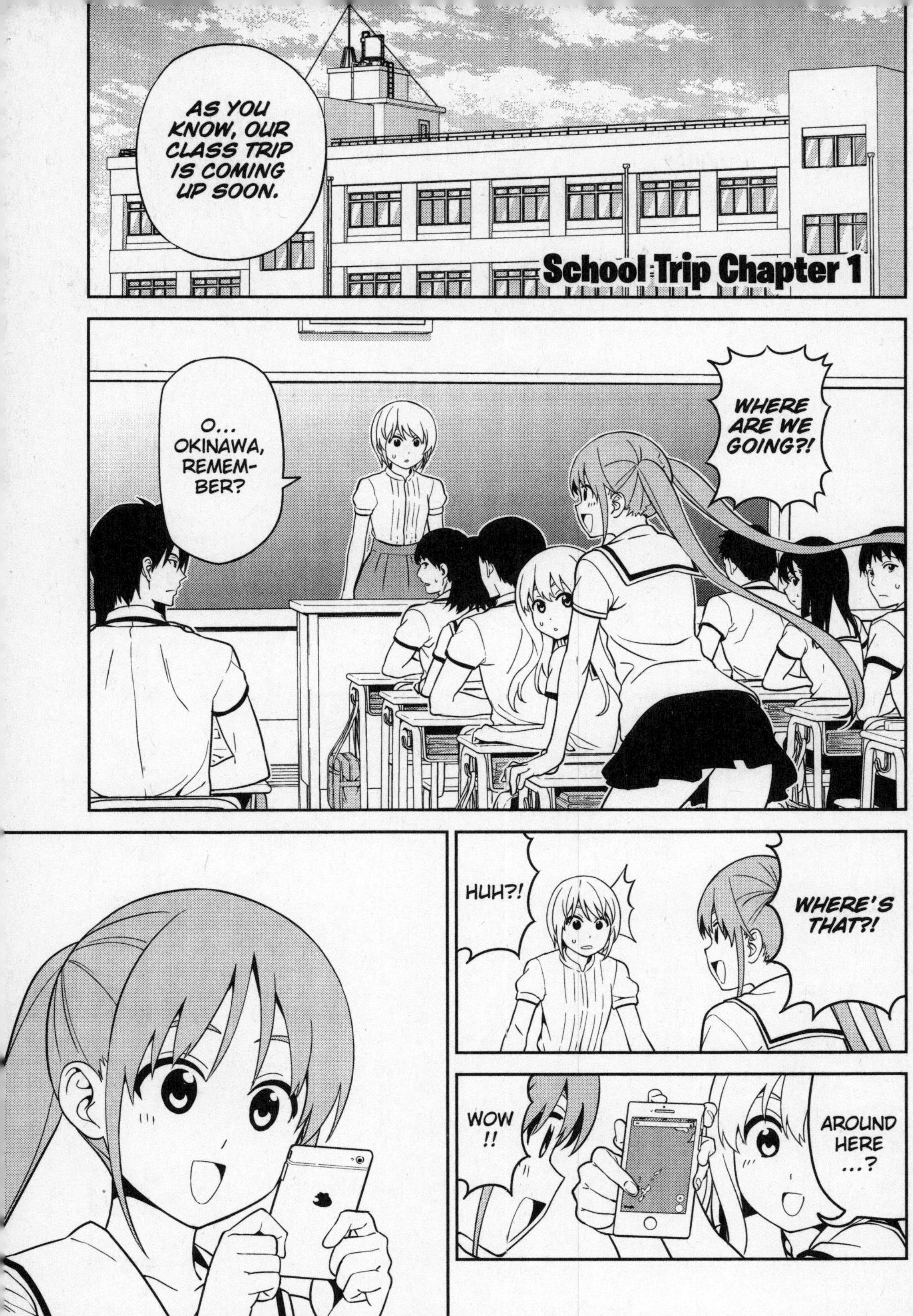
AS YOU KNOW, OUR CLASS TRIP IS COMING UP SOON.
School Trip Chapter 1
WHERE ARE WE GOING?!
O... OKINAWA, REMEMBER?
WHERE'S THAT?!
HUH?!
AROUND HERE ...?
WOW !!

I HAVE NO IDEA WHERE THAT IS!!
WHAT?
WHY ARE WE GOING THERE?!
W... WELL ...
WE'RE GOING TO SWIM IN THE OCEAN...
REALLY ?!
AND THEY HAVE A HUGE AQUARIUM THERE...
OH WOW!!

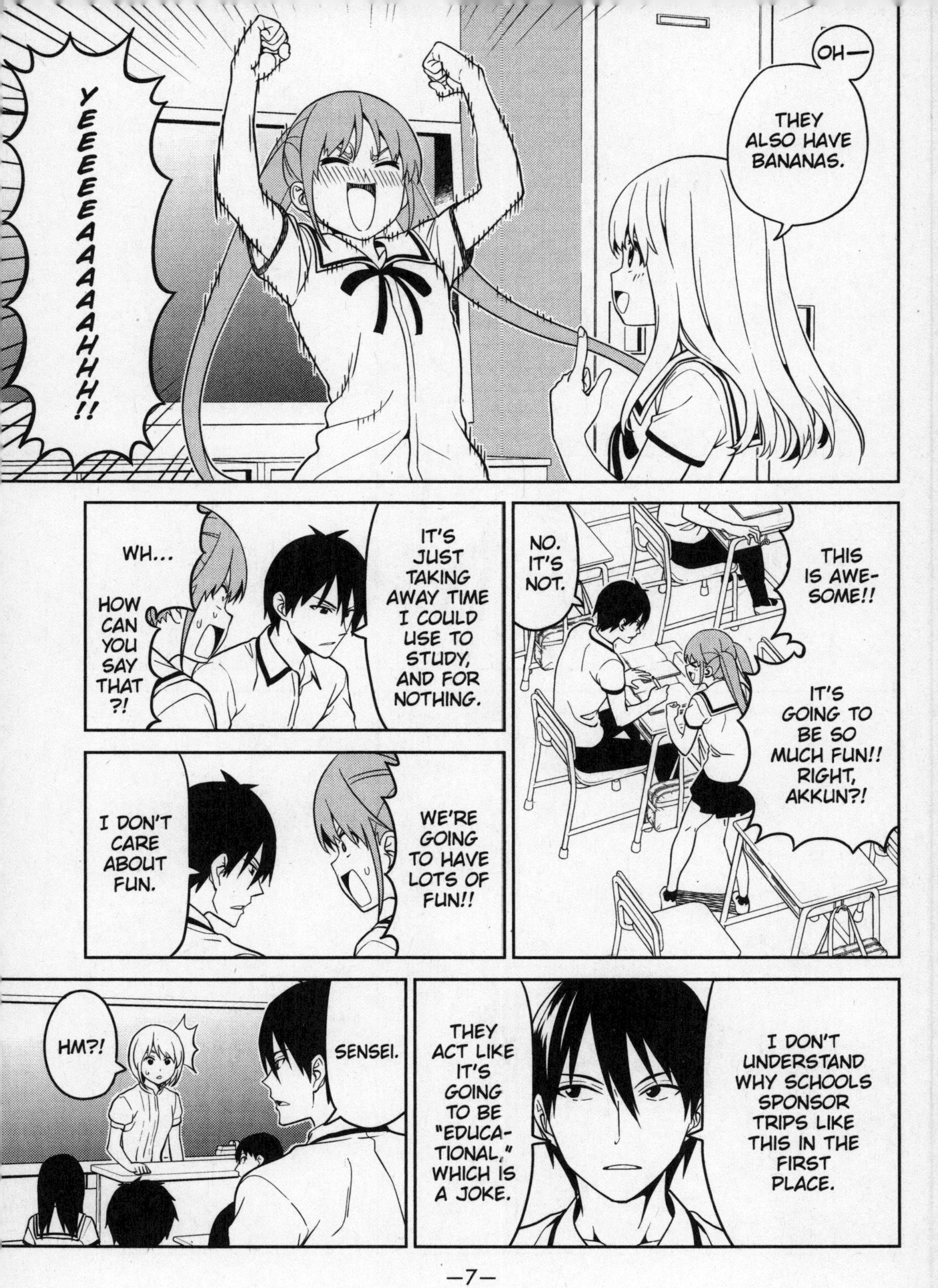
OH—
THEY ALSO HAVE BANANAS.
YEEEEEEAAAAAAAHHHH!!
THIS IS AWE-SOME!!
IT'S GOING TO BE SO MUCH FUN!! RIGHT, AKKUN?!
NO. IT'S NOT.
IT'S JUST TAKING AWAY TIME I COULD USE TO STUDY, AND FOR NOTHING.
WH...
HOW CAN YOU SAY THAT?!
WE'RE GOING TO HAVE LOTS OF FUN!!
I DON'T CARE ABOUT FUN.
I DON'T UNDERSTAND WHY SCHOOLS SPONSOR TRIPS LIKE THIS IN THE FIRST PLACE.
THEY ACT LIKE IT'S GOING TO BE "EDUCA-TIONAL," WHICH IS A JOKE.
SENSEI.
HM?!

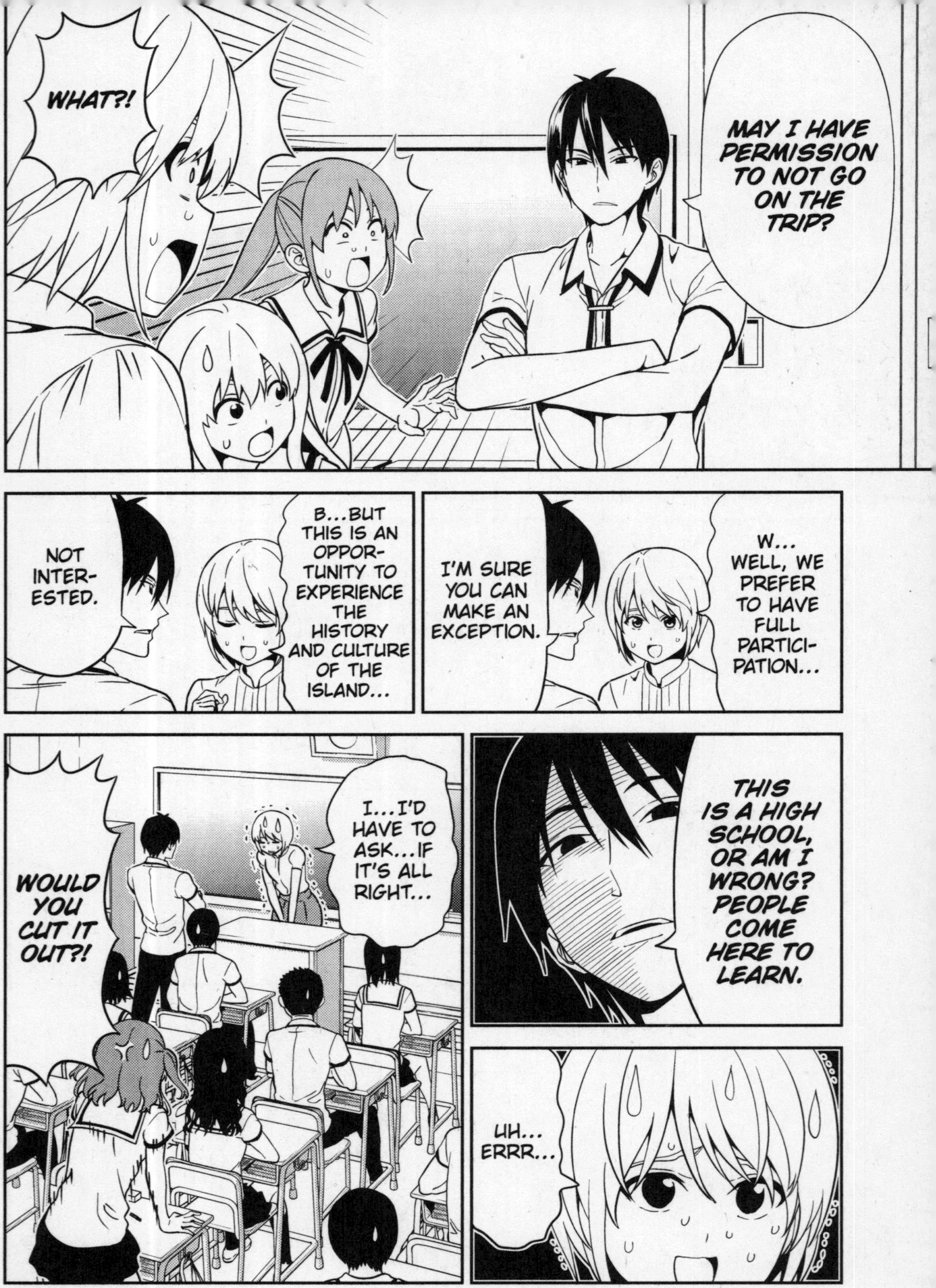
MAY I HAVE PERMISSION TO NOT GO ON THE TRIP?
WHAT?!
W... WELL, WE PREFER TO HAVE FULL PARTICIPATION...
I'M SURE YOU CAN MAKE AN EXCEPTION.
B...BUT THIS IS AN OPPORTUNITY TO EXPERIENCE THE HISTORY AND CULTURE OF THE ISLAND...
NOT INTERESTED.
THIS IS A HIGH SCHOOL, OR AM I WRONG? PEOPLE COME HERE TO LEARN.
UH... ERRR...
I...I'D HAVE TO ASK...IF IT'S ALL RIGHT...
WOULD YOU CUT IT OUT?!

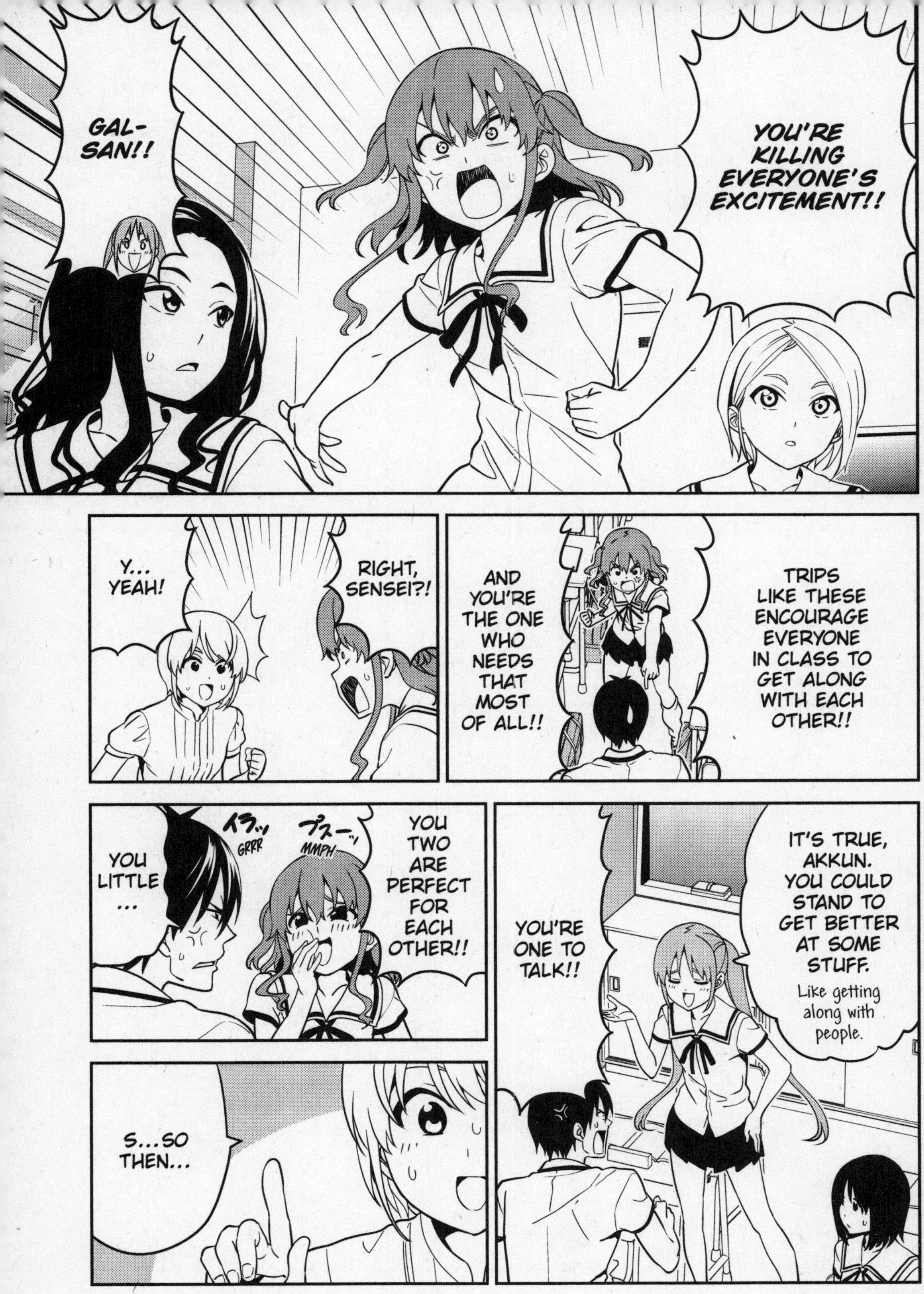
YOU'RE KILLING EVERYONE'S EXCITEMENT!!
GAL-SAN!!
TRIPS LIKE THESE ENCOURAGE EVERYONE IN CLASS TO GET ALONG WITH EACH OTHER!!
AND YOU'RE THE ONE WHO NEEDS THAT MOST OF ALL!!
RIGHT, SENSEI?!
Y... YEAH!
IT'S TRUE, AKKUN. YOU COULD STAND TO GET BETTER AT SOME STUFF.
Like getting along with people.
YOU'RE ONE TO TALK!!
YOU TWO ARE PERFECT FOR EACH OTHER!!
プスーッ
MMPH
イラッ
GRRR
YOU LITTLE ...
S...SO THEN...

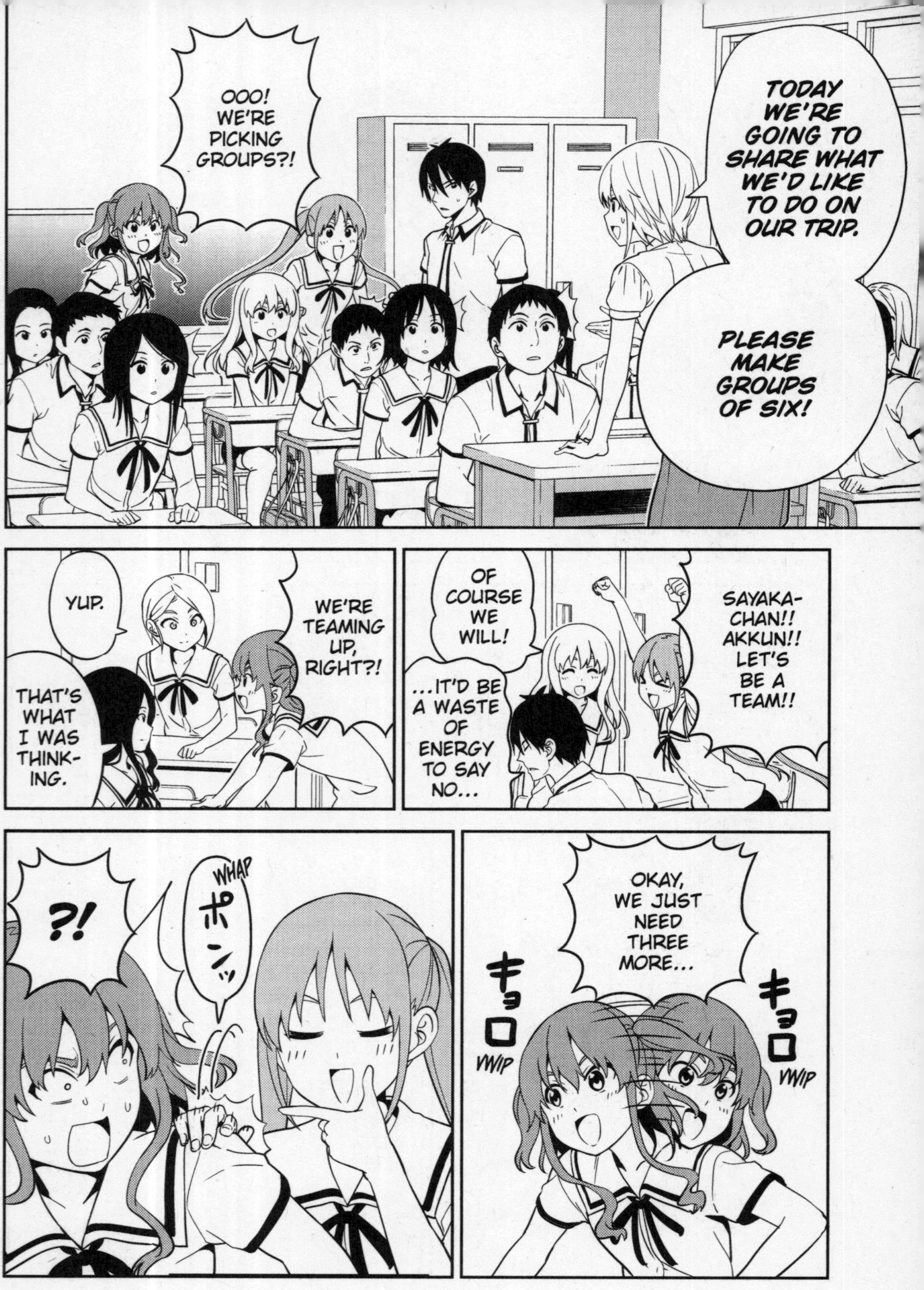
TODAY WE'RE GOING TO SHARE WHAT WE'D LIKE TO DO ON OUR TRIP.
PLEASE MAKE GROUPS OF SIX!
OOO! WE'RE PICKING GROUPS?!
SAYAKA-CHAN!! AKKUN!! LET'S BE A TEAM!!
OF COURSE WE WILL!
...IT'D BE A WASTE OF ENERGY TO SAY NO...
WE'RE TEAMING UP, RIGHT?!
YUP.
THAT'S WHAT I WAS THINKING.
OKAY, WE JUST NEED THREE MORE...
キョロ
VWIP
キョロ
VWIP
ポンッ
WHAP
?!

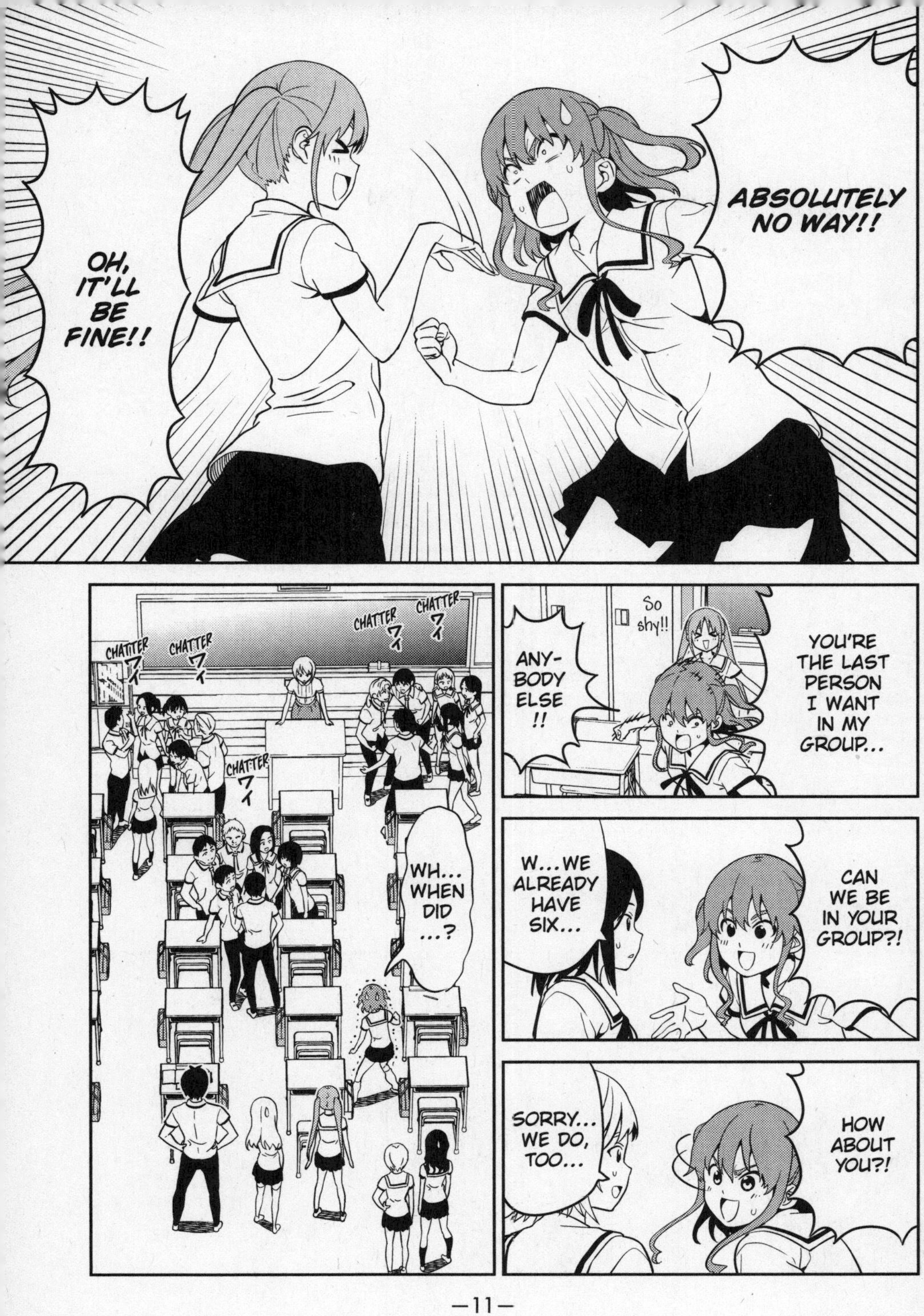
ABSOLUTELY NO WAY!!
OH, IT'LL BE FINE!!
YOU'RE THE LAST PERSON I WANT IN MY GROUP...
So shy!!
ANY-BODY ELSE !!
CAN WE BE IN YOUR GROUP?!
W...WE ALREADY HAVE SIX...
HOW ABOUT YOU?!
SORRY... WE DO, TOO...
CHATTER ワイ
CHATTER ワイ
CHATTER ワイ
CHATTER ワイ
CHATTER ワイ
WH... WHEN DID ...?

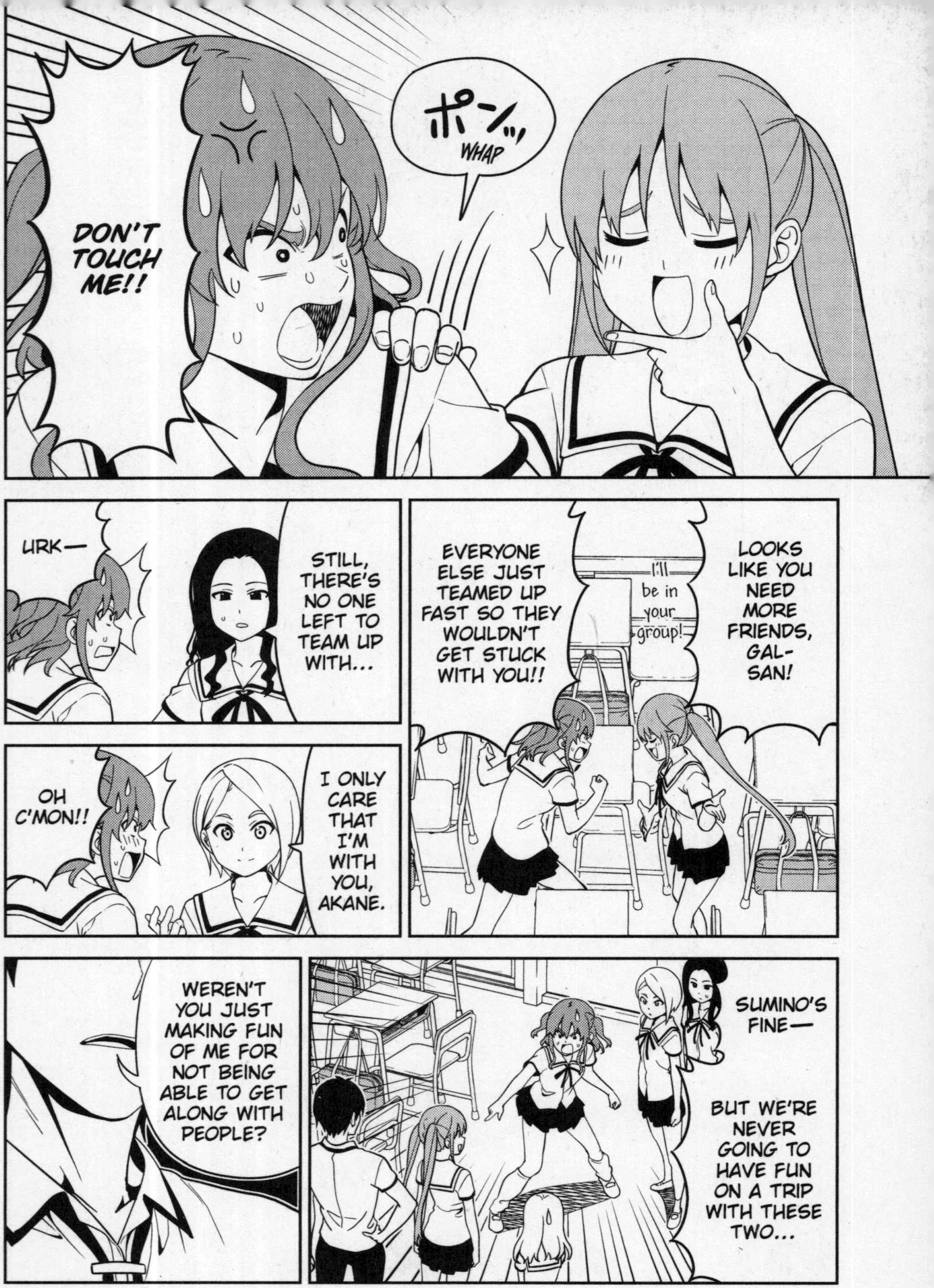
ポーンッ,
WHAP
DON'T TOUCH ME!!
LOOKS LIKE YOU NEED MORE FRIENDS, GAL-SAN!
I'll be in your group!
EVERYONE ELSE JUST TEAMED UP FAST SO THEY WOULDN'T GET STUCK WITH YOU!!
STILL, THERE'S NO ONE LEFT TO TEAM UP WITH...
URK—
I ONLY CARE THAT I'M WITH YOU, AKANE.
OH C'MON!!
SUMINO'S FINE—
BUT WE'RE NEVER GOING TO HAVE FUN ON A TRIP WITH THESE TWO...
WEREN'T YOU JUST MAKING FUN OF ME FOR NOT BEING ABLE TO GET ALONG WITH PEOPLE?

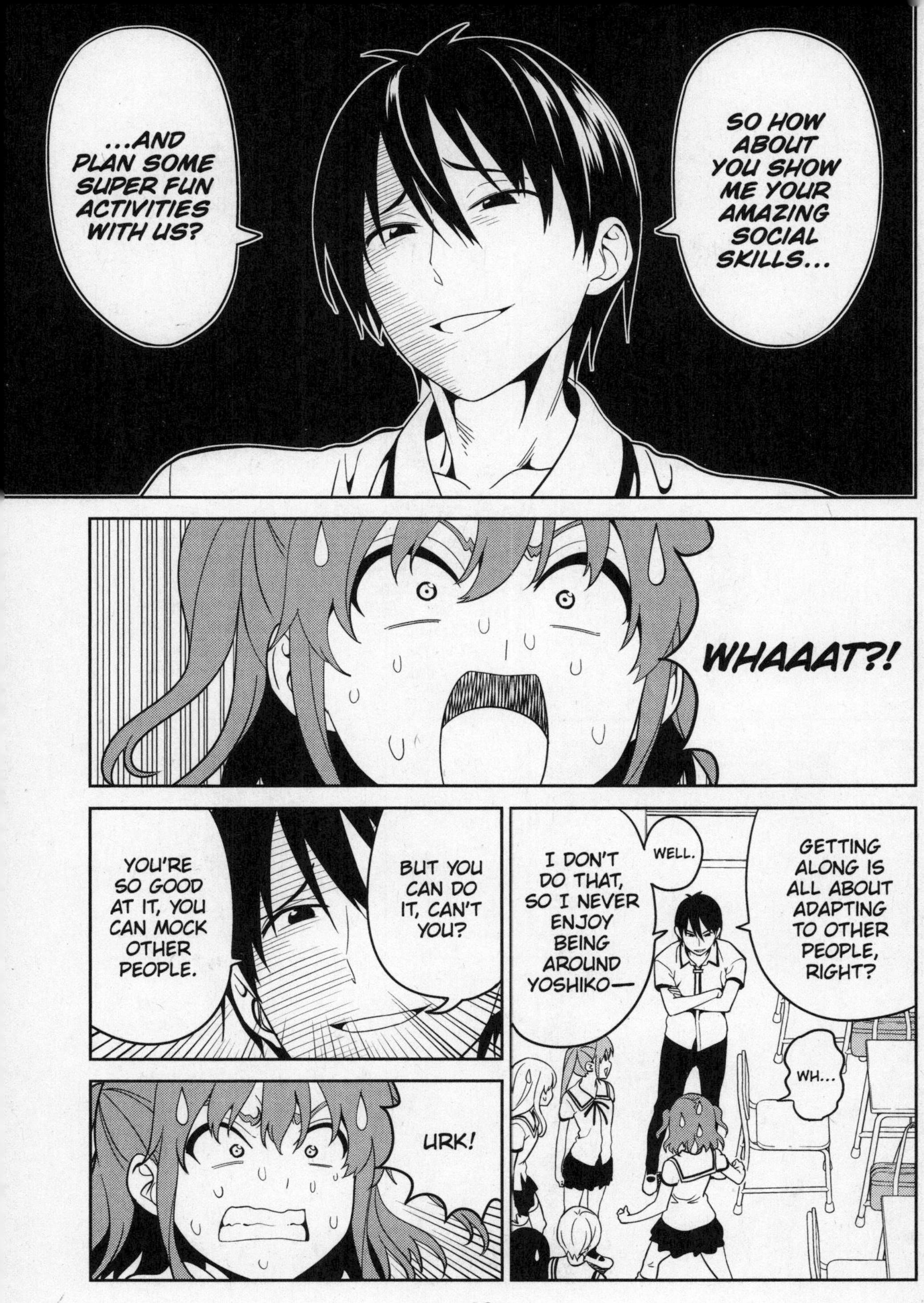
SO HOW ABOUT YOU SHOW ME YOUR AMAZING SOCIAL SKILLS...
...AND PLAN SOME SUPER FUN ACTIVITIES WITH US?
WHAAAT?!
GETTING ALONG IS ALL ABOUT ADAPTING TO OTHER PEOPLE, RIGHT?
WELL.
I DON'T DO THAT, SO I NEVER ENJOY BEING AROUND YOSHIKO—
WH...
BUT YOU CAN DO IT, CAN'T YOU?
YOU'RE SO GOOD AT IT, YOU CAN MOCK OTHER PEOPLE.
URK!

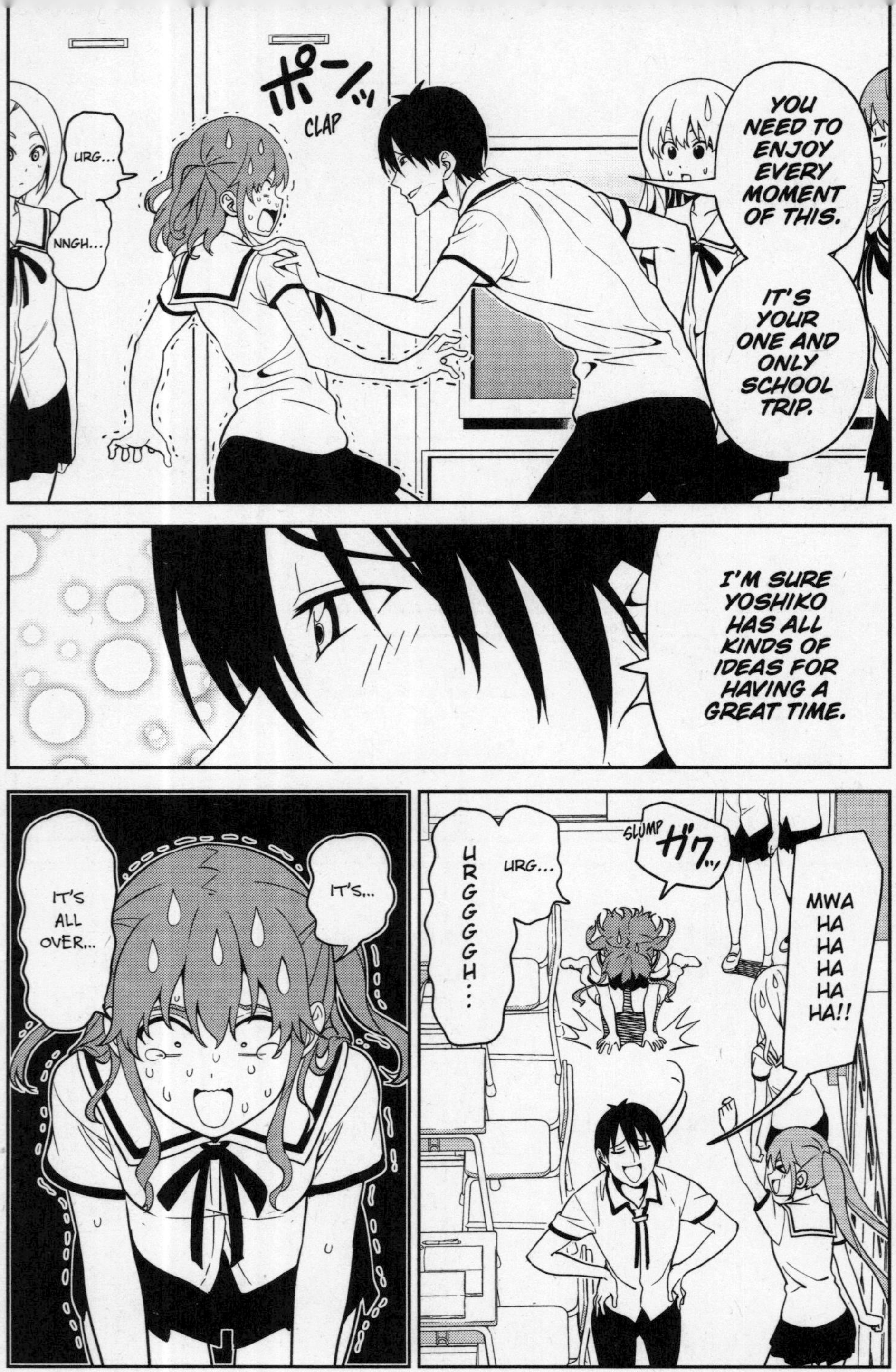
YOU NEED TO ENJOY EVERY MOMENT OF THIS.
IT'S YOUR ONE AND ONLY SCHOOL TRIP.
ポーンッ
CLAP
URG...
NNGH...
I'M SURE YOSHIKO HAS ALL KINDS OF IDEAS FOR HAVING A GREAT TIME.
MWA HA HA HA HA HA!!
ガクッ
SLUMP
URG...
URGGGGH...
IT'S...
IT'S ALL OVER...

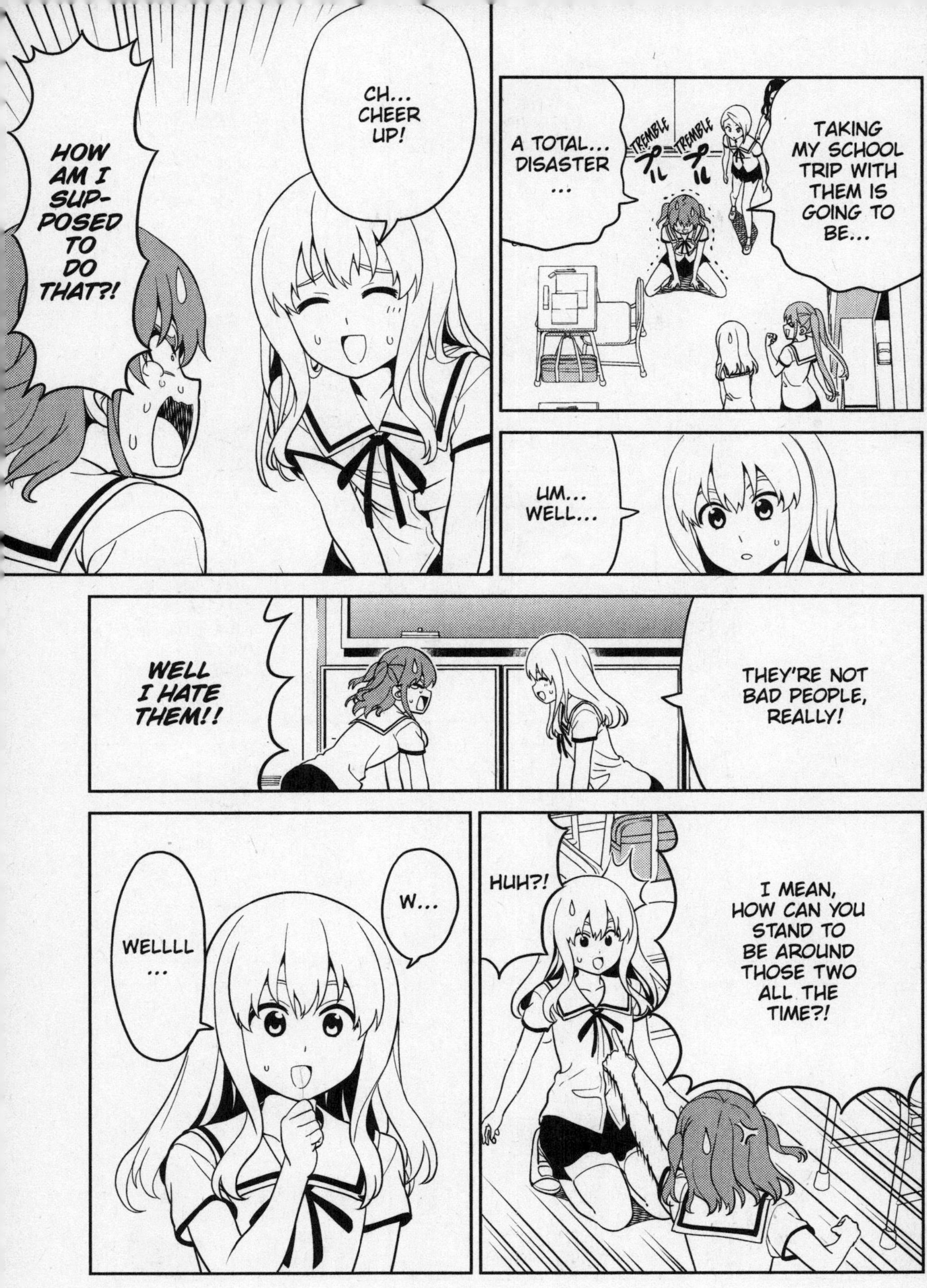
TAKING MY SCHOOL TRIP WITH THEM IS GOING TO BE...
TREMBLE TREMBLE
A TOTAL... DISASTER ...
UM... WELL...
CH... CHEER UP!
HOW AM I SUPPOSED TO DO THAT?!
THEY'RE NOT BAD PEOPLE, REALLY!
WELL I HATE THEM!!
I MEAN, HOW CAN YOU STAND TO BE AROUND THOSE TWO ALL THE TIME?!
HUH?!
W...
WELLLL ...

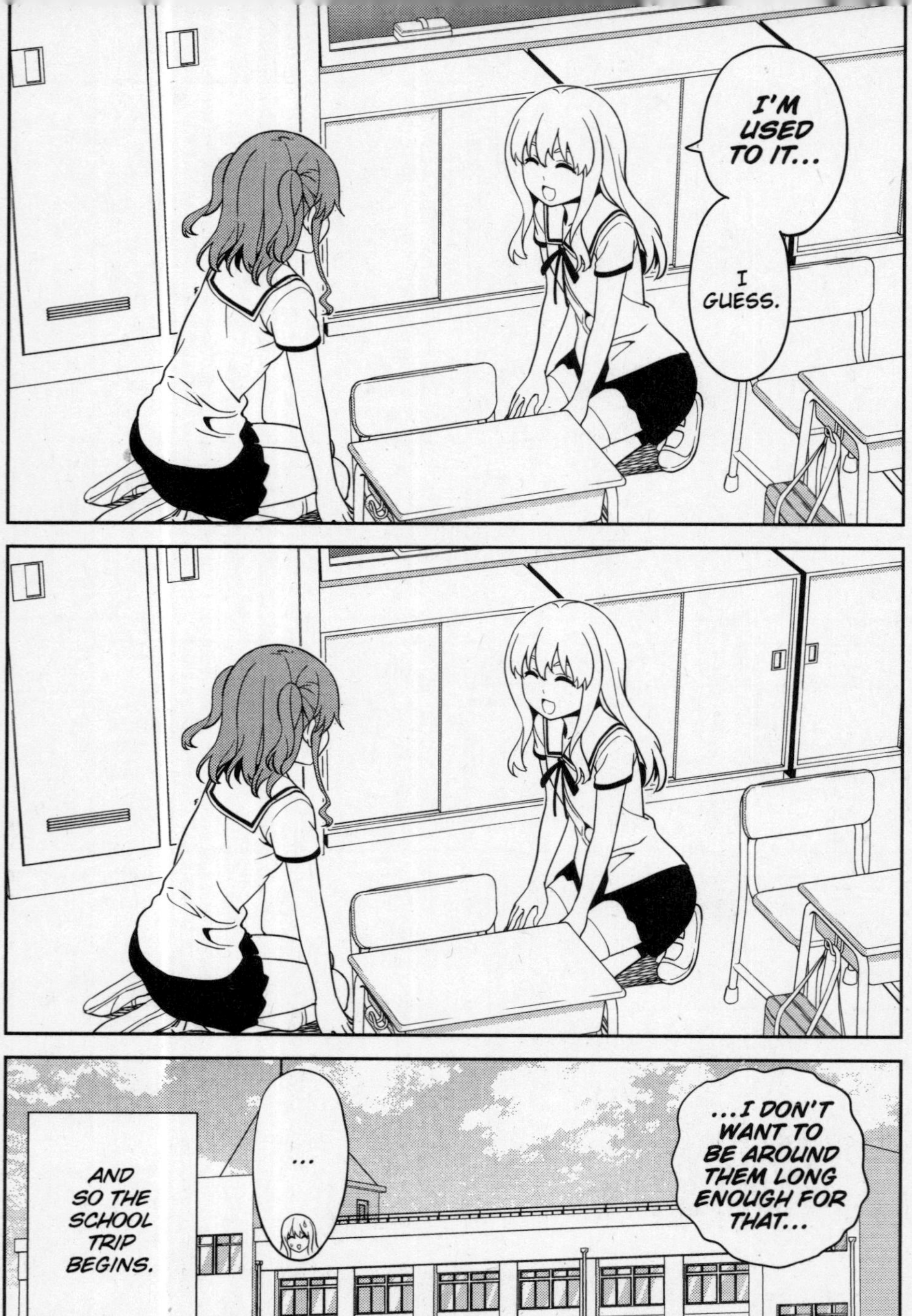
I'M USED TO IT...
I GUESS.
...I DON'T WANT TO BE AROUND THEM LONG ENOUGH FOR THAT...
...
AND SO THE SCHOOL TRIP BEGINS.

I'm Not Giving Up!

A...ARE YOU ALL RIGHT, AKANE...?
I CAN'T LET THEM... RUIN MY SCHOOL TRIP...
I'LL SHOW THEM!! I'M GOING TO HAVE FUN!!
CRYING, THOUGH? REALLY?

(Come on in)

Aho-Girl

\ˈahô͵gərl\ *Japanese, noun.*
A clueless girl.

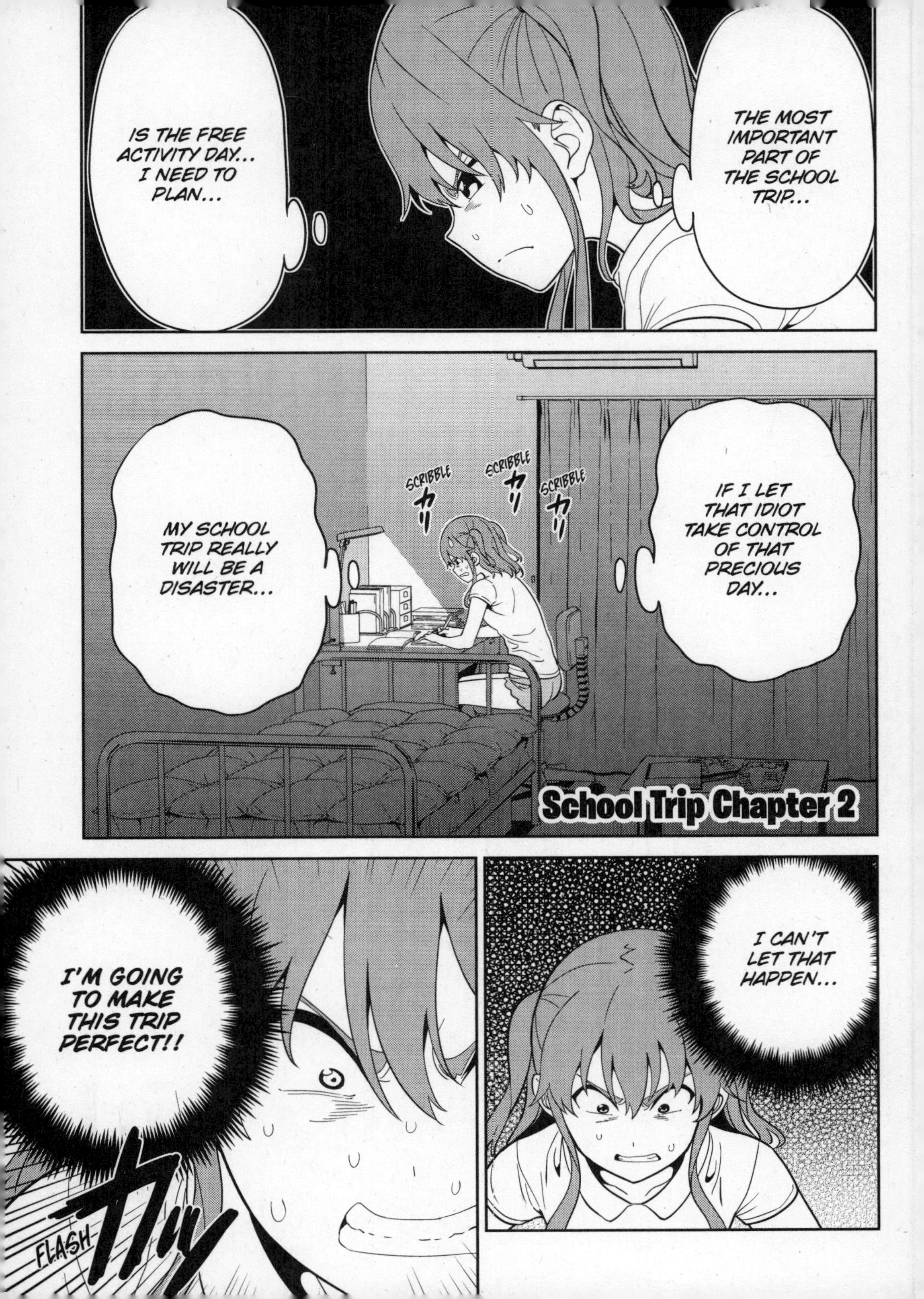
THE MOST IMPORTANT PART OF THE SCHOOL TRIP...
IS THE FREE ACTIVITY DAY... I NEED TO PLAN...
IF I LET THAT IDIOT TAKE CONTROL OF THAT PRECIOUS DAY...
SCRIBBLE カリ
SCRIBBLE カリ
SCRIBBLE カリ
MY SCHOOL TRIP REALLY WILL BE A DISASTER...
School Trip Chapter 2
I CAN'T LET THAT HAPPEN...
I'M GOING TO MAKE THIS TRIP PERFECT!!
FLASH

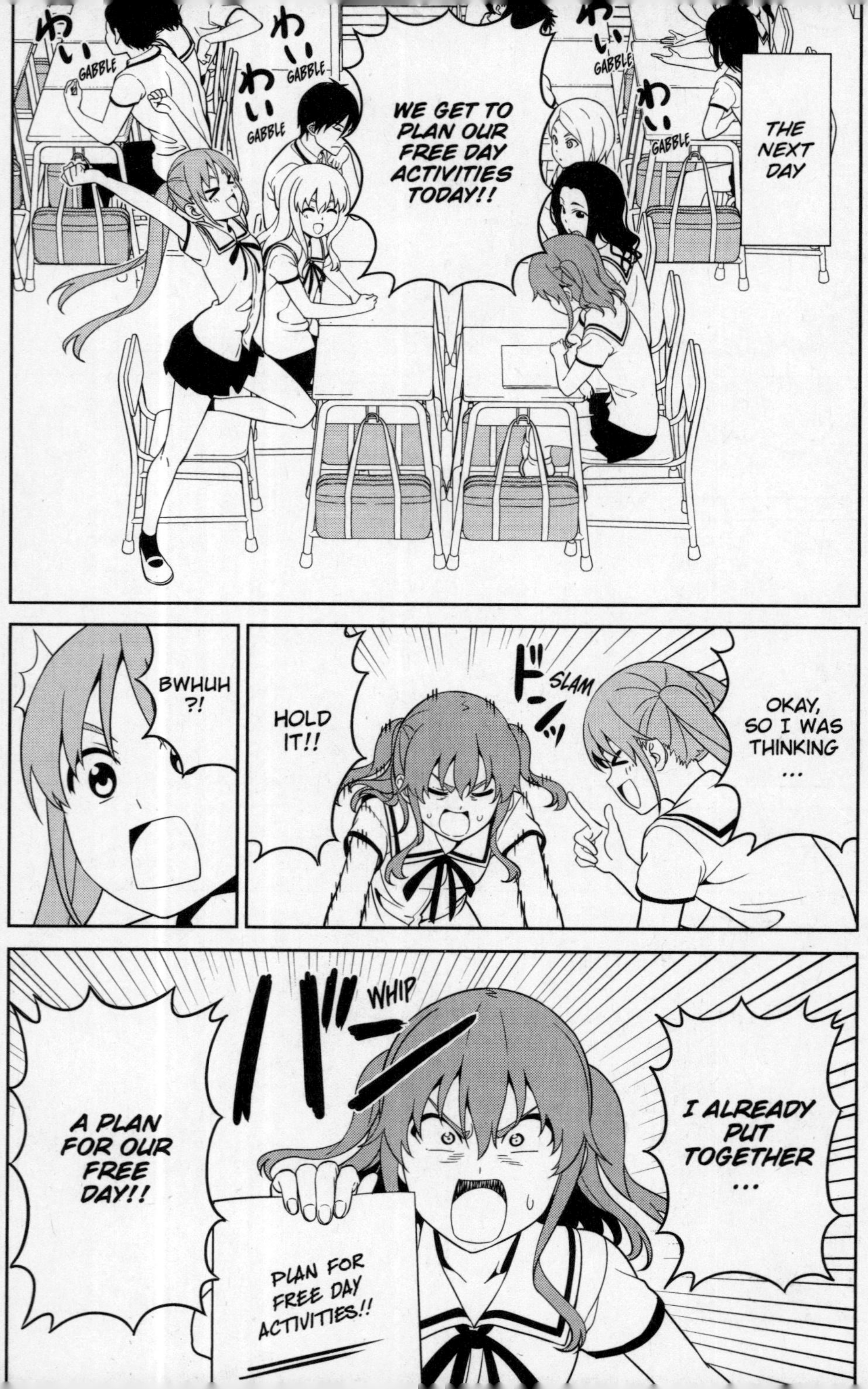
THE NEXT DAY
わい
GABBLE
WE GET TO PLAN OUR FREE DAY ACTIVITIES TODAY!!
わい
GABBLE
わい
GABBLE
わい
GABBLE
OKAY, SO I WAS THINKING ...
ドンッ
SLAM
HOLD IT!!
BWHUH ?!
I ALREADY PUT TOGETHER ...
バー
WHIP
A PLAN FOR OUR FREE DAY!!
PLAN FOR FREE DAY ACTIVITIES!!

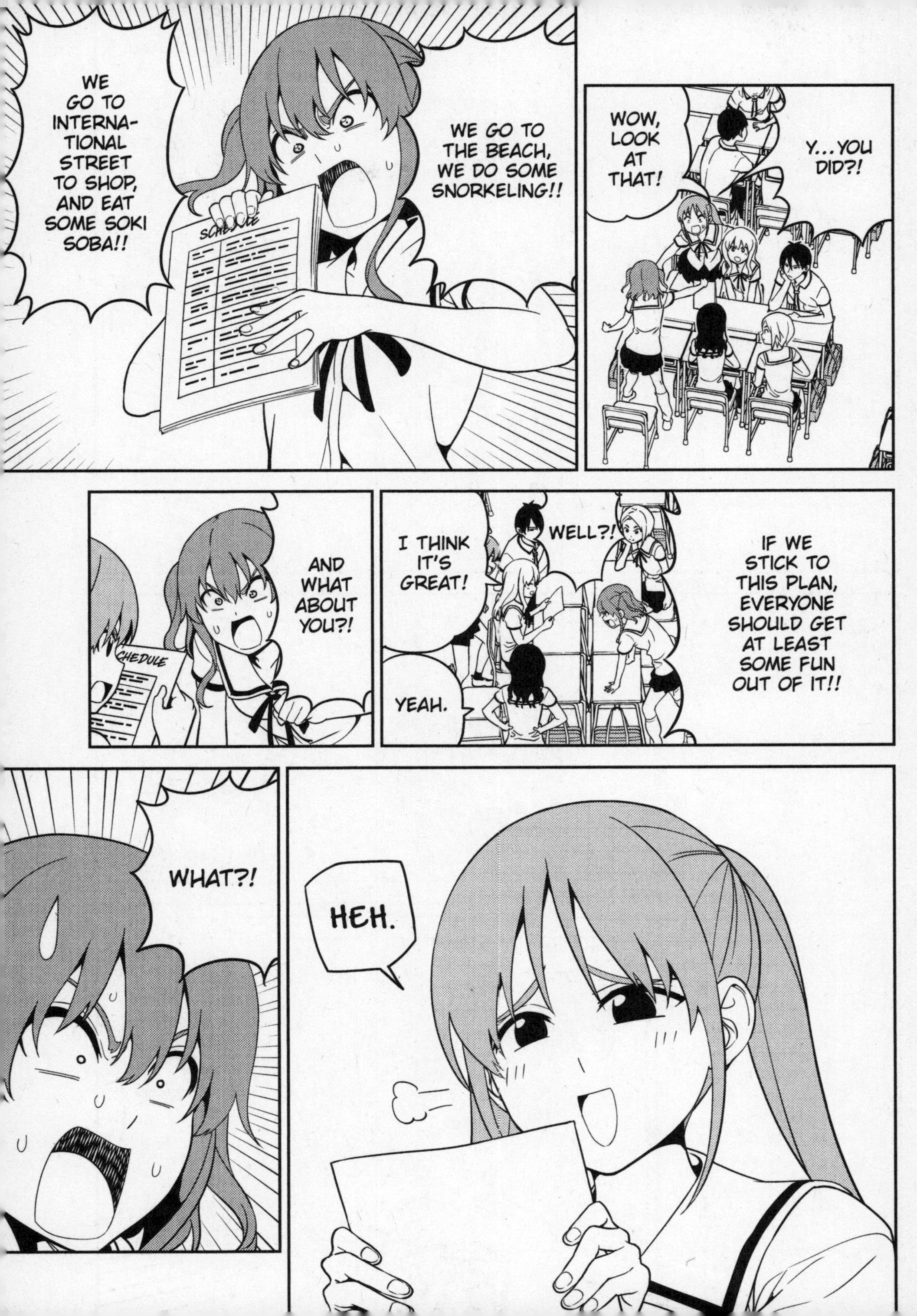
Y…YOU DID?!
WOW, LOOK AT THAT!
WE GO TO THE BEACH, WE DO SOME SNORKELING!!
WE GO TO INTERNA-TIONAL STREET TO SHOP, AND EAT SOME SOKI SOBA!!
SCHEDULE
IF WE STICK TO THIS PLAN, EVERYONE SHOULD GET AT LEAST SOME FUN OUT OF IT!!
WELL?!
I THINK IT'S GREAT!
YEAH.
AND WHAT ABOUT YOU?!
CHEDULE
HEH.
WHAT?!

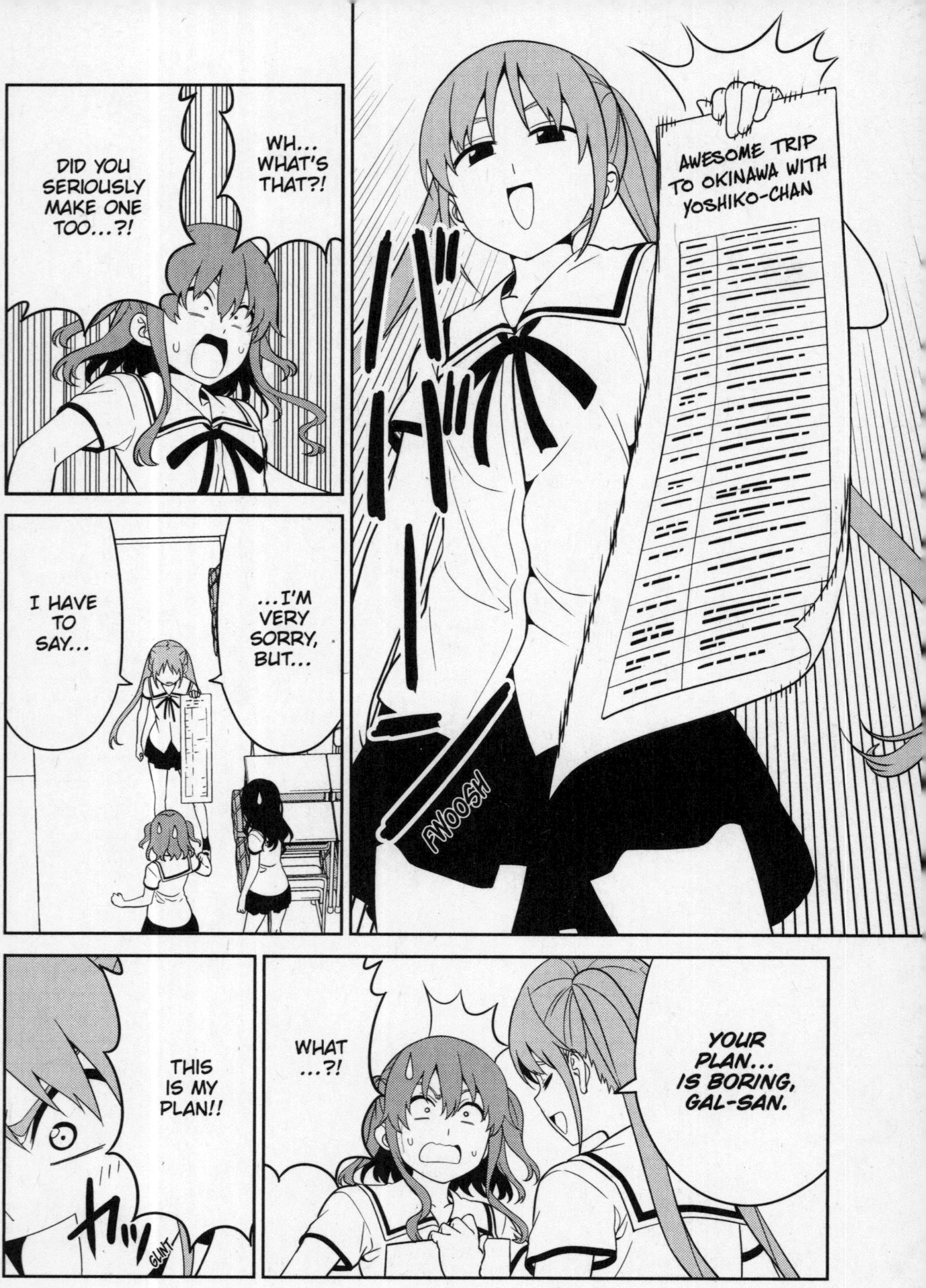
AWESOME TRIP TO OKINAWA WITH YOSHIKO-CHAN
FWOOSH
WH... WHAT'S THAT?!
DID YOU SERIOUSLY MAKE ONE TOO...?!
...I'M VERY SORRY, BUT...
I HAVE TO SAY...
YOUR PLAN... IS BORING, GAL-SAN.
WHAT ...?!
THIS IS MY PLAN!!
GLINT

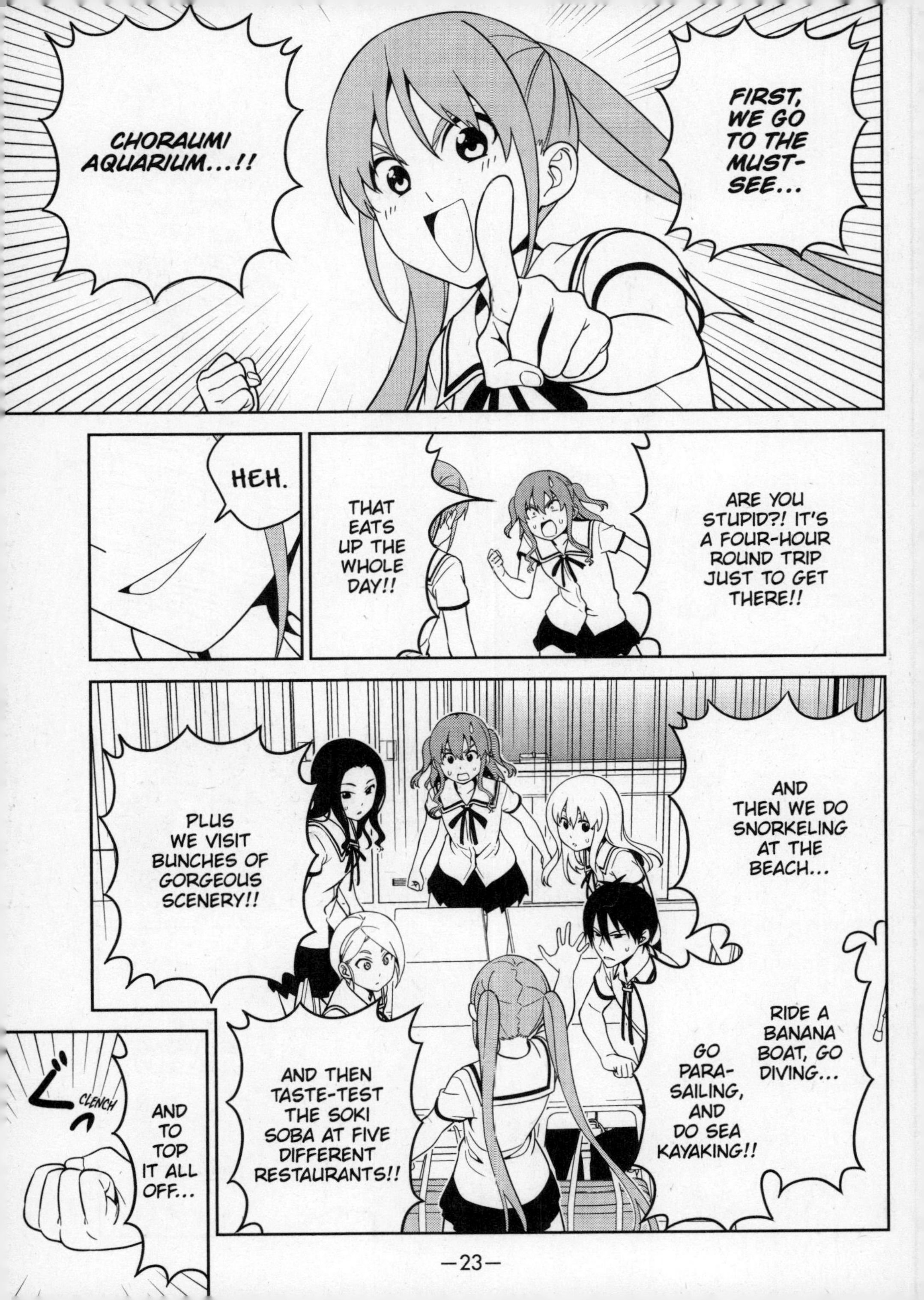
FIRST, WE GO TO THE MUST-SEE...
CHORAUMI AQUARIUM...!!
ARE YOU STUPID?! IT'S A FOUR-HOUR ROUND TRIP JUST TO GET THERE!!
THAT EATS UP THE WHOLE DAY!!
HEH.
AND THEN WE DO SNORKELING AT THE BEACH...
RIDE A BANANA BOAT, GO DIVING...
GO PARA-SAILING, AND DO SEA KAYAKING!!
PLUS WE VISIT BUNCHES OF GORGEOUS SCENERY!!
AND THEN TASTE-TEST THE SOKI SOBA AT FIVE DIFFERENT RESTAURANTS!!
CLENCH
AND TO TOP IT ALL OFF...

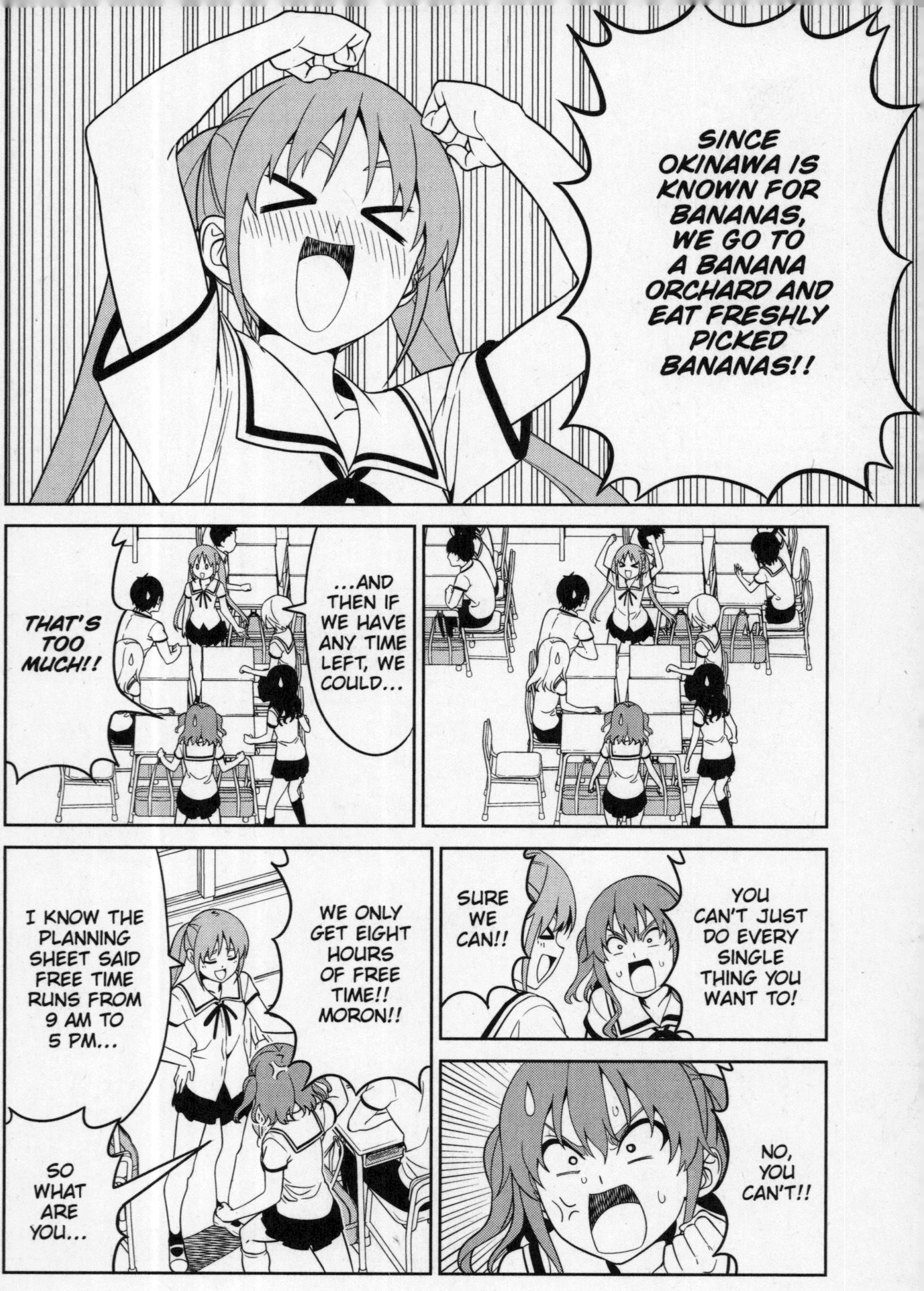
SINCE OKINAWA IS KNOWN FOR BANANAS, WE GO TO A BANANA ORCHARD AND EAT FRESHLY PICKED BANANAS!!
...AND THEN IF WE HAVE ANY TIME LEFT, WE COULD...
THAT'S TOO MUCH!!
YOU CAN'T JUST DO EVERY SINGLE THING YOU WANT TO!
SURE WE CAN!!
NO, YOU CAN'T!!
WE ONLY GET EIGHT HOURS OF FREE TIME!! MORON!!
I KNOW THE PLANNING SHEET SAID FREE TIME RUNS FROM 9 AM TO 5 PM...
SO WHAT ARE YOU...

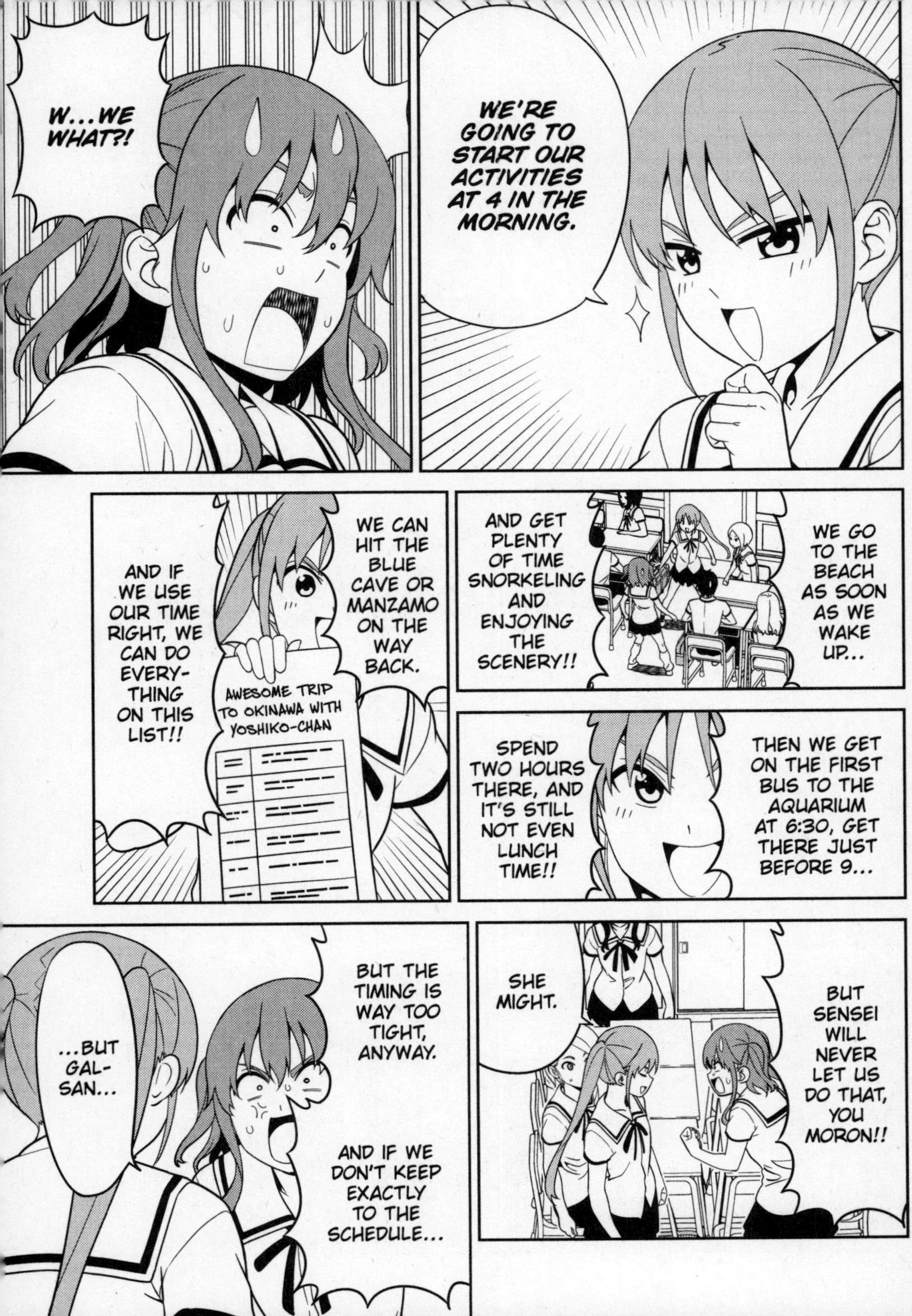
WE'RE GOING TO START OUR ACTIVITIES AT 4 IN THE MORNING.
W...WE WHAT?!
WE GO TO THE BEACH AS SOON AS WE WAKE UP...
AND GET PLENTY OF TIME SNORKELING AND ENJOYING THE SCENERY!!
THEN WE GET ON THE FIRST BUS TO THE AQUARIUM AT 6:30, GET THERE JUST BEFORE 9...
SPEND TWO HOURS THERE, AND IT'S STILL NOT EVEN LUNCH TIME!!
WE CAN HIT THE BLUE CAVE OR MANZAMO ON THE WAY BACK.
AND IF WE USE OUR TIME RIGHT, WE CAN DO EVERY-THING ON THIS LIST!!
AWESOME TRIP TO OKINAWA WITH YOSHIKO-CHAN
BUT SENSEI WILL NEVER LET US DO THAT, YOU MORON!!
SHE MIGHT.
BUT THE TIMING IS WAY TOO TIGHT, ANYWAY.
AND IF WE DON'T KEEP EXACTLY TO THE SCHEDULE...
...BUT GAL-SAN...

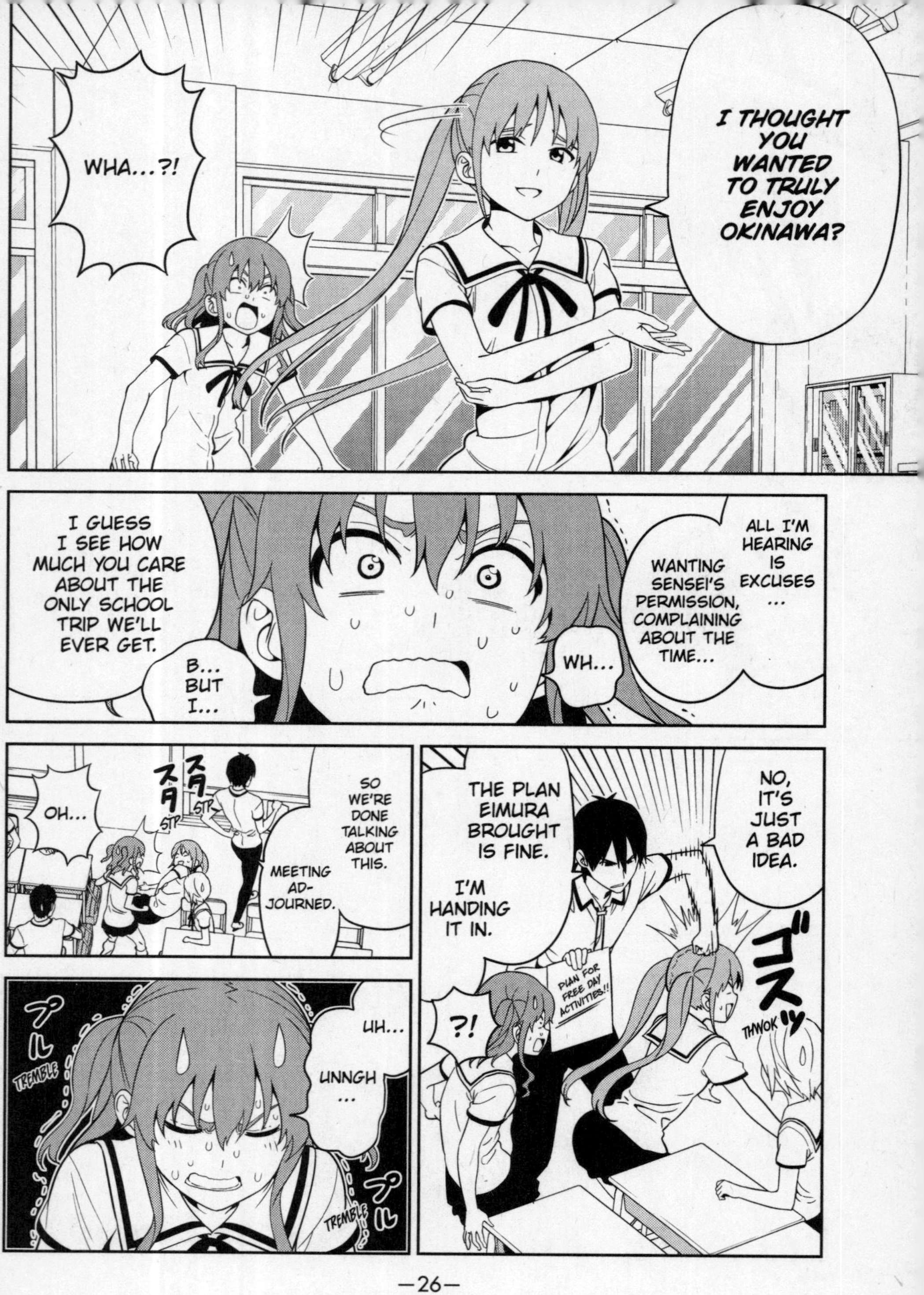
I THOUGHT YOU WANTED TO TRULY ENJOY OKINAWA?
WHA...?!
ALL I'M HEARING IS EXCUSES ...
WANTING SENSEI'S PERMISSION, COMPLAINING ABOUT THE TIME...
WH...
I GUESS I SEE HOW MUCH YOU CARE ABOUT THE ONLY SCHOOL TRIP WE'LL EVER GET.
B... BUT I...
NO, IT'S JUST A BAD IDEA.
THE PLAN EIMURA BROUGHT IS FINE.
I'M HANDING IT IN.
ゴスッ
THWOK
PLAN FOR FREE DAY ACTIVITIES!!
?!
SO WE'RE DONE TALKING ABOUT THIS.
スタ
STP
スタ
STP
MEETING AD-JOURNED.
OH...
UH...
UNNGH ...
プル
TREMBLE
プル
TREMBLE

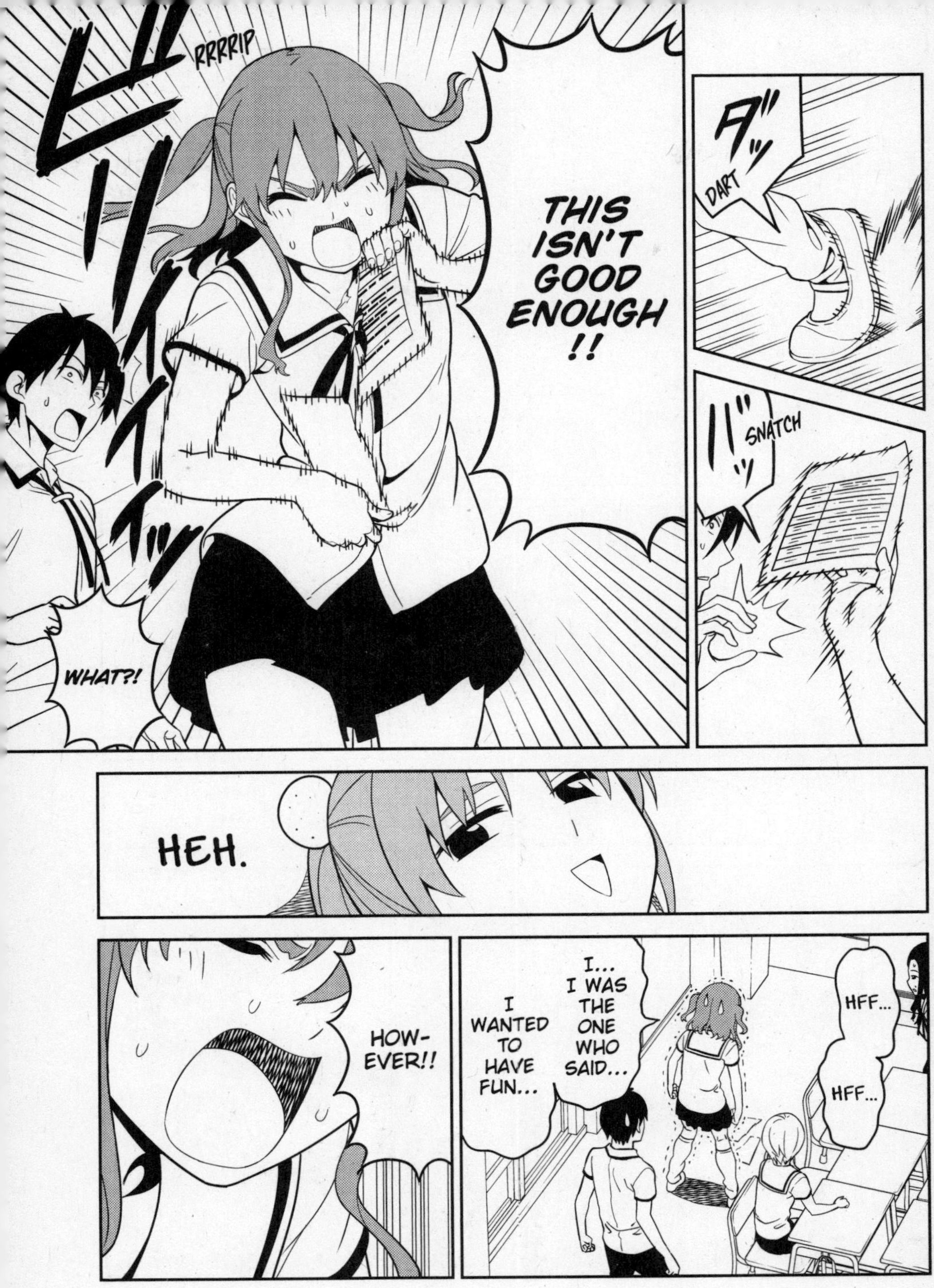
ダッ
DART
バッ
SNATCH
RRRRIP
THIS ISN'T GOOD ENOUGH!!
WHAT?!
HEH.
HFF...
HFF...
I... I WAS THE ONE WHO SAID...
I WANTED TO HAVE FUN...
HOW-EVER!!

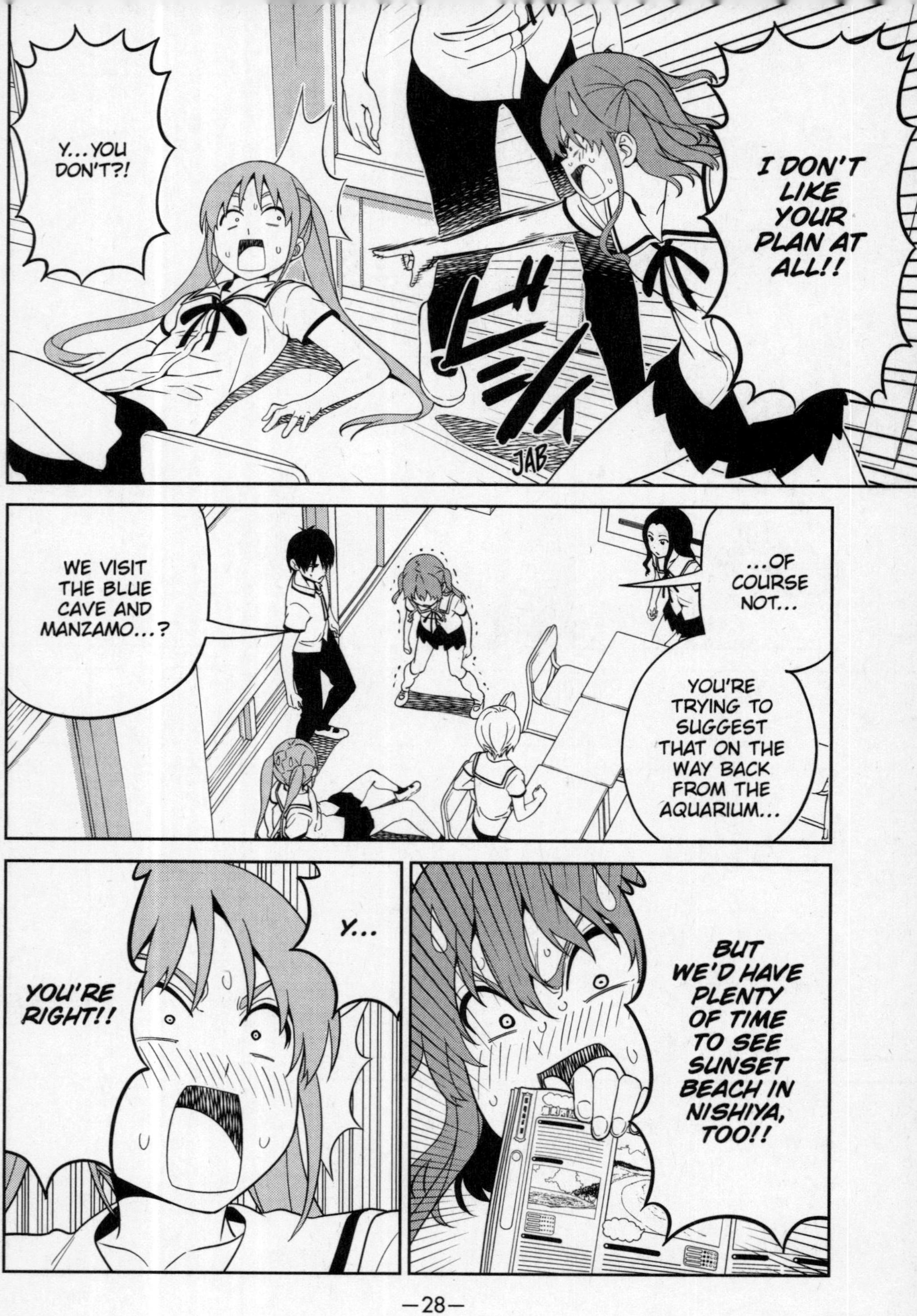

I DON'T LIKE YOUR PLAN AT ALL!!
Y...YOU DON'T?!
ビシィ
JAB
...OF COURSE NOT...
YOU'RE TRYING TO SUGGEST THAT ON THE WAY BACK FROM THE AQUARIUM...
WE VISIT THE BLUE CAVE AND MANZAMO...?
BUT WE'D HAVE PLENTY OF TIME TO SEE SUNSET BEACH IN NISHIYA, TOO!!
Y...
YOU'RE RIGHT!!

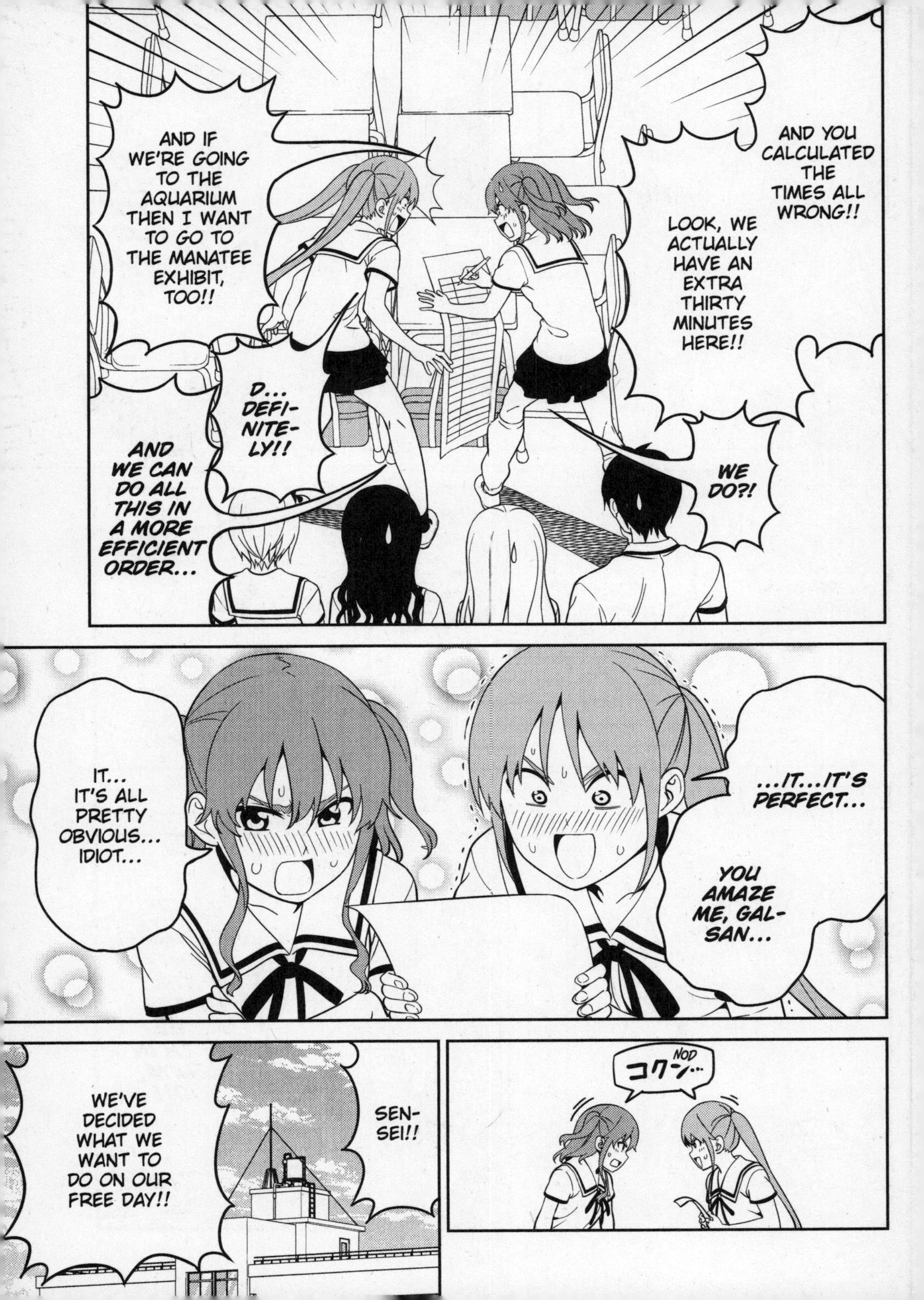
AND YOU CALCULATED THE TIMES ALL WRONG!!
LOOK, WE ACTUALLY HAVE AN EXTRA THIRTY MINUTES HERE!!
AND IF WE'RE GOING TO THE AQUARIUM THEN I WANT TO GO TO THE MANATEE EXHIBIT, TOO!!
WE DO?!
D... DEFI-NITE-LY!!
AND WE CAN DO ALL THIS IN A MORE EFFICIENT ORDER...
...IT...IT'S PERFECT...
YOU AMAZE ME, GAL-SAN...
IT... IT'S ALL PRETTY OBVIOUS... IDIOT...
NOD
コクン…
SEN-SEI!!
WE'VE DECIDED WHAT WE WANT TO DO ON OUR FREE DAY!!

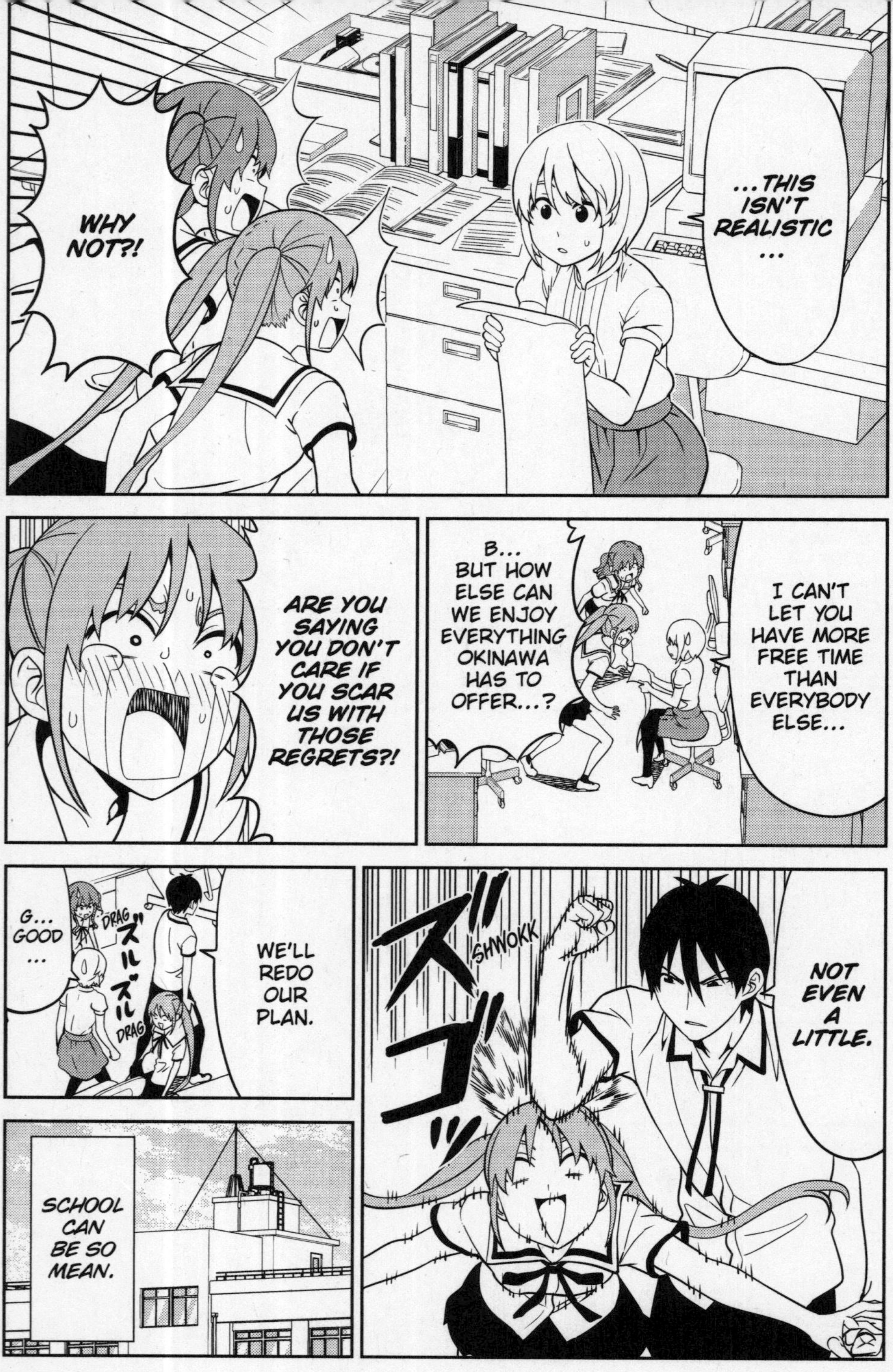
...THIS ISN'T REALISTIC ...
WHY NOT?!
I CAN'T LET YOU HAVE MORE FREE TIME THAN EVERYBODY ELSE...
B... BUT HOW ELSE CAN WE ENJOY EVERYTHING OKINAWA HAS TO OFFER...?
ARE YOU SAYING YOU DON'T CARE IF YOU SCAR US WITH THOSE REGRETS?!
NOT EVEN A LITTLE.
ズゴッ
SHWOKK
WE'LL REDO OUR PLAN.
DRAG
ズルズル
DRAG
G... GOOD ...
SCHOOL CAN BE SO MEAN.

I'm Gonna Do What I Want

NOW WHAT DO WE DO...?! OUR TRIP IS...
HEH.
DON'T YOU SEE ...?
WE'LL JUST DO IT IN SECRET!!
ARE YOU SERIOUS ?!

(Reggae > sandy beaches >>)

Aho-Girl

\ˈahô͵gərl\ *Japanese, noun.*
A clueless girl.

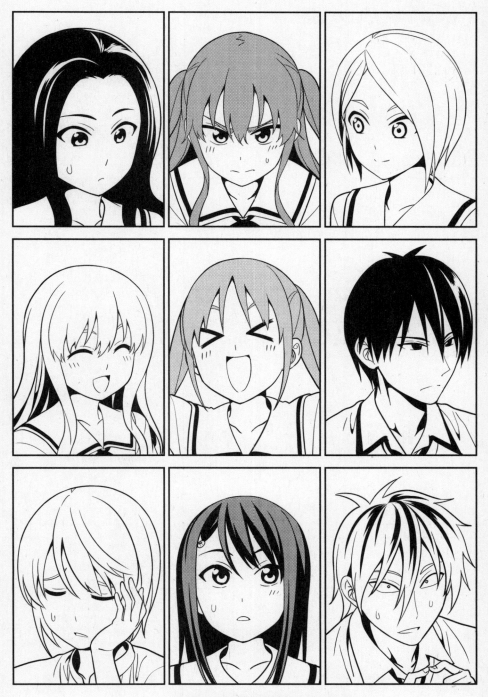

School Trip Chapter 3

Cut-away

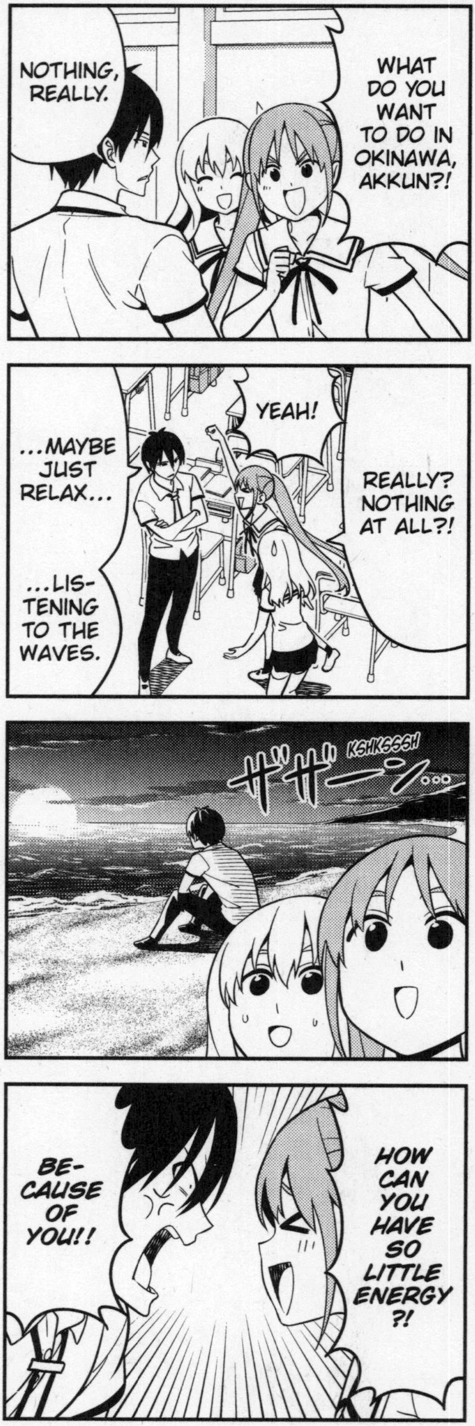
WHAT DO YOU WANT TO DO IN OKINAWA, AKKUN?!
NOTHING, REALLY.
REALLY? NOTHING AT ALL?!
YEAH!
...MAYBE JUST RELAX...
...LIS-TENING TO THE WAVES.
KSHKSSSH
ザザーン…
HOW CAN YOU HAVE SO LITTLE ENERGY?!
BE-CAUSE OF YOU!!

Sure Is

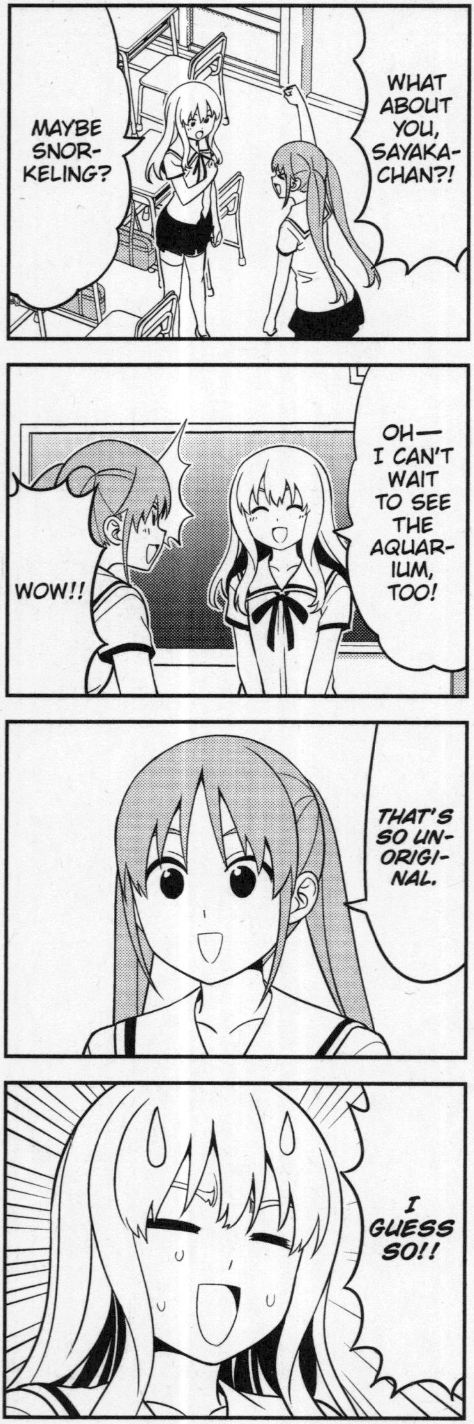
WHAT ABOUT YOU, SAYAKA-CHAN?!
MAYBE SNOR-KELING?
OH— I CAN'T WAIT TO SEE THE AQUAR-IUM, TOO!
WOW!!
THAT'S SO UN-ORIGI-NAL.
I GUESS SO!!

It Just Slipped Out!!

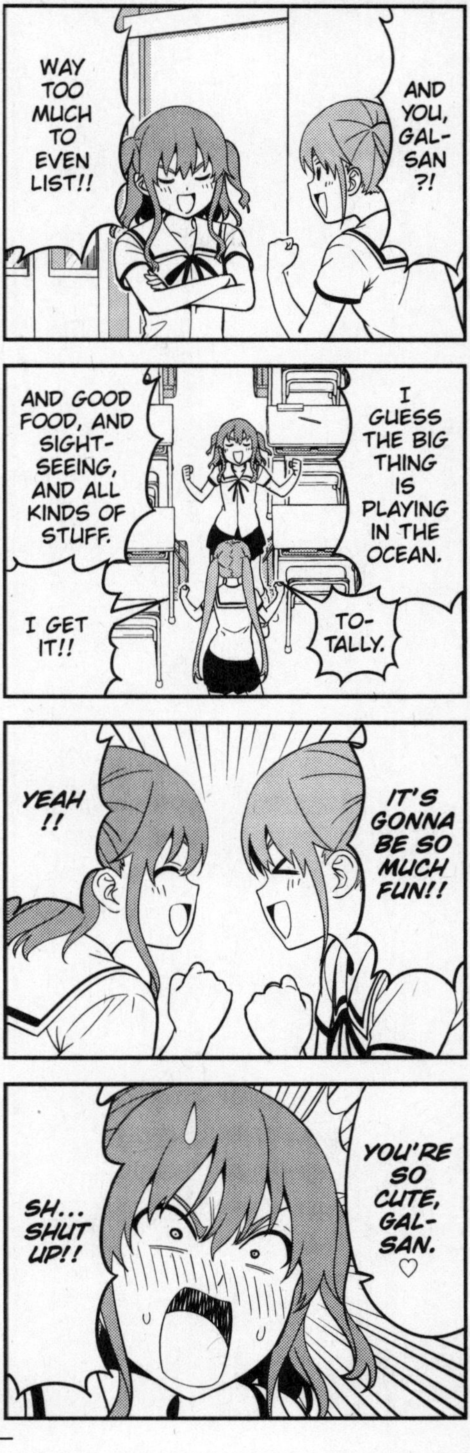
AND YOU, GAL-SAN?!
WAY TOO MUCH TO EVEN LIST!!
I GUESS THE BIG THING IS PLAYING IN THE OCEAN.
AND GOOD FOOD, AND SIGHT-SEEING, AND ALL KINDS OF STUFF.
TO-TALLY.
I GET IT!!
IT'S GONNA BE SO MUCH FUN!!
YEAH!!
YOU'RE SO CUTE, GAL-SAN. ♡
SH... SHUT UP!!

It...It Just Slipped Out!!

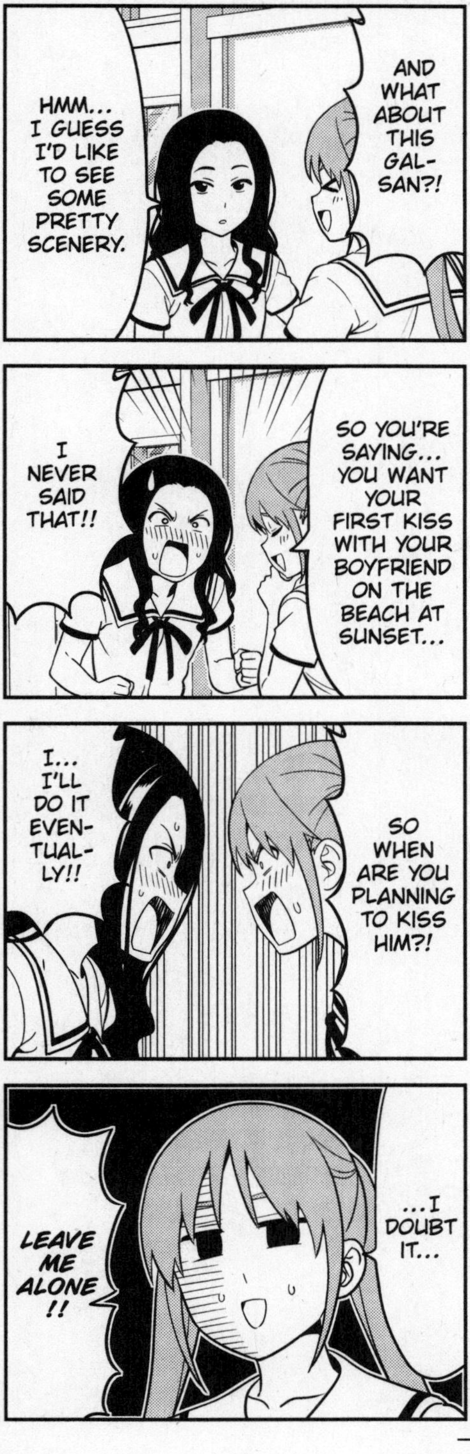
AND WHAT ABOUT THIS GAL-SAN?!
HMM... I GUESS I'D LIKE TO SEE SOME PRETTY SCENERY.
SO YOU'RE SAYING... YOU WANT YOUR FIRST KISS WITH YOUR BOYFRIEND ON THE BEACH AT SUNSET...
I NEVER SAID THAT!!
SO WHEN ARE YOU PLANNING TO KISS HIM?!
I... I'LL DO IT EVEN-TUAL-LY!!
...I DOUBT IT...
LEAVE ME ALONE!!

Soon?! MUCH Better?!

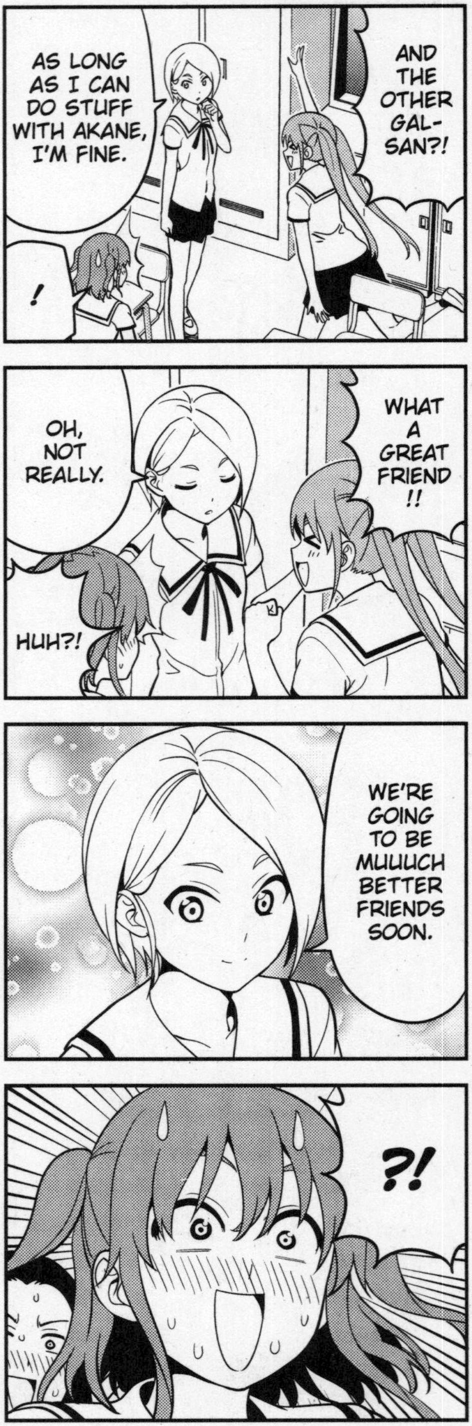
AND THE OTHER GAL-SAN?!
AS LONG AS I CAN DO STUFF WITH AKANE, I'M FINE.
!
WHAT A GREAT FRIEND!!
OH, NOT REALLY.
HUH?!
WE'RE GOING TO BE MUUUCH BETTER FRIENDS SOON.
?!

Clueless

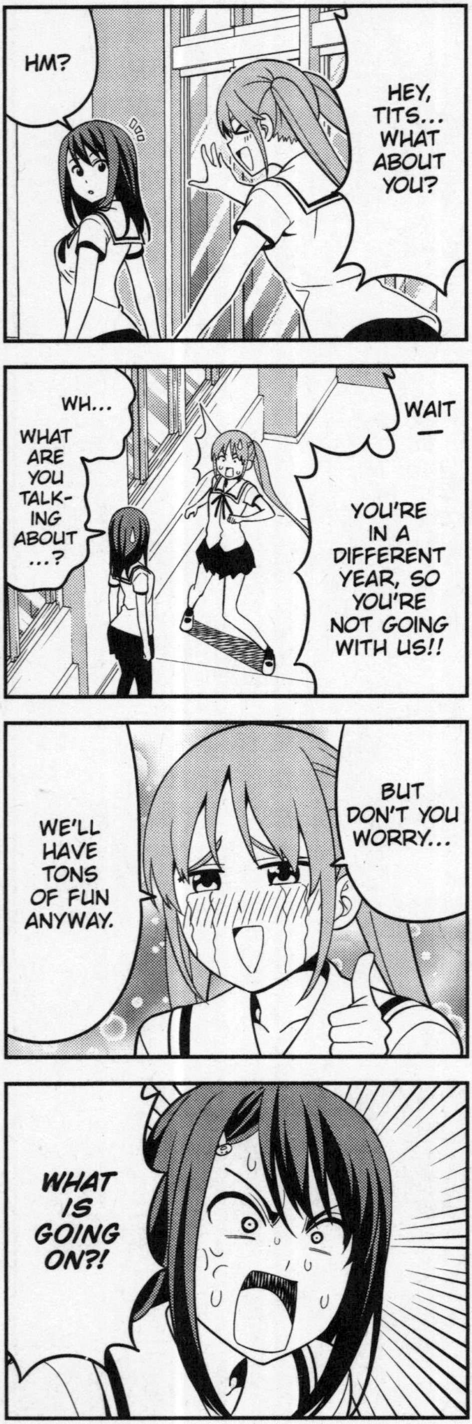
HEY, TITS... WHAT ABOUT YOU?
HM?
WAIT—
YOU'RE IN A DIFFERENT YEAR, SO YOU'RE NOT GOING WITH US!!
WH... WHAT ARE YOU TALKING ABOUT...?
BUT DON'T YOU WORRY...
WE'LL HAVE TONS OF FUN ANYWAY.
WHAT IS GOING ON?!

I'm Gonna Be Honest

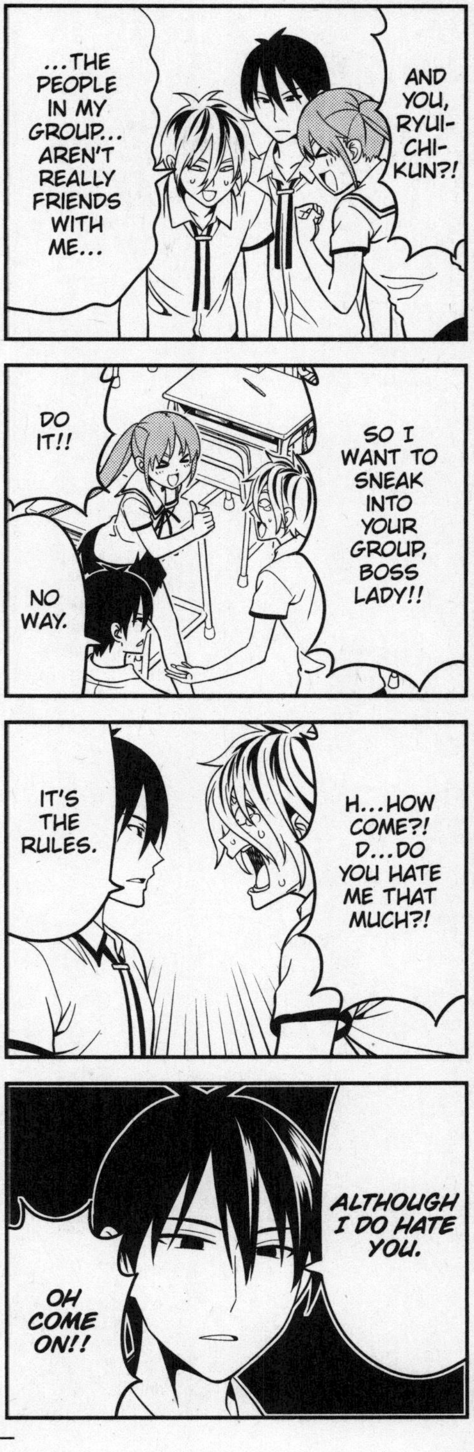
AND YOU, RYUI-CHI-KUN?!
...THE PEOPLE IN MY GROUP... AREN'T REALLY FRIENDS WITH ME...
SO I WANT TO SNEAK INTO YOUR GROUP, BOSS LADY!!
DO IT!!
NO WAY.
H...HOW COME?! D...DO YOU HATE ME THAT MUCH?!
IT'S THE RULES.
ALTHOUGH I DO HATE YOU.
OH COME ON!!

It's My Specialty

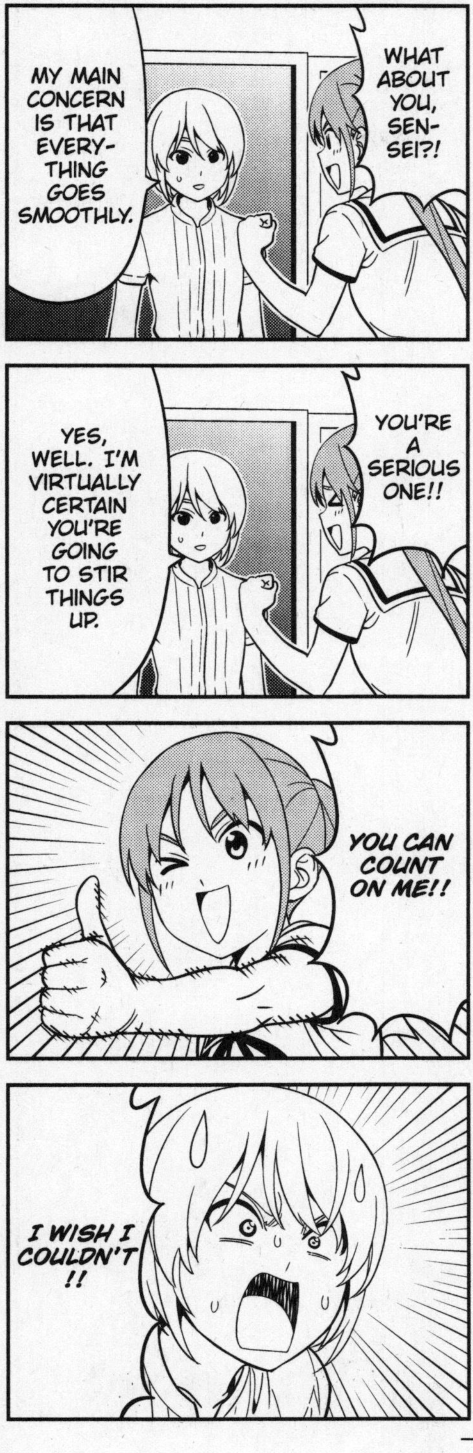
WHAT ABOUT YOU, SEN-SEI?!
MY MAIN CONCERN IS THAT EVERY-THING GOES SMOOTHLY.
YOU'RE A SERIOUS ONE!!
YES, WELL. I'M VIRTUALLY CERTAIN YOU'RE GOING TO STIR THINGS UP.
YOU CAN COUNT ON ME!!
I WISH I COULDN'T !!

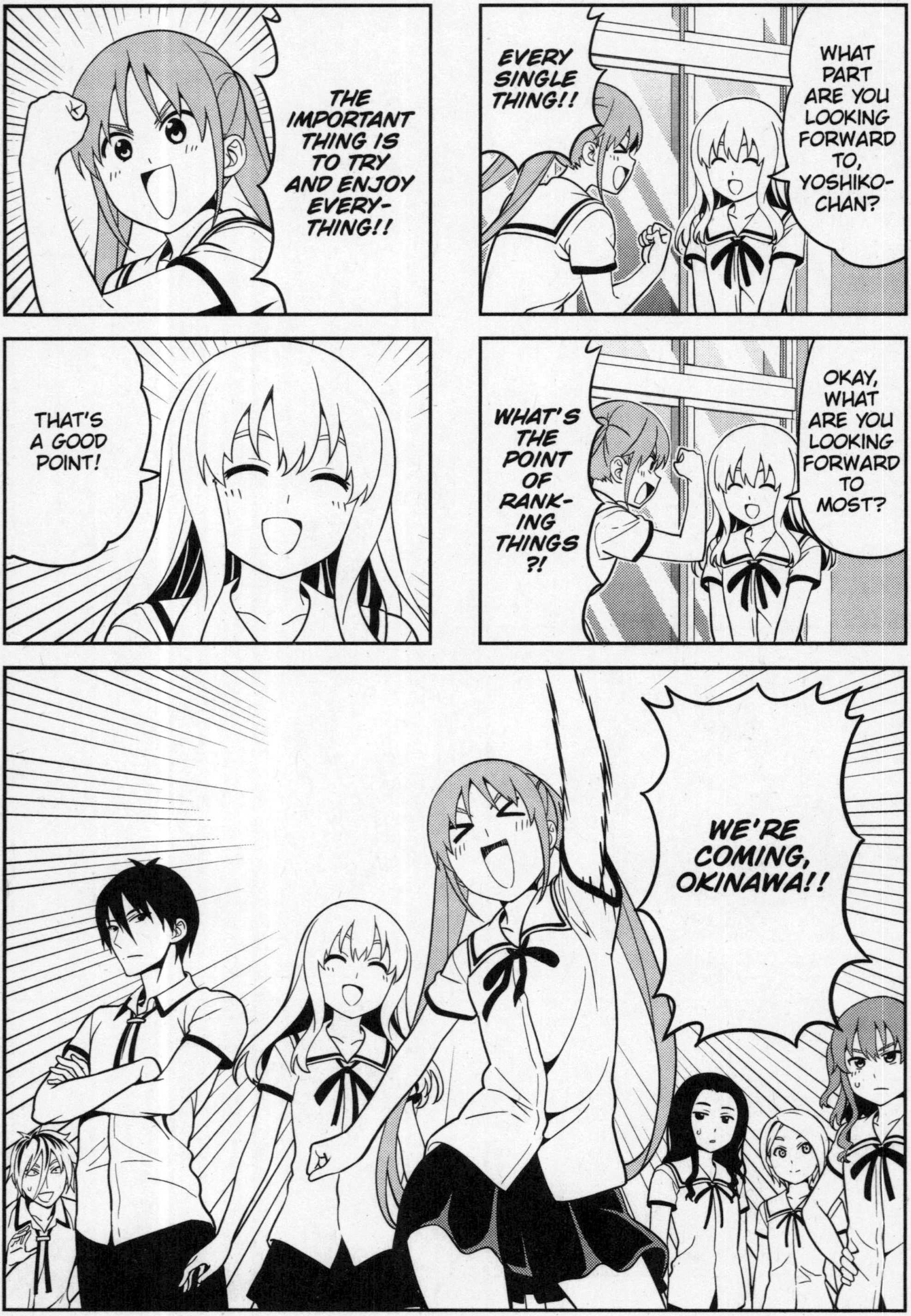
WHAT PART ARE YOU LOOKING FORWARD TO, YOSHIKO-CHAN?
EVERY SINGLE THING!!
THE IMPORTANT THING IS TO TRY AND ENJOY EVERY-THING!!
OKAY, WHAT ARE YOU LOOKING FORWARD TO MOST?
WHAT'S THE POINT OF RANK-ING THINGS?!
THAT'S A GOOD POINT!
WE'RE COMING, OKINAWA!!

All Packed

どっさり
HEAP
READY!!

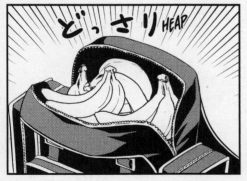

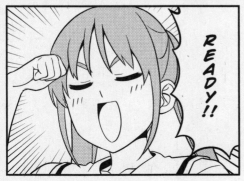

(So hot, my heart's burning up)

Aho-Girl

\\'ahô͵gərl\\ *Japanese, noun.*
A clueless girl.

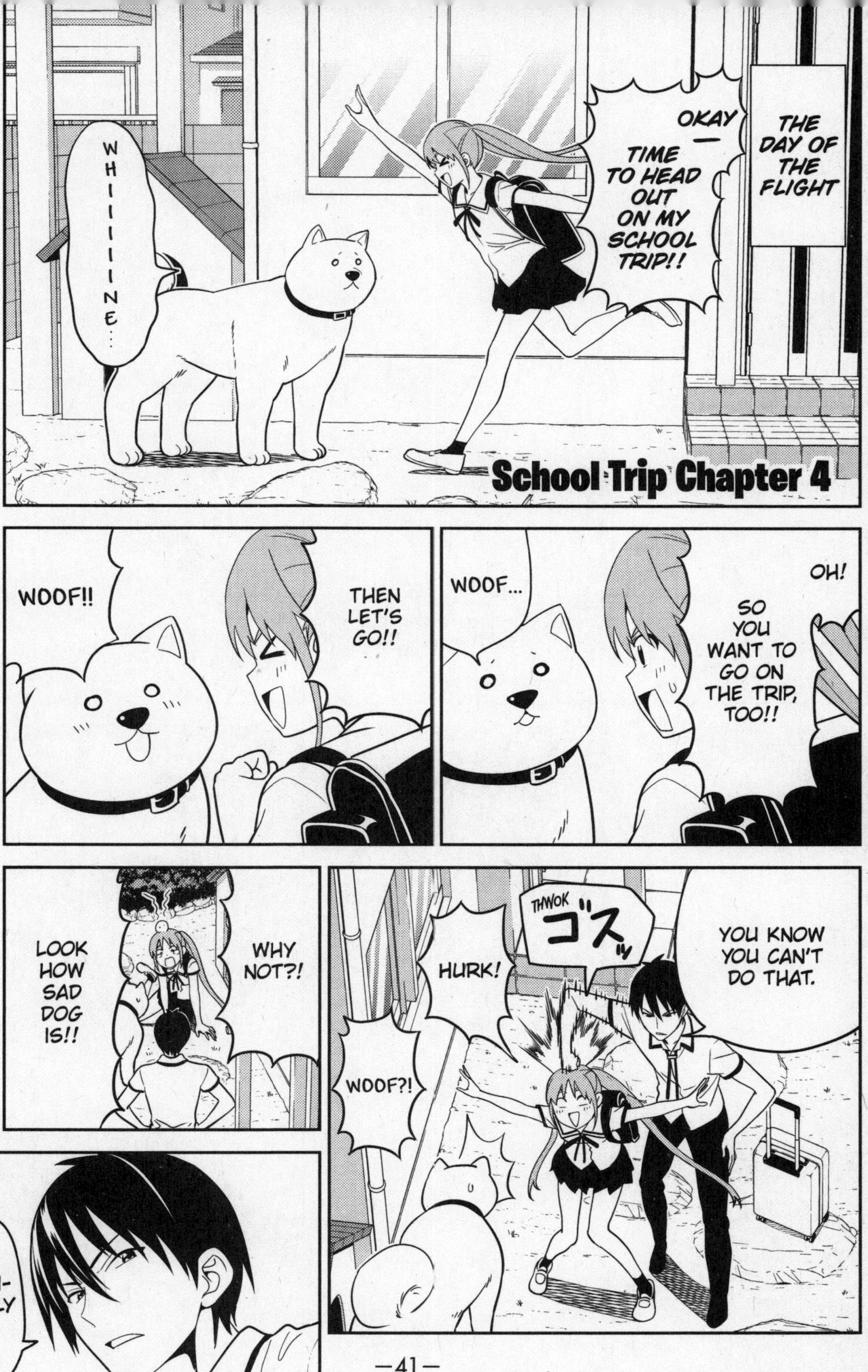
THE DAY OF THE FLIGHT
OKAY — TIME TO HEAD OUT ON MY SCHOOL TRIP!!
WHIIIIIINE...
School Trip Chapter 4
OH! SO YOU WANT TO GO ON THE TRIP, TOO!!
WOOF...
THEN LET'S GO!!
WOOF!!
YOU KNOW YOU CAN'T DO THAT.
THWOK ゴスッ
HURK!
WOOF?!
WHY NOT?!
LOOK HOW SAD DOG IS!!
SERI-OUSLY?!

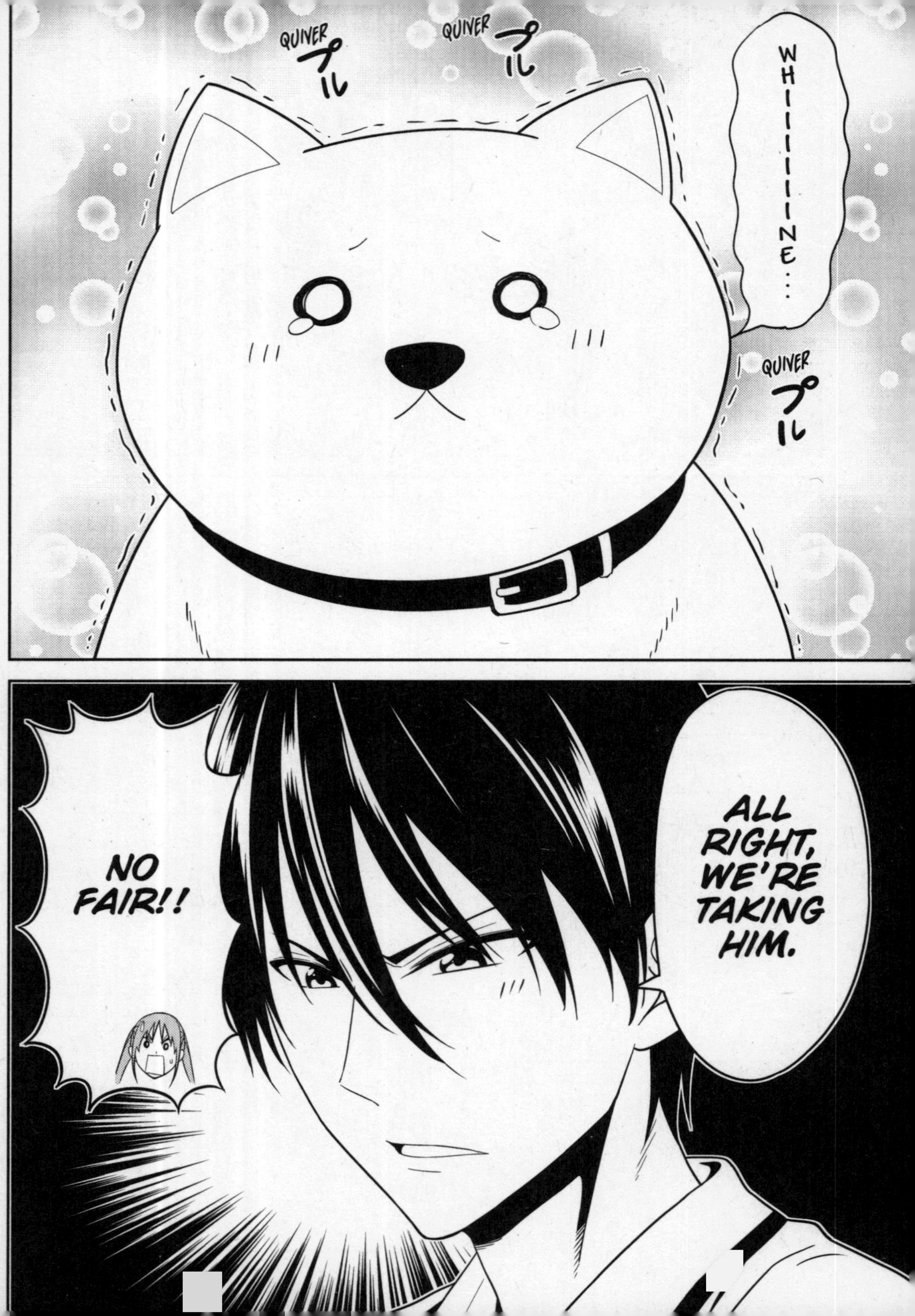
WHIIIIIINE...
QUIVER プル
QUIVER プル
QUIVER プル
ALL RIGHT, WE'RE TAKING HIM.
NO FAIR!!

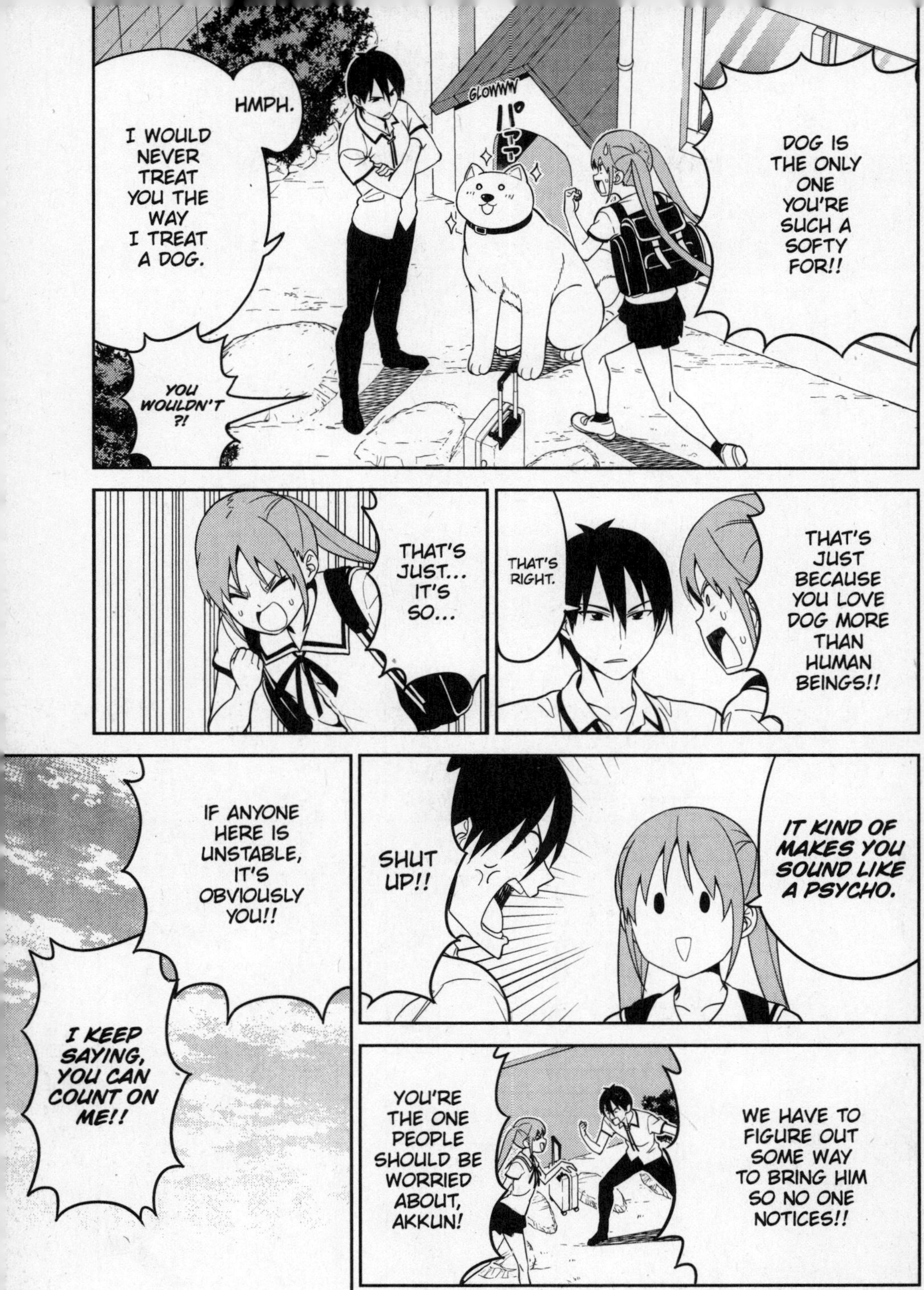
DOG IS THE ONLY ONE YOU'RE SUCH A SOFTY FOR!!
GLOWWW
HMPH.
I WOULD NEVER TREAT YOU THE WAY I TREAT A DOG.
YOU WOULDN'T ?!
THAT'S JUST BECAUSE YOU LOVE DOG MORE THAN HUMAN BEINGS!!
THAT'S RIGHT.
THAT'S JUST... IT'S SO...
IT KIND OF MAKES YOU SOUND LIKE A PSYCHO.
SHUT UP!!
WE HAVE TO FIGURE OUT SOME WAY TO BRING HIM SO NO ONE NOTICES!!
YOU'RE THE ONE PEOPLE SHOULD BE WORRIED ABOUT, AKKUN!
IF ANYONE HERE IS UNSTABLE, IT'S OBVIOUSLY YOU!!
I KEEP SAYING, YOU CAN COUNT ON ME!!

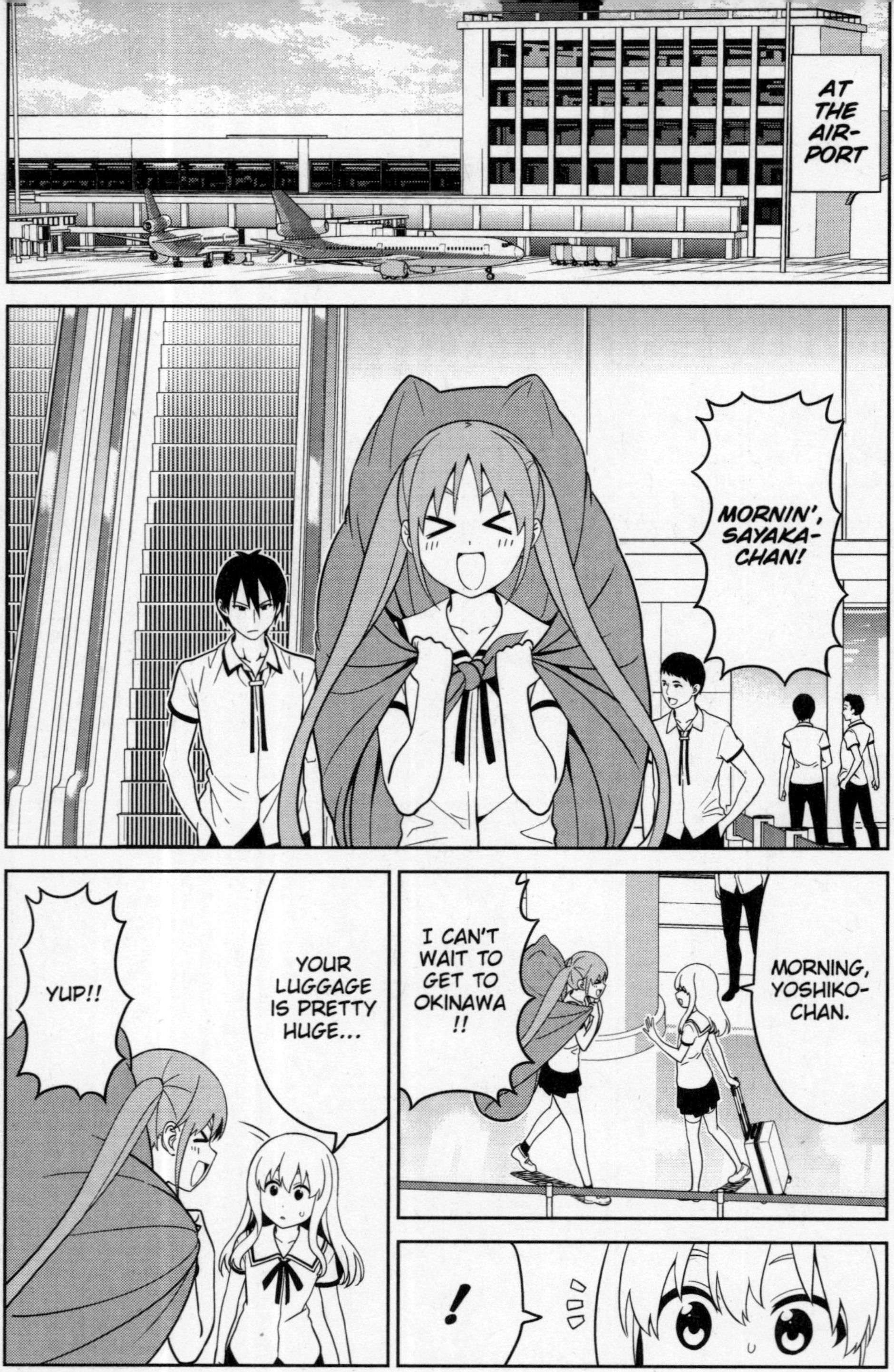
AT THE AIR-PORT
MORNIN', SAYAKA-CHAN!
MORNING, YOSHIKO-CHAN.
I CAN'T WAIT TO GET TO OKINAWA !!
!
YOUR LUGGAGE IS PRETTY HUGE...
YUP!!

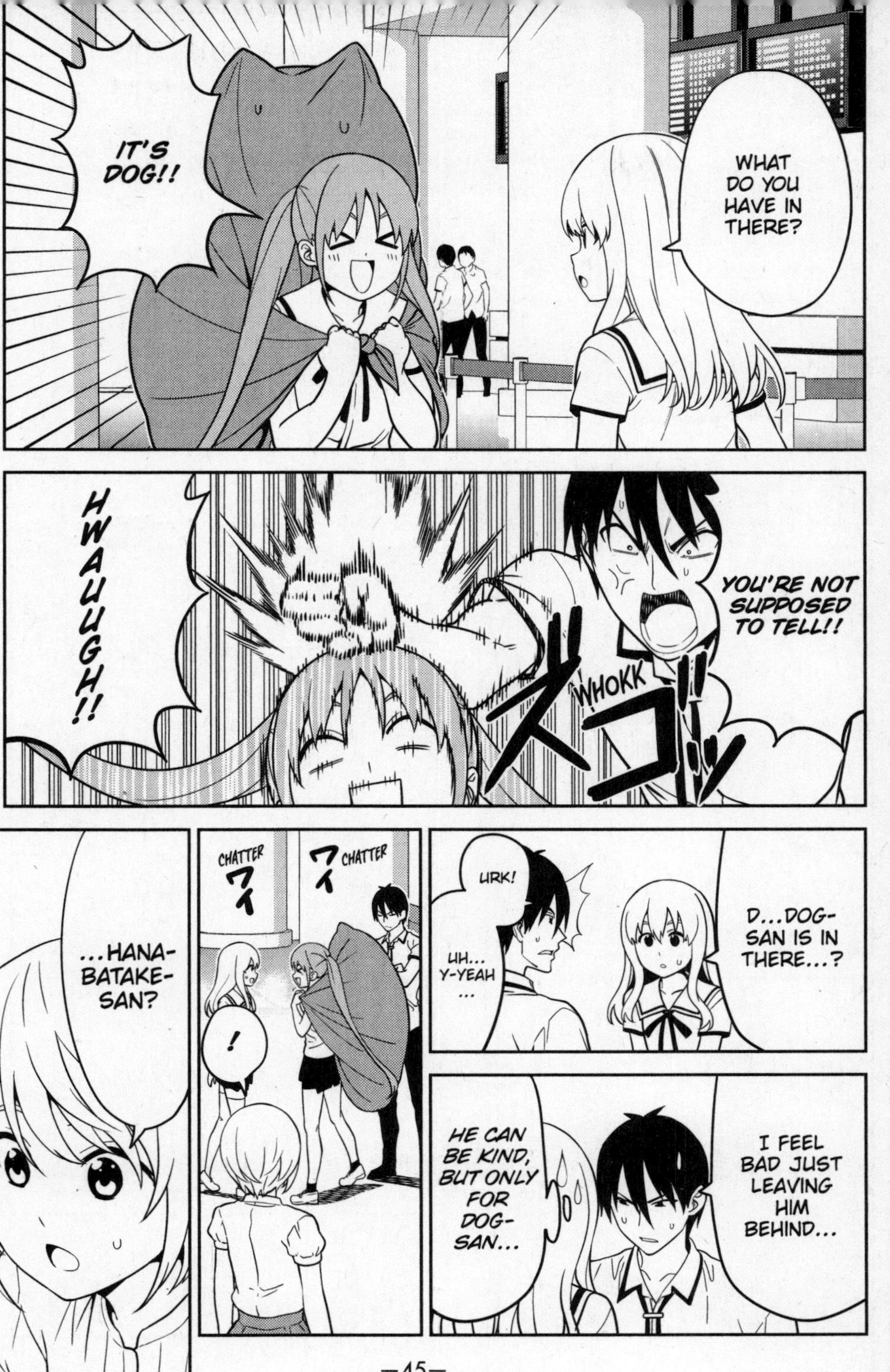
WHAT DO YOU HAVE IN THERE?
IT'S DOG!!
YOU'RE NOT SUPPOSED TO TELL!!
WHOKK
HWAUUGH!!
D...DOG-SAN IS IN THERE...?
URK!
UH... Y-YEAH ...
I FEEL BAD JUST LEAVING HIM BEHIND...
HE CAN BE KIND, BUT ONLY FOR DOG-SAN...
ワイ CHATTER
ワイ CHATTER
!
...HANA-BATAKE-SAN?

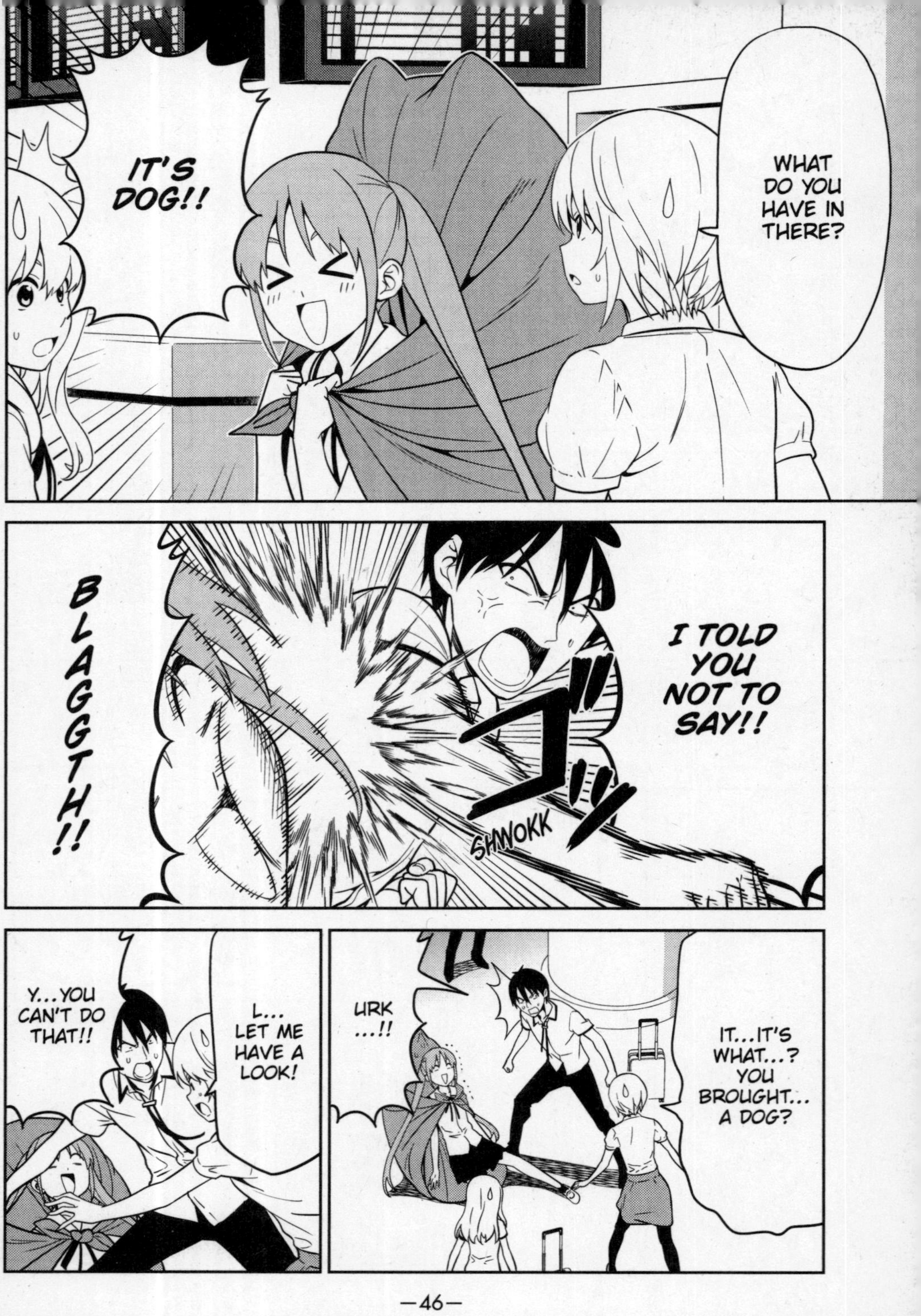
WHAT DO YOU HAVE IN THERE?
IT'S DOG!!
I TOLD YOU NOT TO SAY!!
BLAGGTH!!
SHNOKK
IT...IT'S WHAT...? YOU BROUGHT... A DOG?
URK ...!!
L... LET ME HAVE A LOOK!
Y...YOU CAN'T DO THAT!!

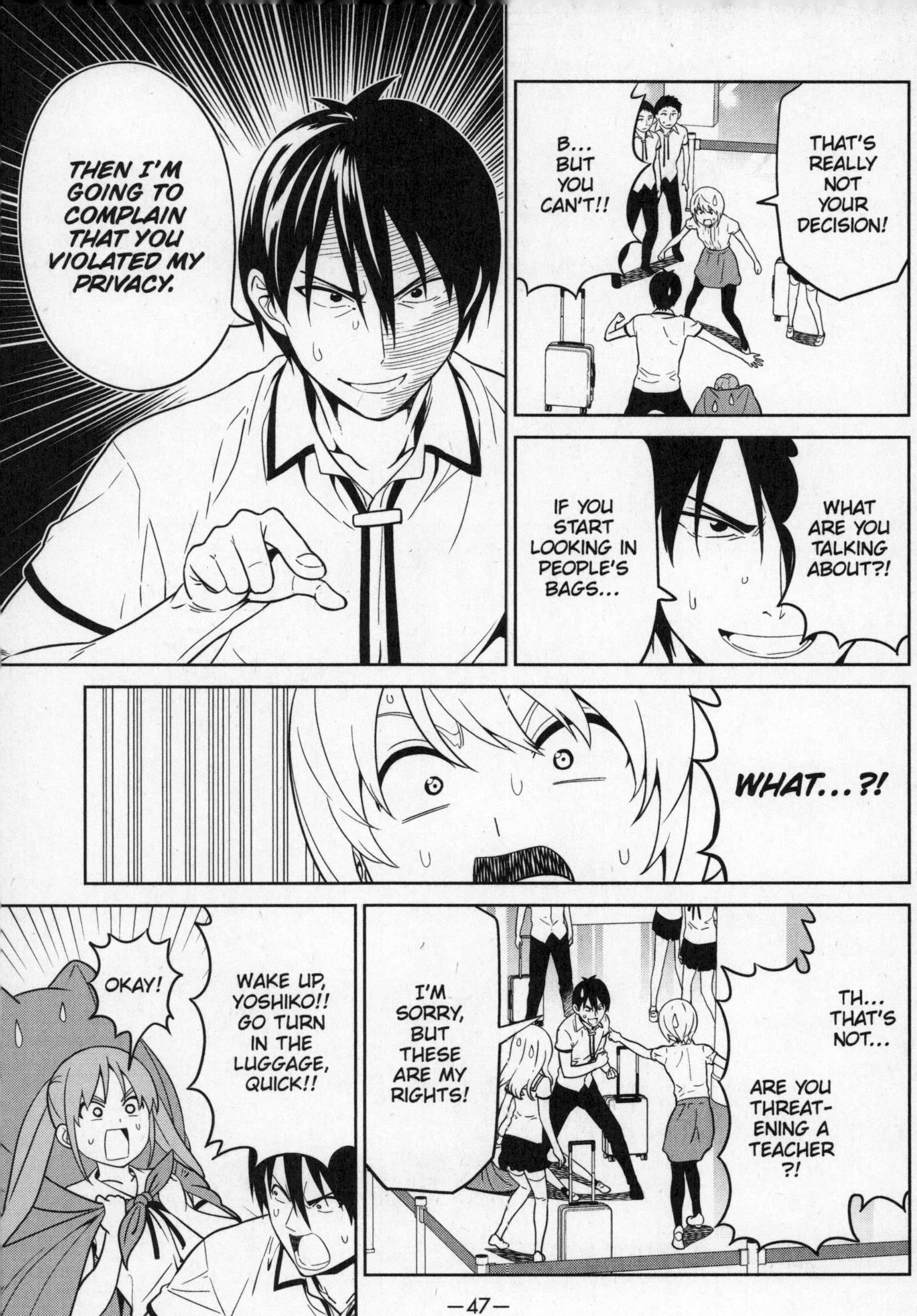
THAT'S REALLY NOT YOUR DECISION!
B... BUT YOU CAN'T!!
WHAT ARE YOU TALKING ABOUT?!
IF YOU START LOOKING IN PEOPLE'S BAGS...
THEN I'M GOING TO COMPLAIN THAT YOU VIOLATED MY PRIVACY.
WHAT...?!
TH... THAT'S NOT...
ARE YOU THREAT-ENING A TEACHER?!
I'M SORRY, BUT THESE ARE MY RIGHTS!
WAKE UP, YOSHIKO!! GO TURN IN THE LUGGAGE, QUICK!!
OKAY!

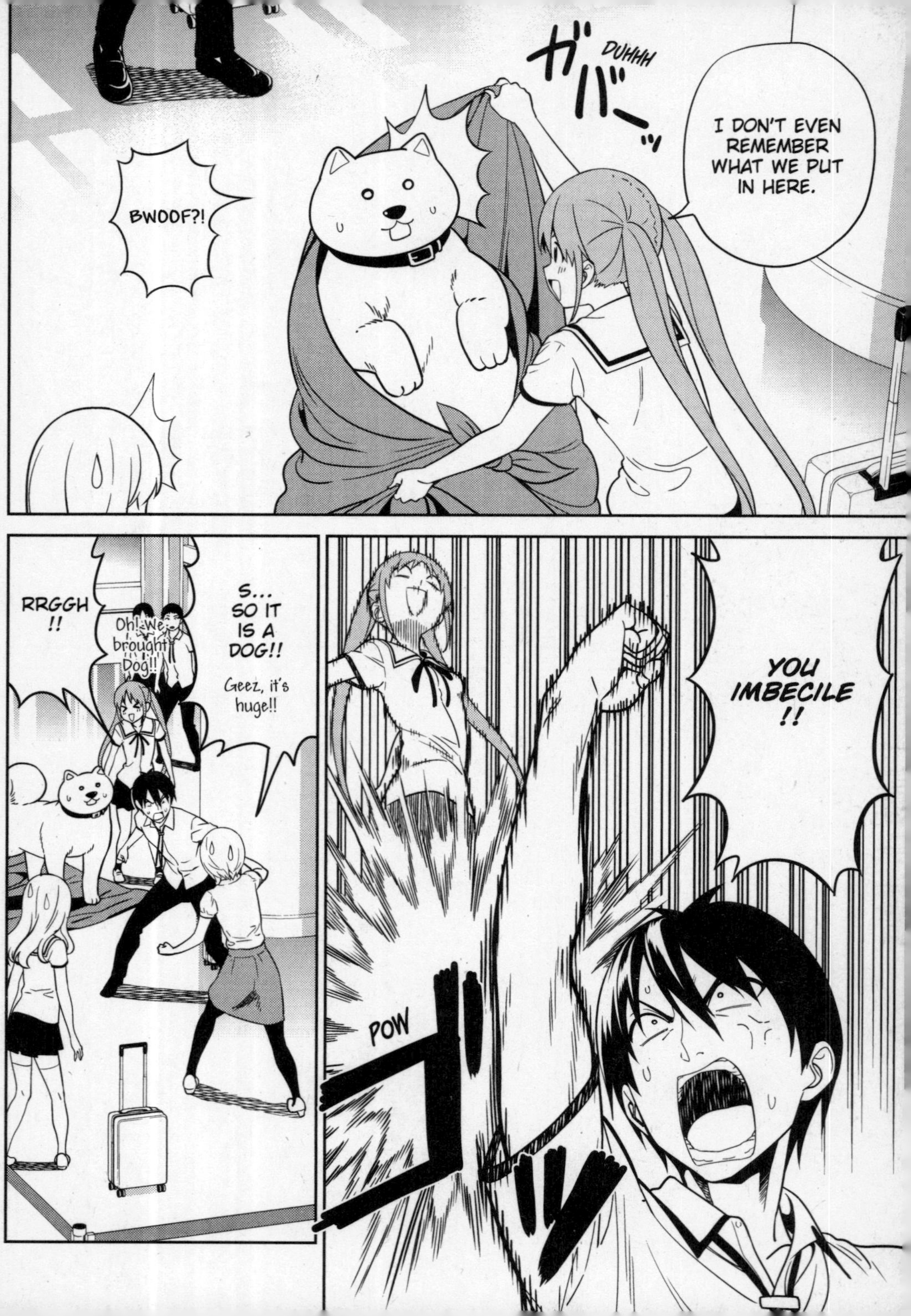ガバーッ
DUHHH
I DON'T EVEN REMEMBER WHAT WE PUT IN HERE.
BWOOF?!
YOU IMBECILE !!
ゴッ
POW
S... SO IT IS A DOG!!
Geez, it's huge!!
Oh! We brought Dog!!
RRGGH !!

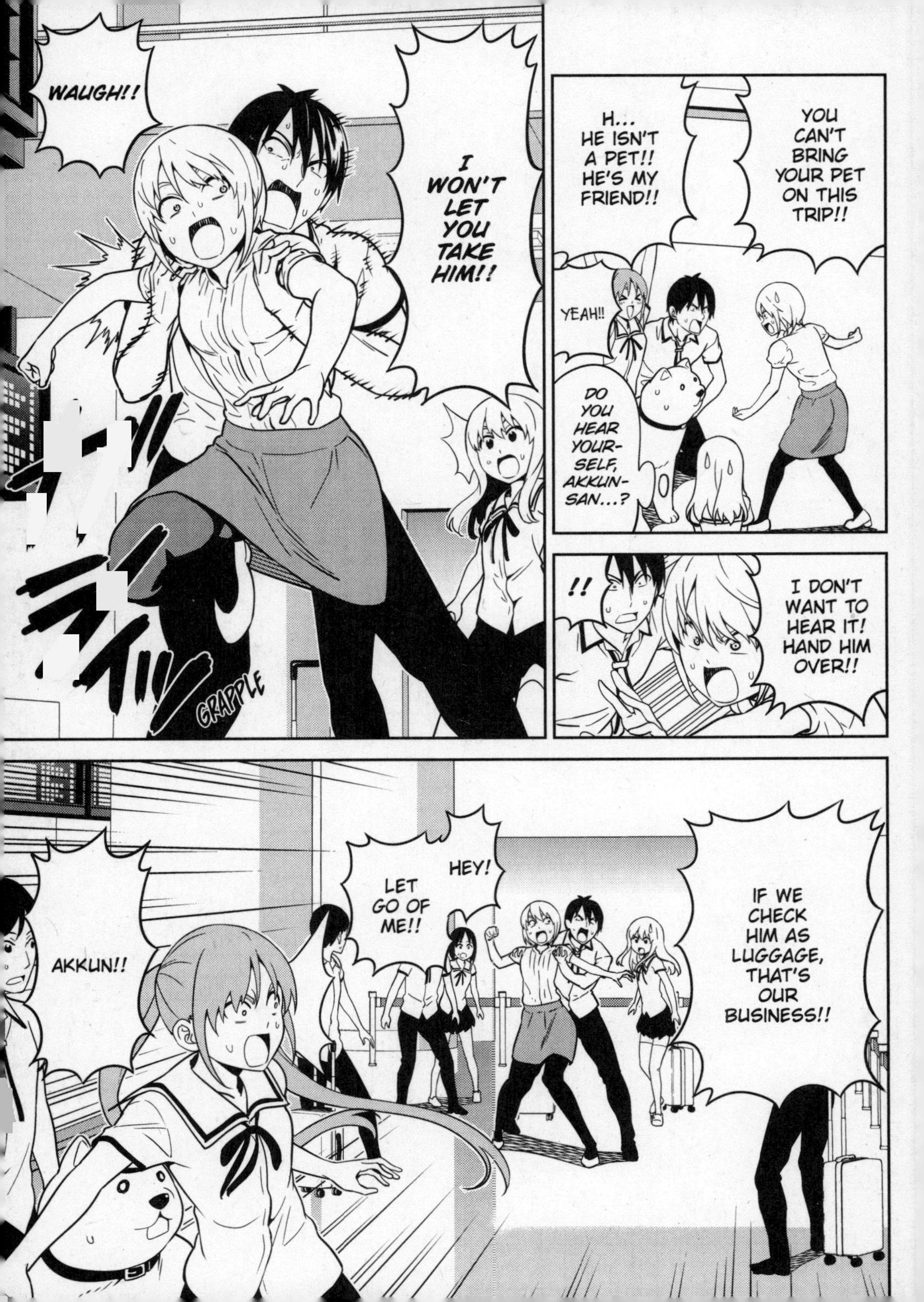
YOU CAN'T BRING YOUR PET ON THIS TRIP!!
H... HE ISN'T A PET!! HE'S MY FRIEND!!
YEAH!!
DO YOU HEAR YOURSELF, AKKUN-SAN...?
I DON'T WANT TO HEAR IT! HAND HIM OVER!!
!!
I WON'T LET YOU TAKE HIM!!
WAUGH!!
GRAPPLE
IF WE CHECK HIM AS LUGGAGE, THAT'S OUR BUSINESS!!
HEY!
LET GO OF ME!!
AKKUN!!

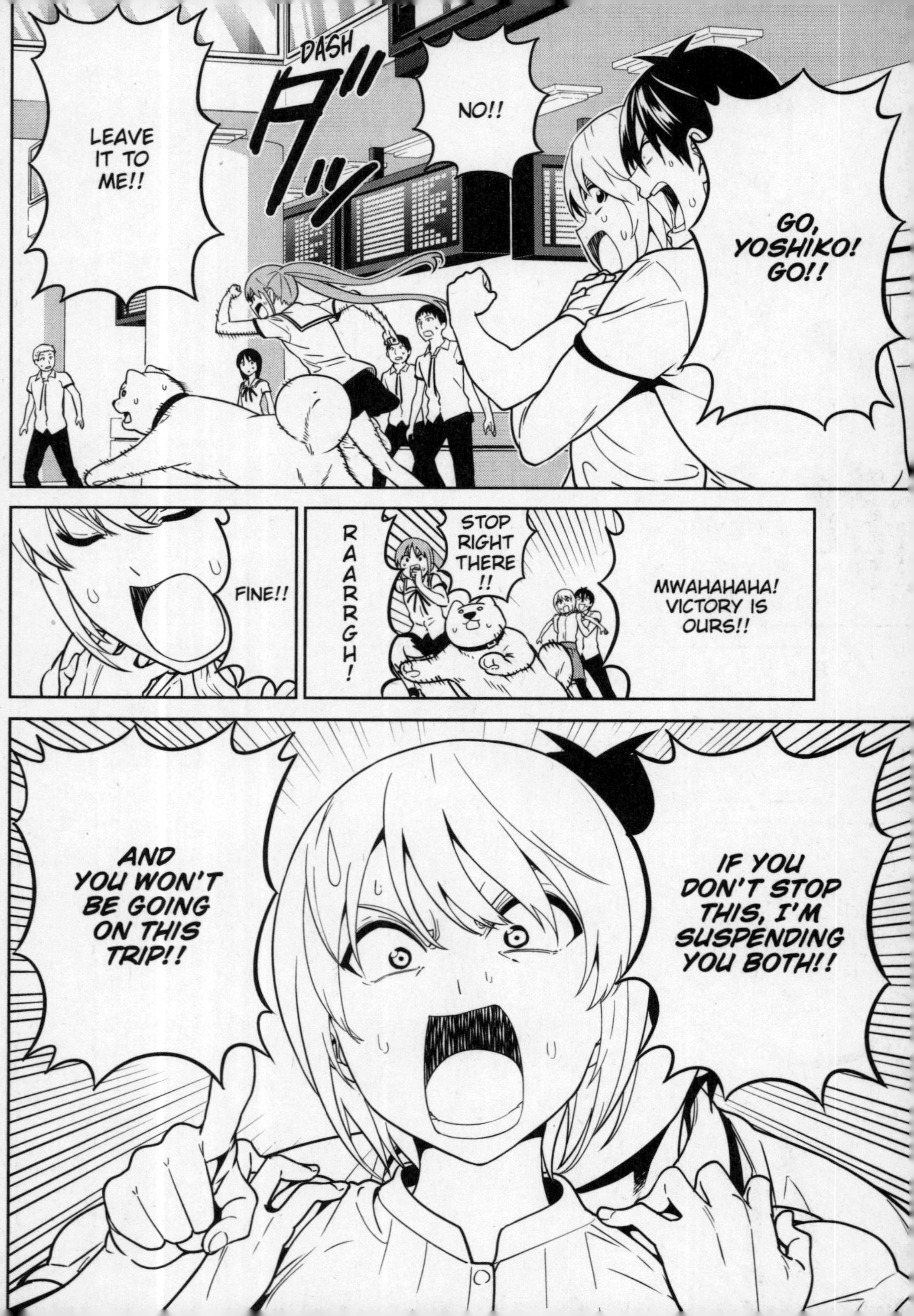
GO, YOSHIKO! GO!!
NO!!
DASH
LEAVE IT TO ME!!
MWAHAHAHA! VICTORY IS OURS!!
STOP RIGHT THERE!!
RAAARRGH!
FINE!!
IF YOU DON'T STOP THIS, I'M SUSPENDING YOU BOTH!!
AND YOU WON'T BE GOING ON THIS TRIP!!

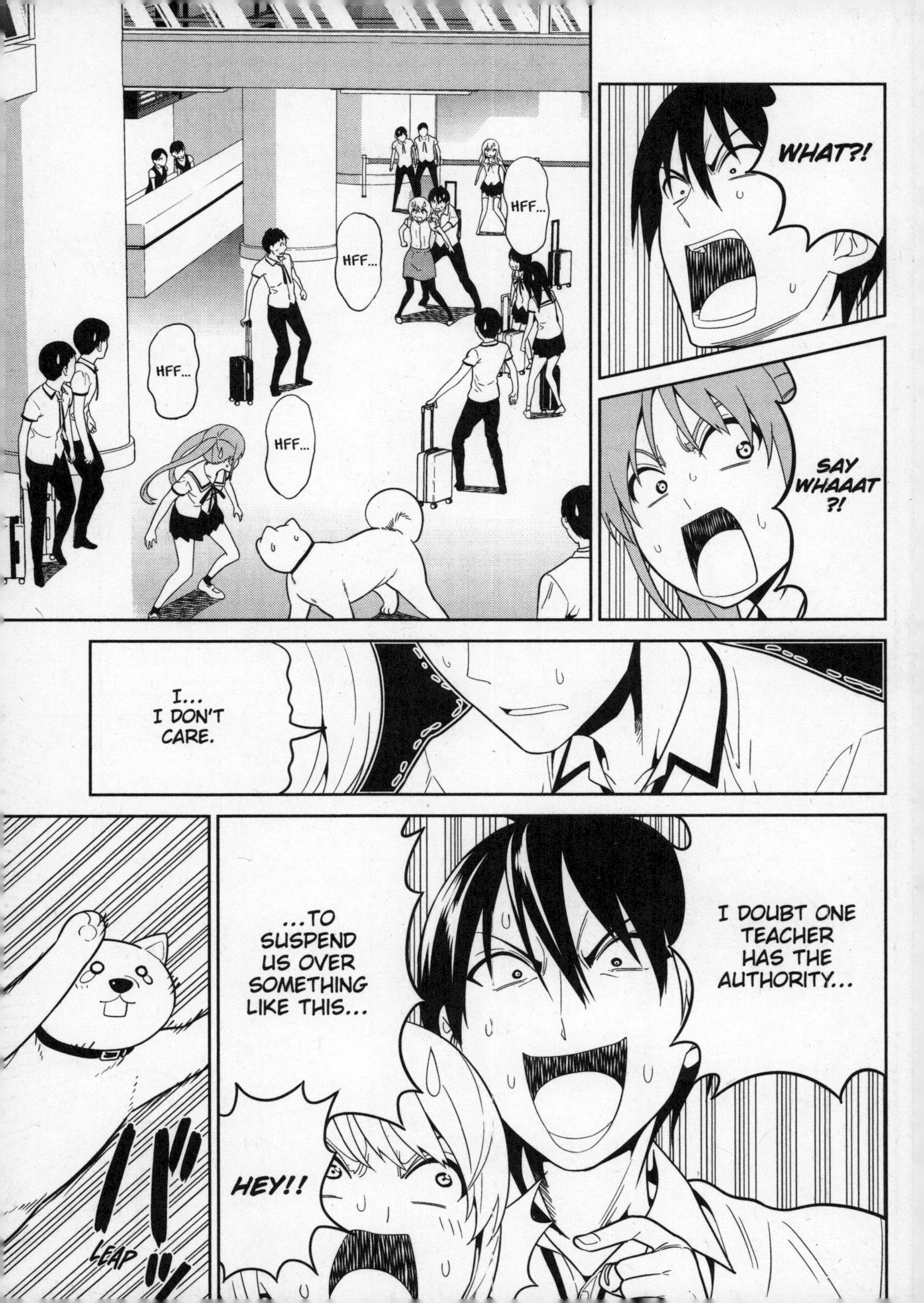
WHAT?!
SAY WHAAAT?!
HFF...
HFF...
HFF...
HFF...
I... I DON'T CARE.
I DOUBT ONE TEACHER HAS THE AUTHORITY...
...TO SUSPEND US OVER SOMETHING LIKE THIS...
HEY!!
LEAP

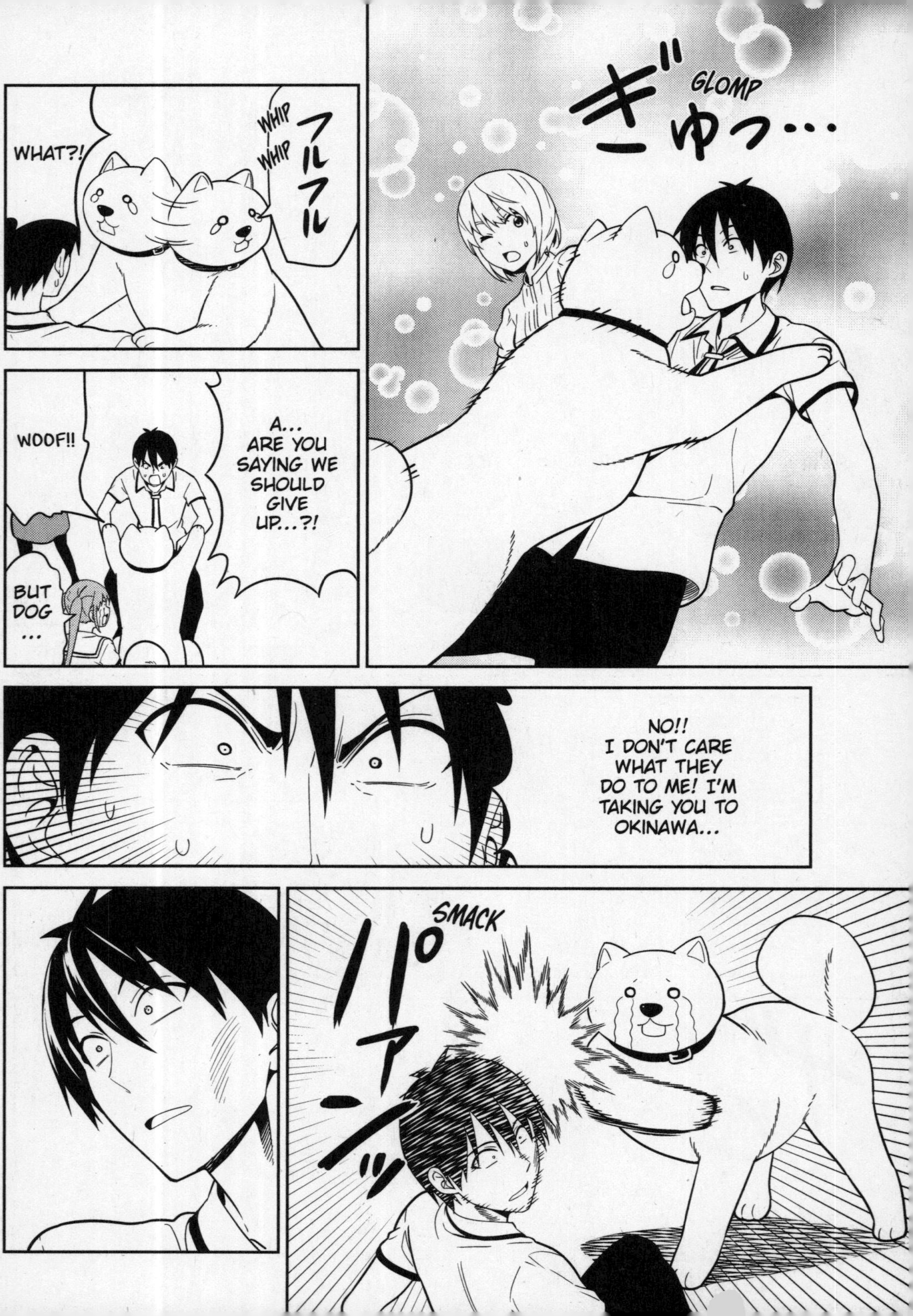
ぎゅっ…
GLOMP
WHIP WHIP
フルフル
WHAT?!
A... ARE YOU SAYING WE SHOULD GIVE UP...?!
WOOF!!
BUT DOG...
NO!! I DON'T CARE WHAT THEY DO TO ME! I'M TAKING YOU TO OKINAWA...
SMACK
パァーッ

WOOF...

...ARE YOU... SAYING I...I NEED TO TAKE CARE...OF MYSELF...?

OH, DOG...

I'M SORRY...

...NNGH...

HWHEEEN

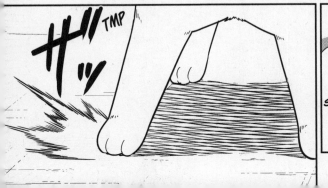

TMP

I'M SORRY...

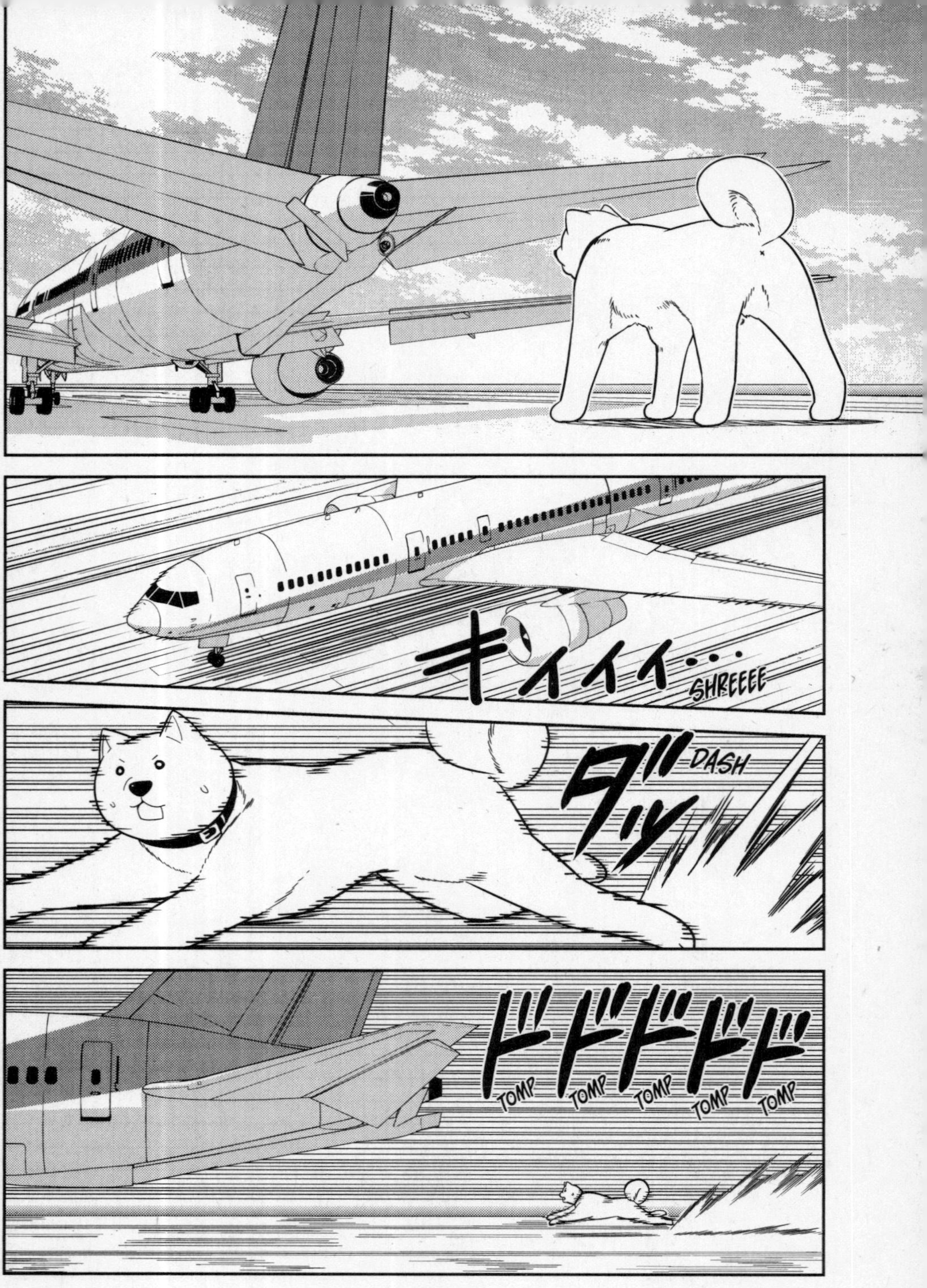
キィィィ…
SHREEEE
ダッ
DASH
ドドドドドド
TOMP
TOMP
TOMP
TOMP
TOMP

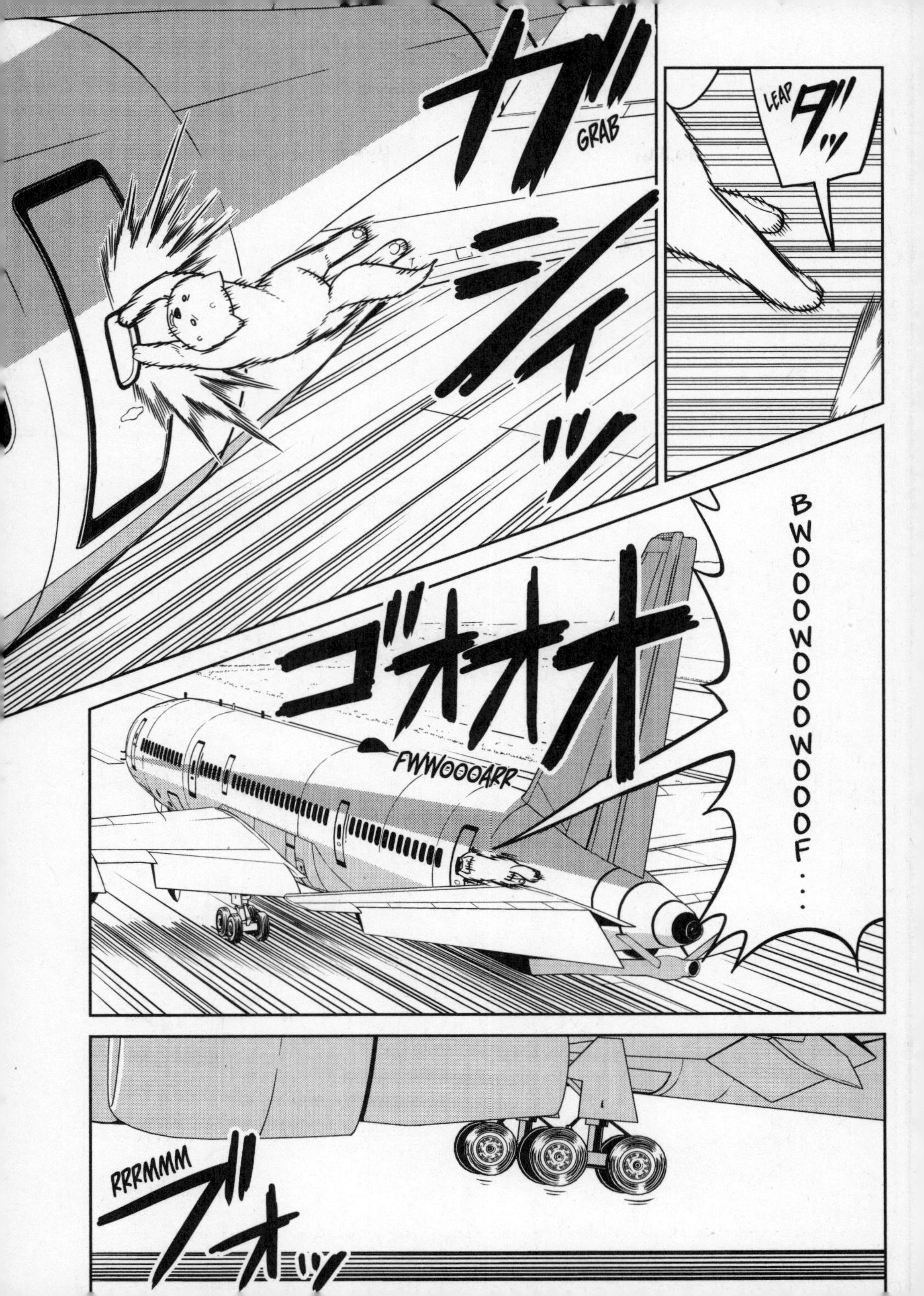
LEAP
ダッ
ガシィッ
GRAB
BWOOOWOOOOWOOOOF...
ゴオオオ
FWWOOOARR
RRRMMM
ブオッ

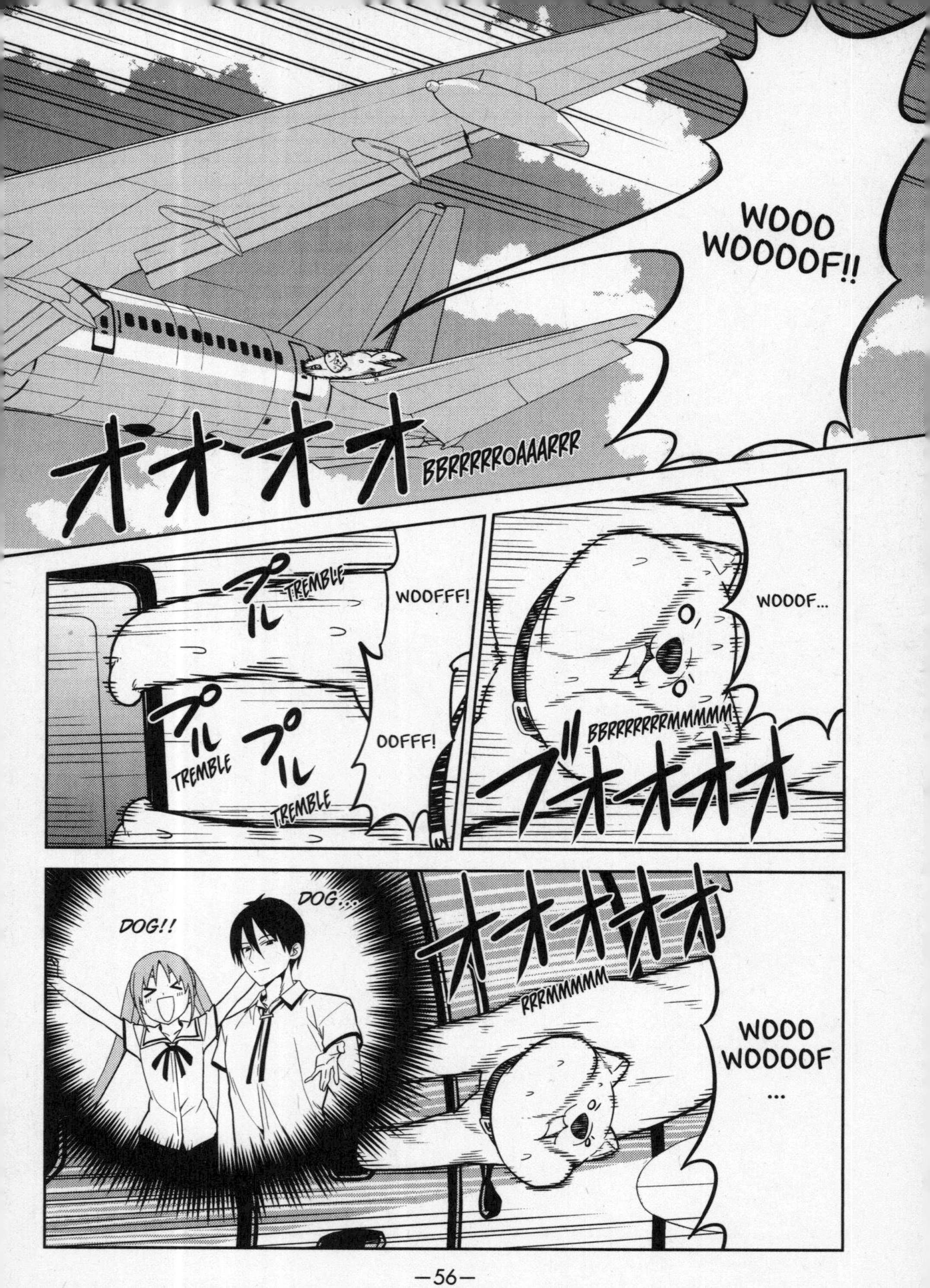
WOOO WOOOOF!!
オオオオ
BBRRRRROAAARRR
WOOOF...
ブオオオオ
BBRRRRRRMMMMM
WOOFFF!
OOFFF!
プル
TREMBLE
プル
TREMBLE
プル
TREMBLE
WOOO WOOOOF ...
オオオオオ
RRRMMMMM
DOG...
DOG!!

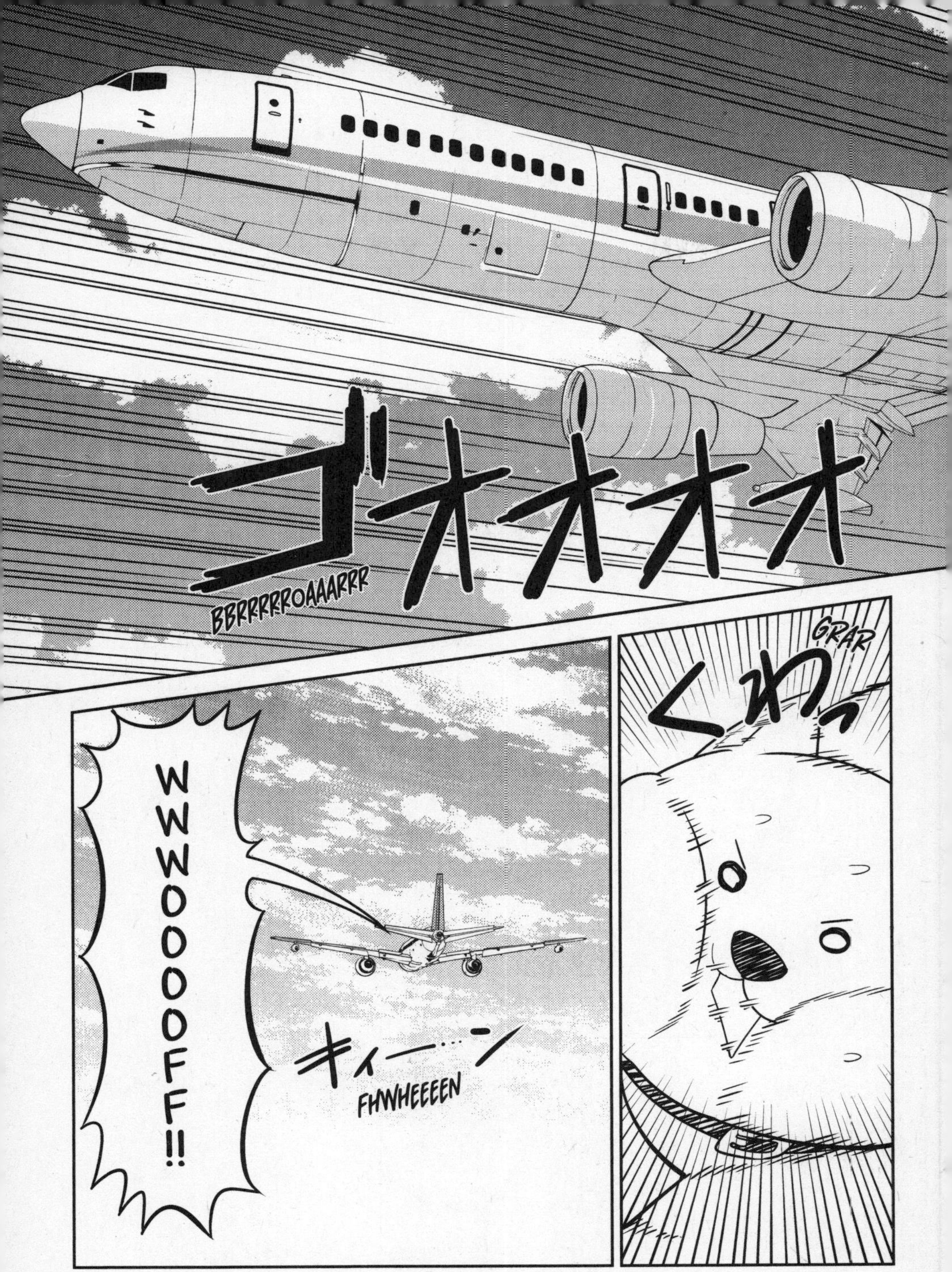
ゴオオオオ
BBRRRRROAAARRR
くわっ
GRAR
WWWOOOOOOFF!!
キィー…ン
FHWHEEEEN

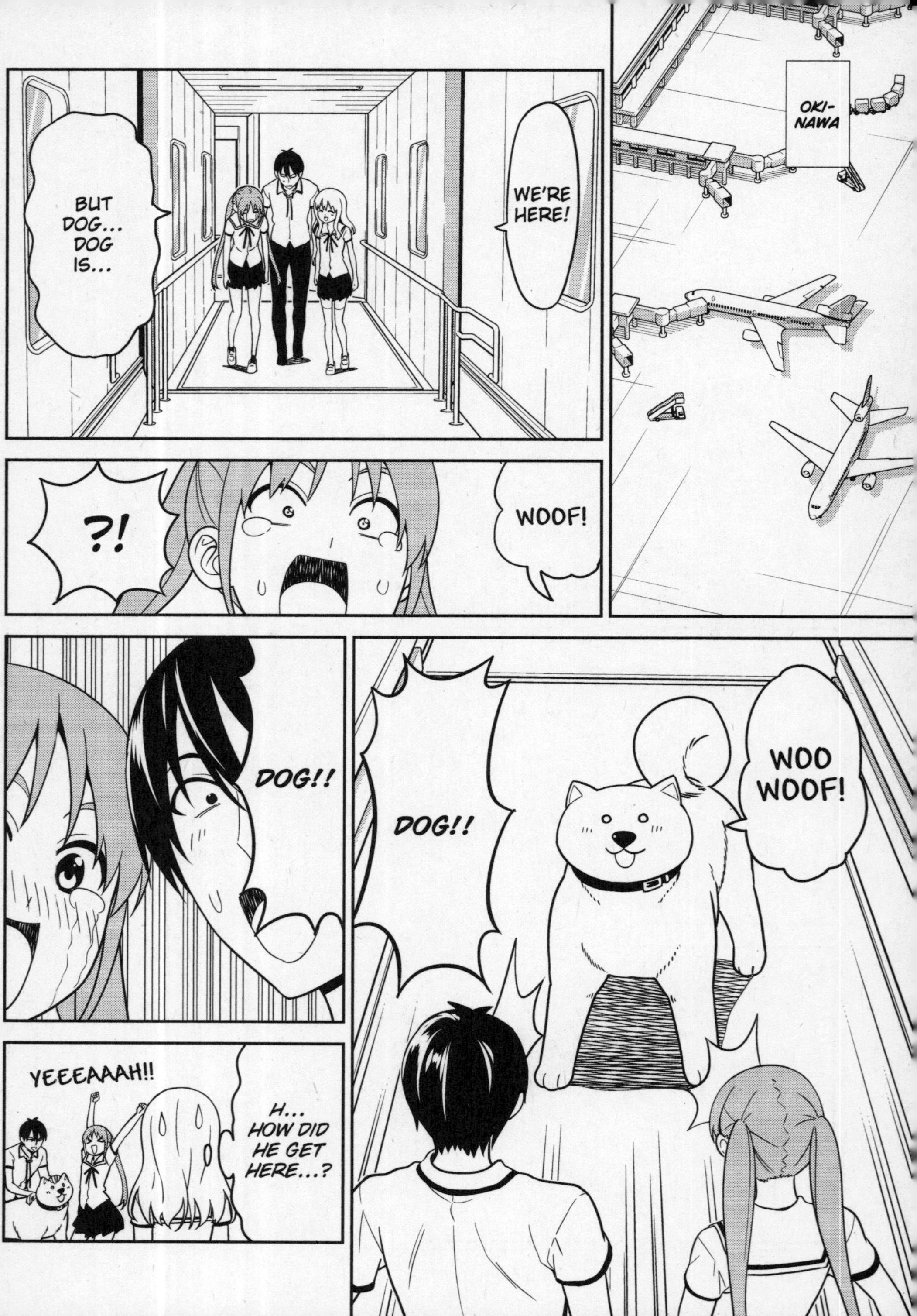
OKI-NAWA
WE'RE HERE!
BUT DOG... DOG IS...
WOOF!
?!
WOO WOOF!
DOG!!
DOG!!
YEEEAAAH!!
H... HOW DID HE GET HERE...?

All You Need Is Can-do Spirit

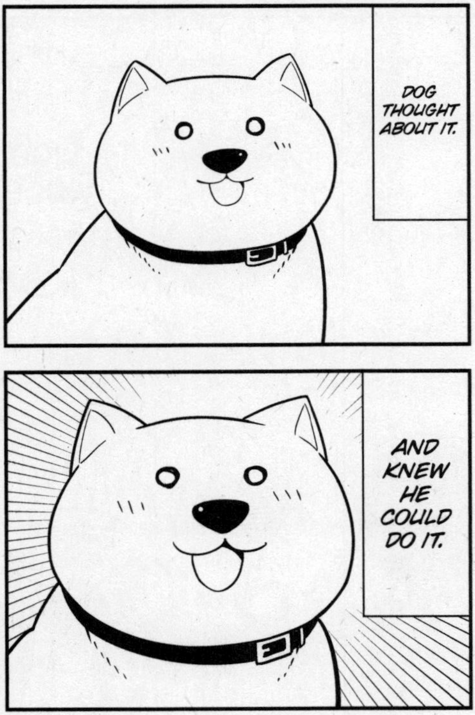
DOG THOUGHT ABOUT IT.
AND KNEW HE COULD DO IT.

(Falling like rain in the night, watch, the Perseid)

Aho-Girl

\ˈahôˌgərl\ *Japanese, noun.*
A clueless girl.

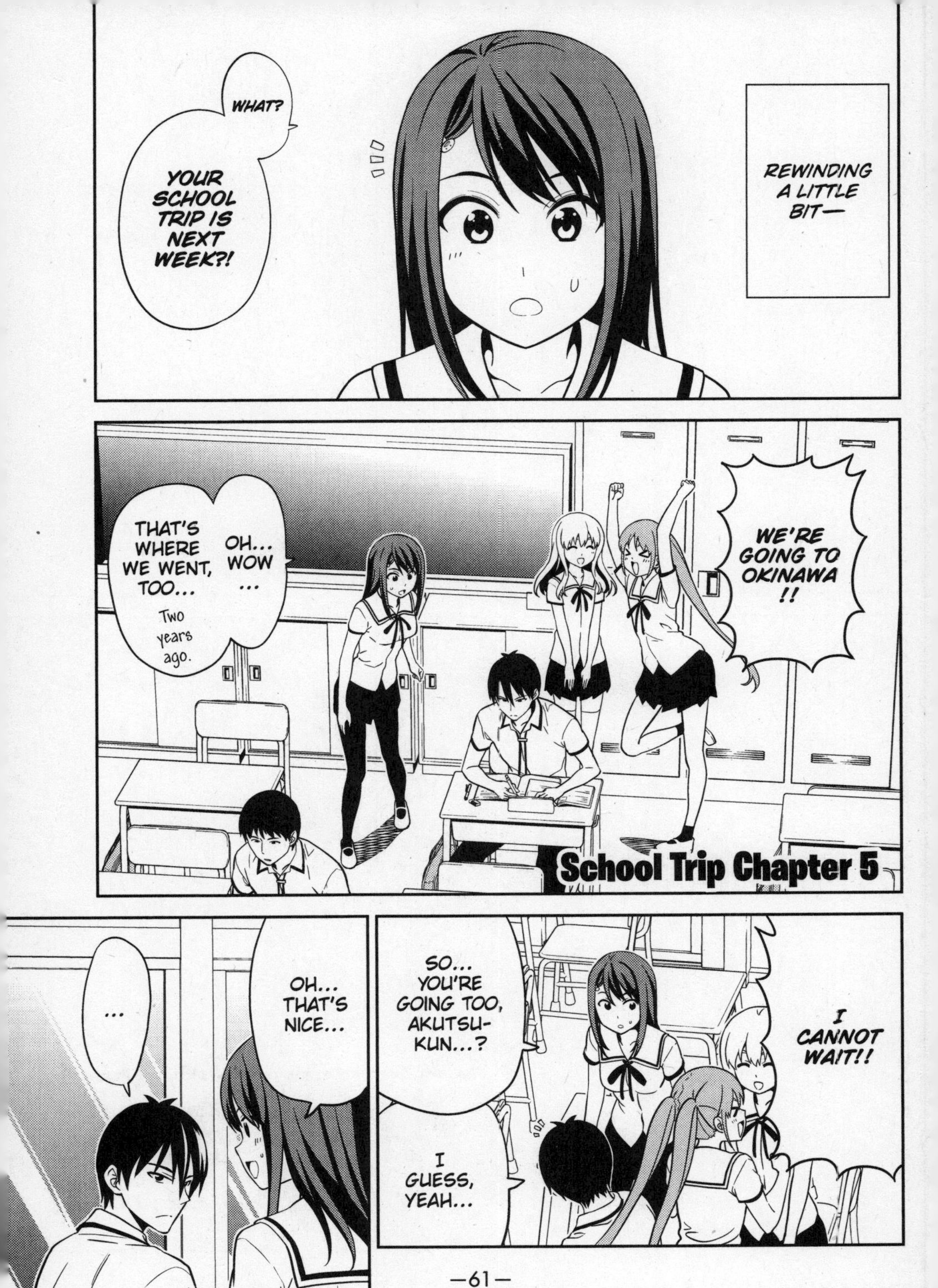
REWINDING A LITTLE BIT—
WHAT?
YOUR SCHOOL TRIP IS NEXT WEEK?!
WE'RE GOING TO OKINAWA!!
OH... WOW...
THAT'S WHERE WE WENT, TOO...
Two years ago.
School Trip Chapter 5
I CANNOT WAIT!!
SO... YOU'RE GOING TOO, AKUTSU-KUN...?
I GUESS, YEAH...
OH... THAT'S NICE...
...

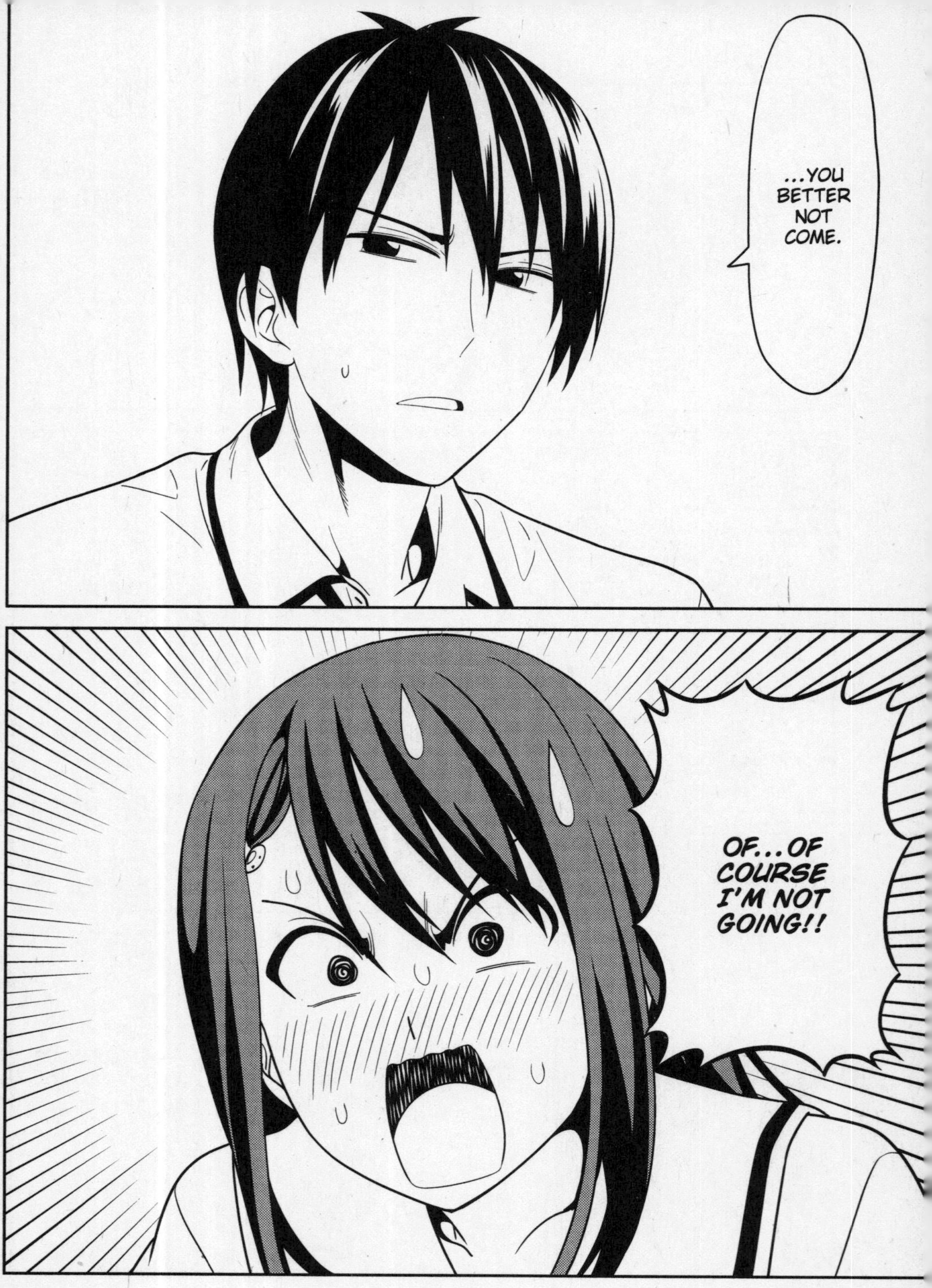
...YOU BETTER NOT COME.
OF...OF COURSE I'M NOT GOING!!

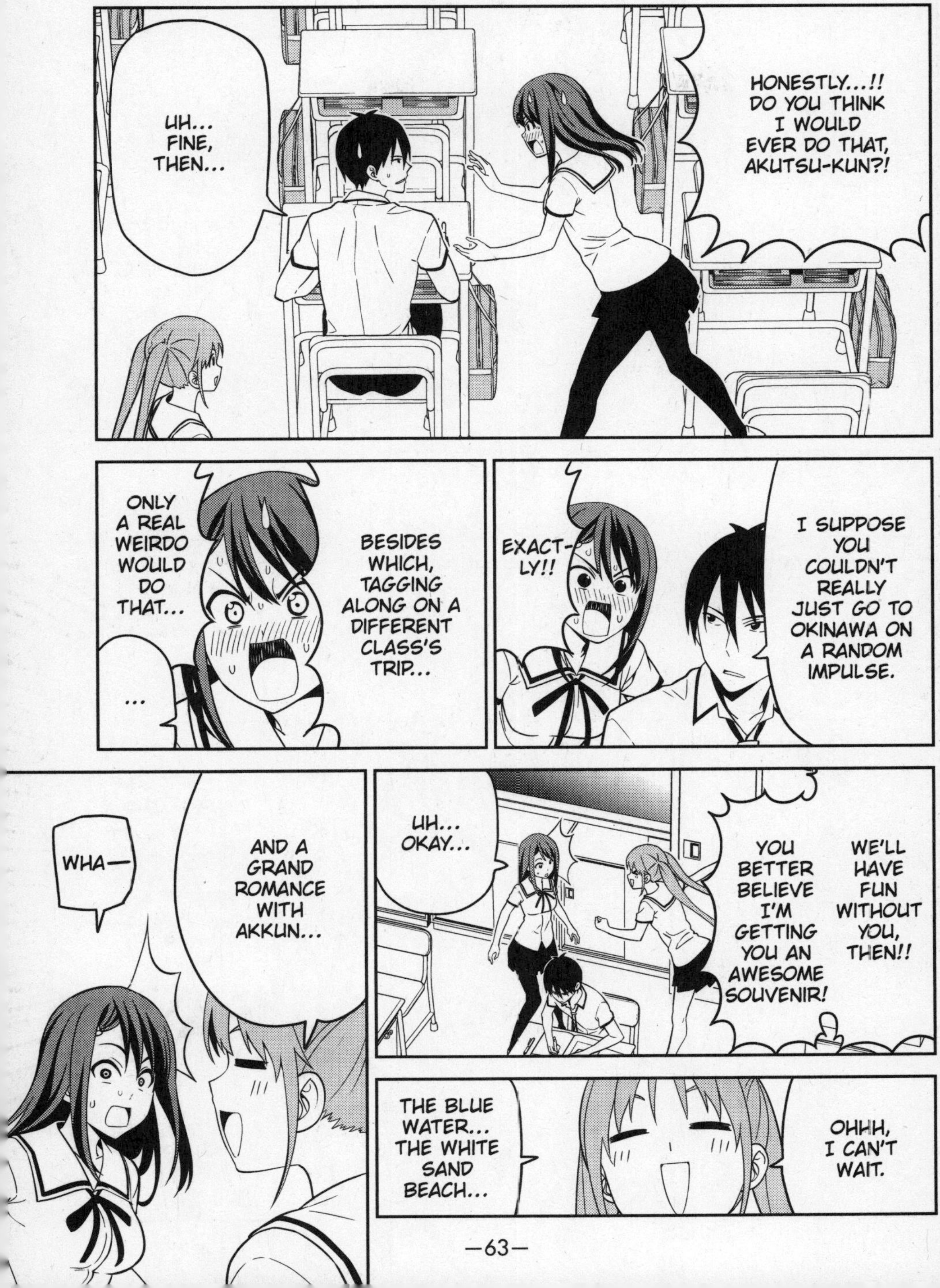
HONESTLY...!! DO YOU THINK I WOULD EVER DO THAT, AKUTSU-KUN?!
UH... FINE, THEN...
I SUPPOSE YOU COULDN'T REALLY JUST GO TO OKINAWA ON A RANDOM IMPULSE.
EXACT-LY!!
BESIDES WHICH, TAGGING ALONG ON A DIFFERENT CLASS'S TRIP...
ONLY A REAL WEIRDO WOULD DO THAT...
...
WE'LL HAVE FUN WITHOUT YOU, THEN!!
YOU BETTER BELIEVE I'M GETTING YOU AN AWESOME SOUVENIR!
UH... OKAY...
OHHH, I CAN'T WAIT.
THE BLUE WATER... THE WHITE SAND BEACH...
AND A GRAND ROMANCE WITH AKKUN...
WHA—

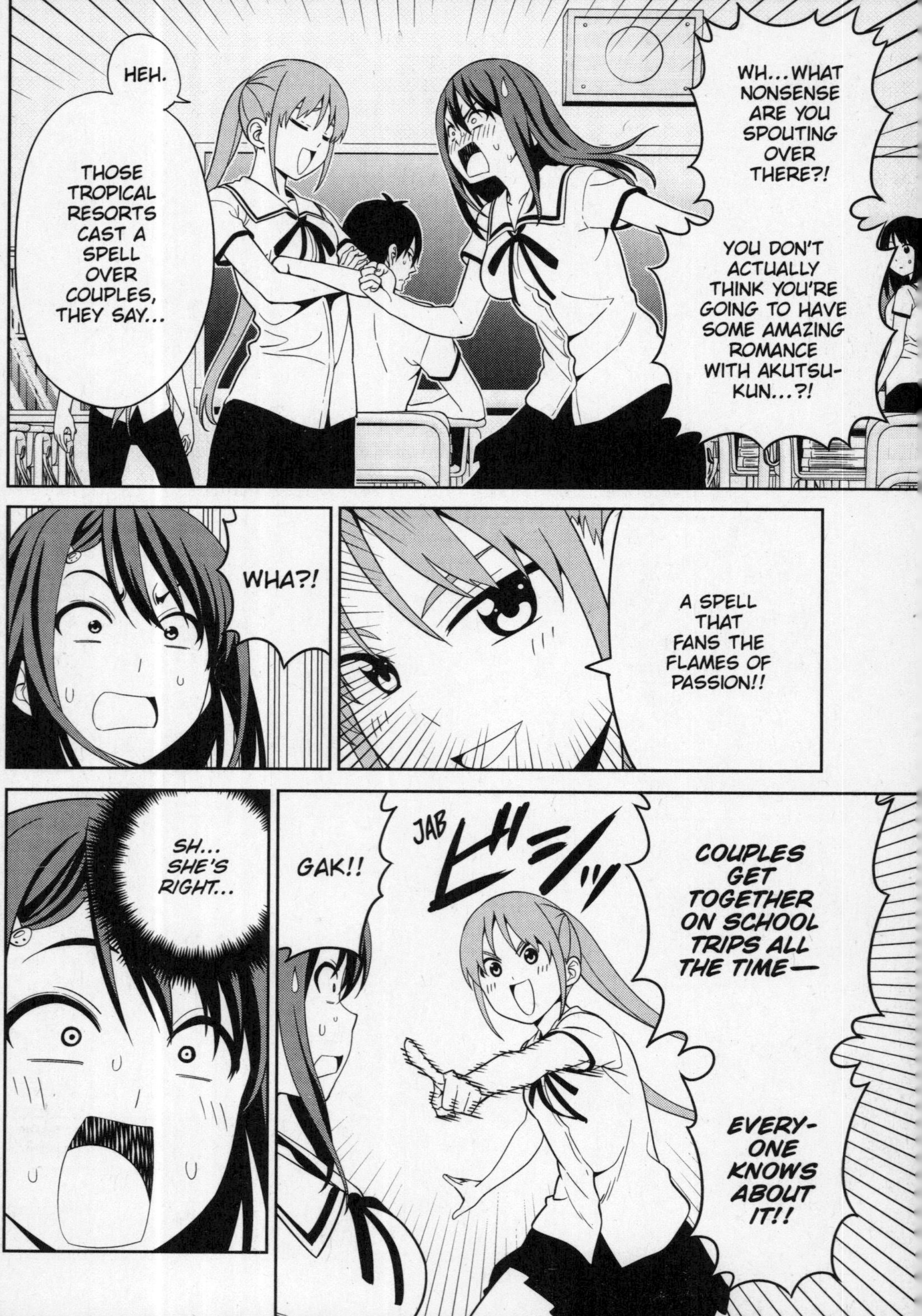
WH...WHAT NONSENSE ARE YOU SPOUTING OVER THERE?!
YOU DON'T ACTUALLY THINK YOU'RE GOING TO HAVE SOME AMAZING ROMANCE WITH AKUTSU-KUN...?!
HEH.
THOSE TROPICAL RESORTS CAST A SPELL OVER COUPLES, THEY SAY...
A SPELL THAT FANS THE FLAMES OF PASSION!!
WHA?!
COUPLES GET TOGETHER ON SCHOOL TRIPS ALL THE TIME—
EVERY-ONE KNOWS ABOUT IT!!
JAB
GAK!!
SH... SHE'S RIGHT...

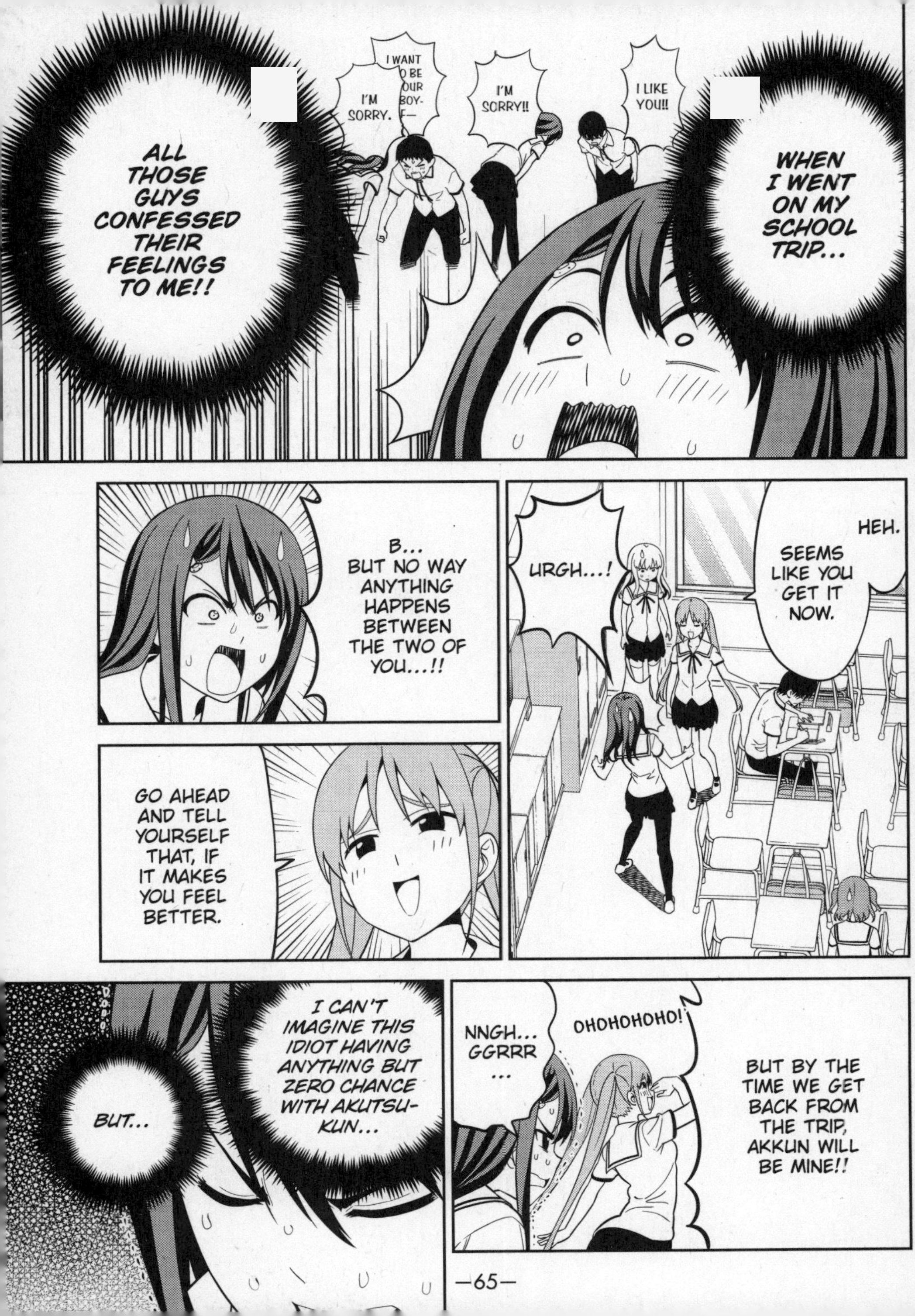
WHEN I WENT ON MY SCHOOL TRIP...
I LIKE YOU!!
I'M SORRY!!
I WANT O BE OUR BOY- F—
I'M SORRY.
ALL THOSE GUYS CONFESSED THEIR FEELINGS TO ME!!
HEH.
SEEMS LIKE YOU GET IT NOW.
URGH...!
B... BUT NO WAY ANYTHING HAPPENS BETWEEN THE TWO OF YOU...!!
GO AHEAD AND TELL YOURSELF THAT, IF IT MAKES YOU FEEL BETTER.
OHOHOHOHO!
BUT BY THE TIME WE GET BACK FROM THE TRIP, AKKUN WILL BE MINE!!
NNGH... GGRRR ...
I CAN'T IMAGINE THIS IDIOT HAVING ANYTHING BUT ZERO CHANCE WITH AKUTSU-KUN...
BUT...

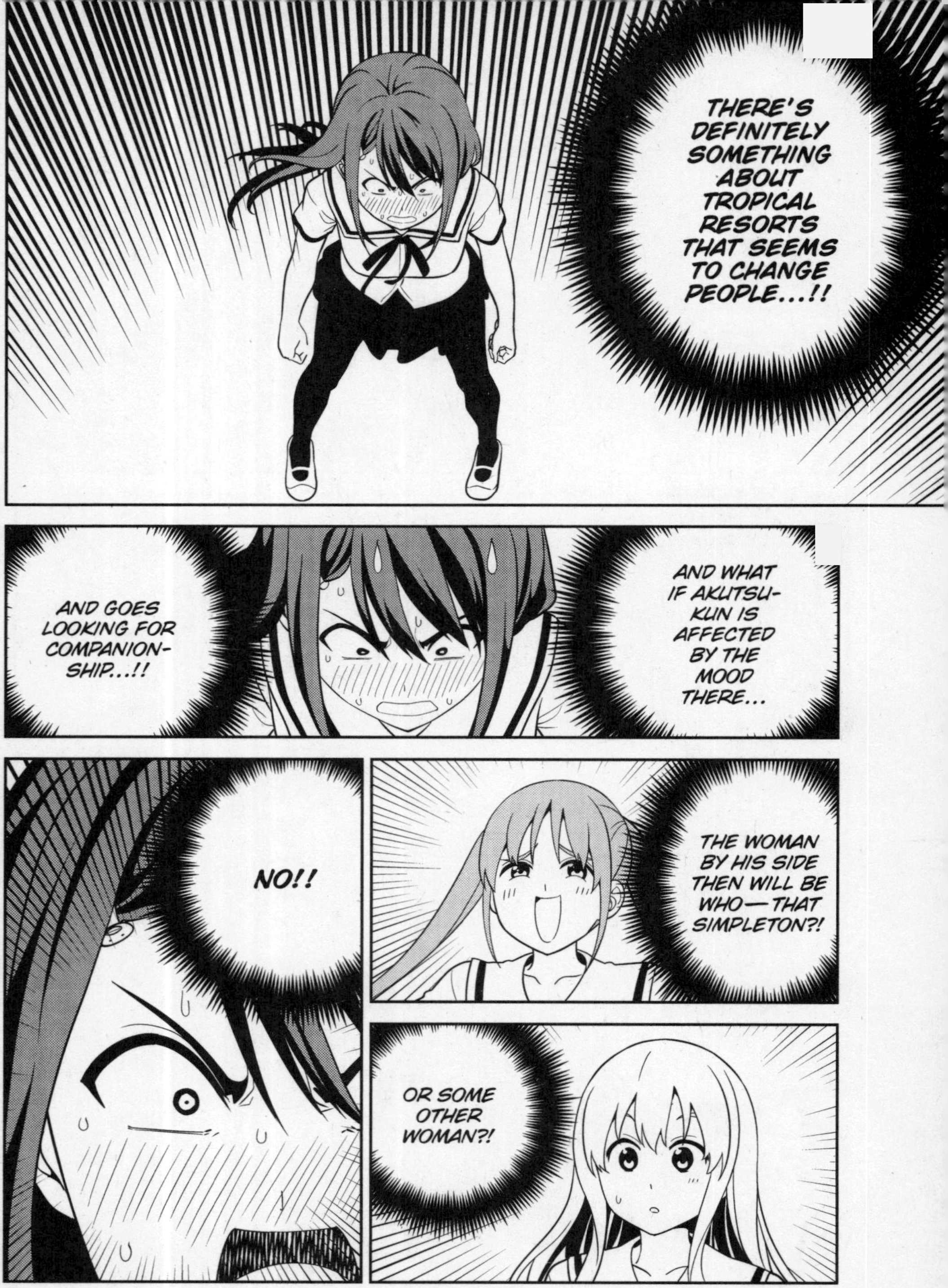
THERE'S DEFINITELY SOMETHING ABOUT TROPICAL RESORTS THAT SEEMS TO CHANGE PEOPLE...!!
AND WHAT IF AKUTSU-KUN IS AFFECTED BY THE MOOD THERE...
AND GOES LOOKING FOR COMPANION-SHIP...!!
THE WOMAN BY HIS SIDE THEN WILL BE WHO—THAT SIMPLETON?!
OR SOME OTHER WOMAN?!
NO!!

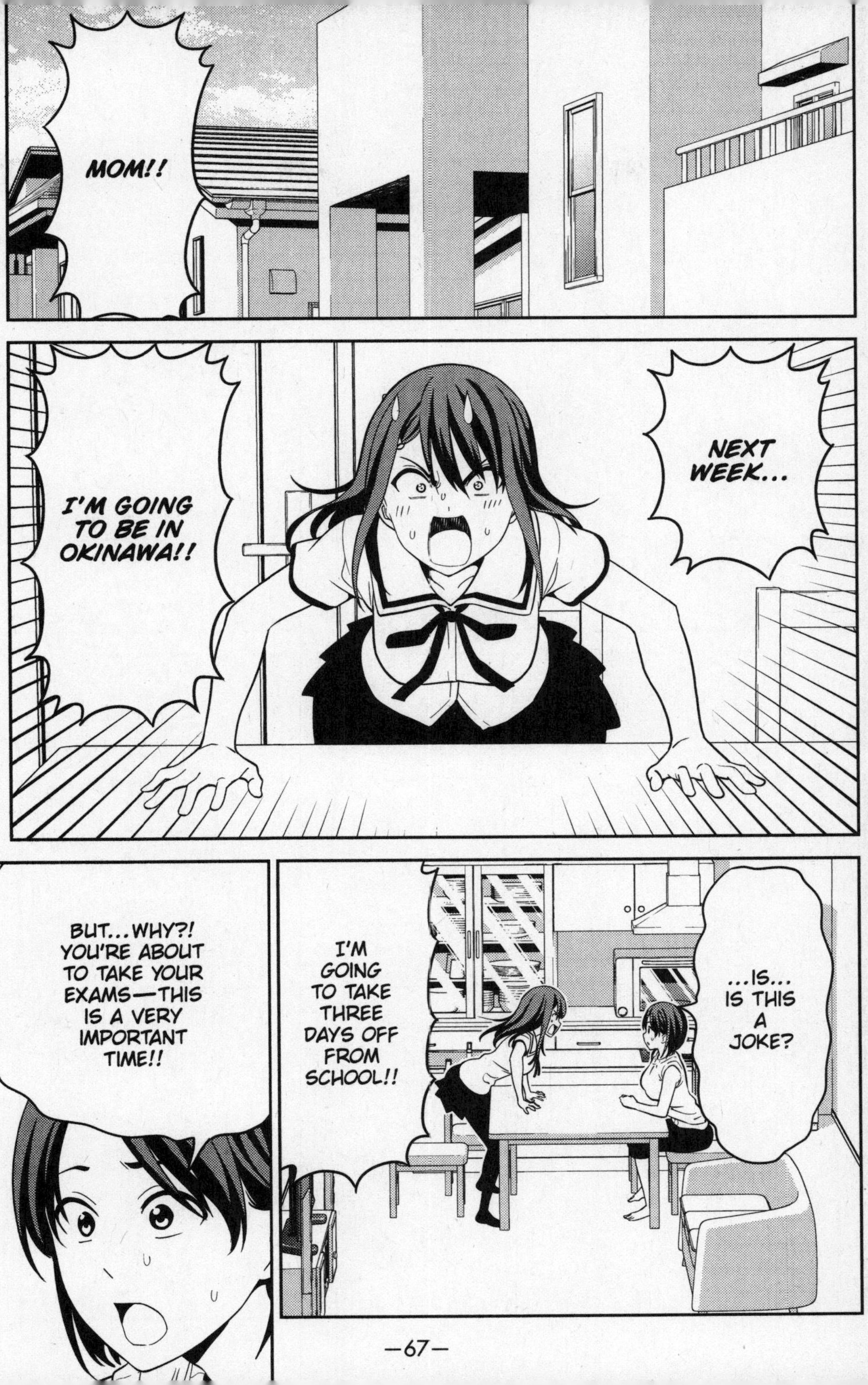
MOM!!
NEXT WEEK...
I'M GOING TO BE IN OKINAWA!!
...IS... IS THIS A JOKE?
I'M GOING TO TAKE THREE DAYS OFF FROM SCHOOL!!
BUT...WHY?! YOU'RE ABOUT TO TAKE YOUR EXAMS—THIS IS A VERY IMPORTANT TIME!!

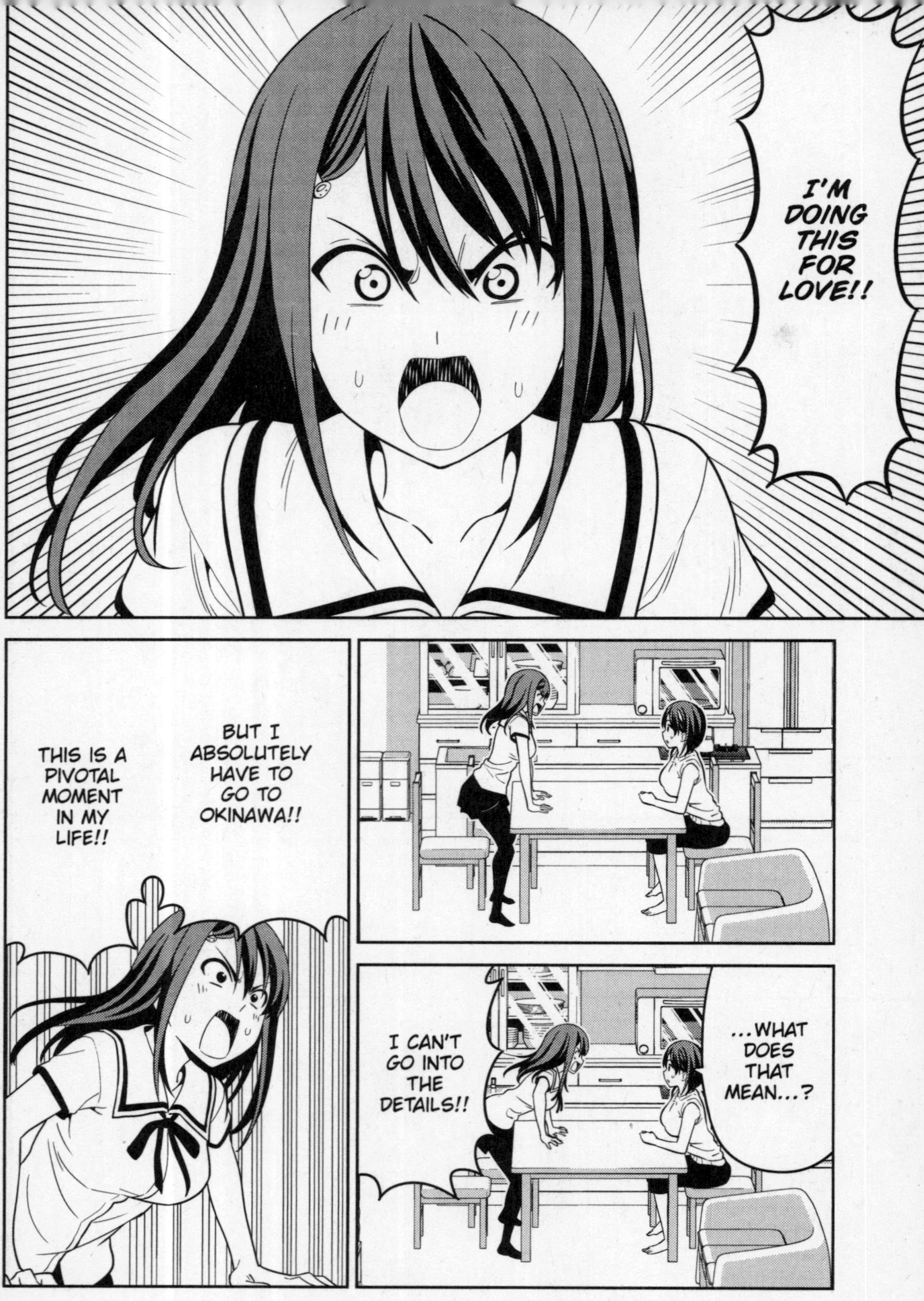
I'M DOING THIS FOR LOVE!!
...WHAT DOES THAT MEAN...?
I CAN'T GO INTO THE DETAILS!!
BUT I ABSOLUTELY HAVE TO GO TO OKINAWA!!
THIS IS A PIVOTAL MOMENT IN MY LIFE!!

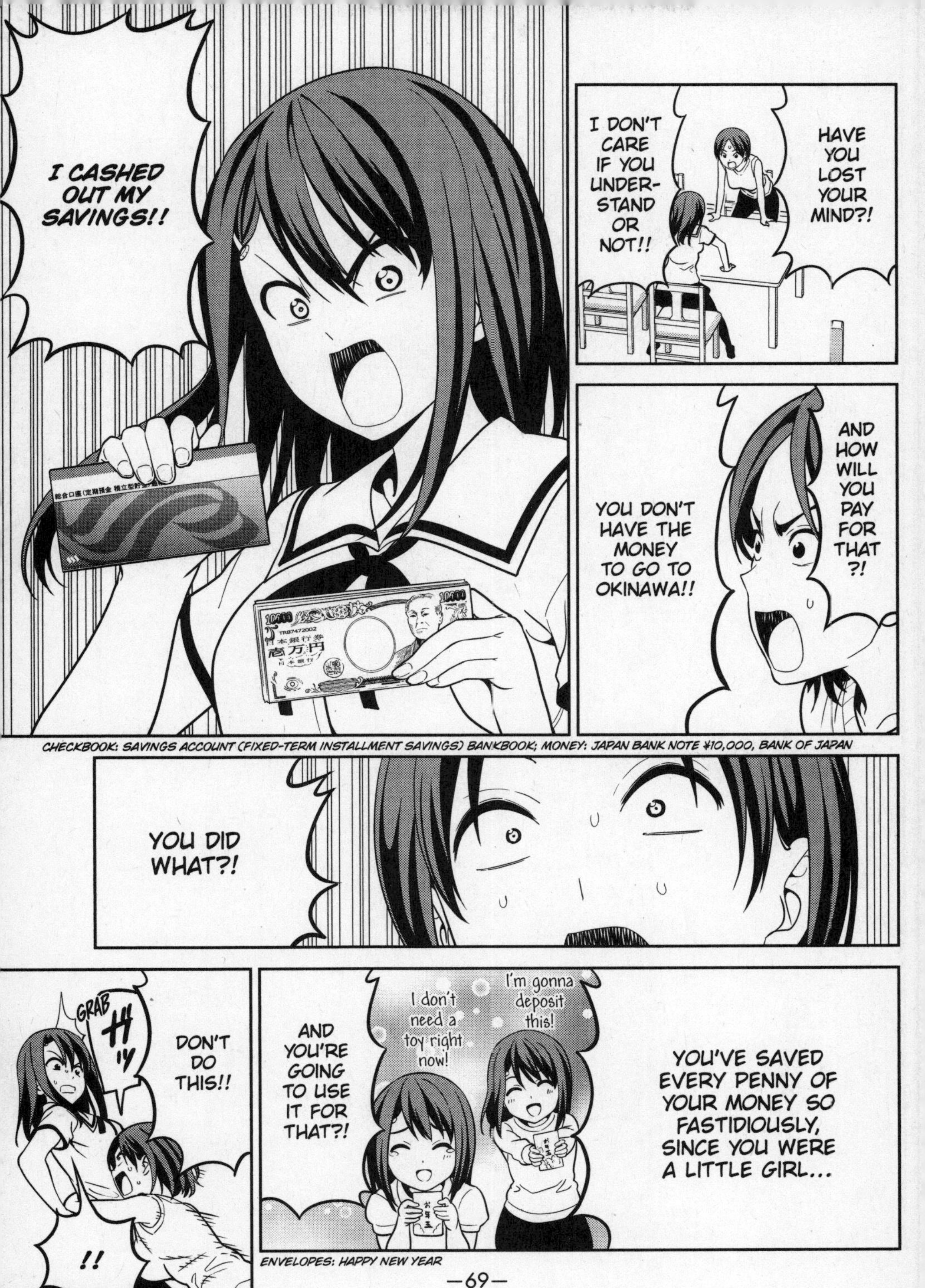
HAVE YOU LOST YOUR MIND?!
I DON'T CARE IF YOU UNDER-STAND OR NOT!!
AND HOW WILL YOU PAY FOR THAT?!
YOU DON'T HAVE THE MONEY TO GO TO OKINAWA!!
I CASHED OUT MY SAVINGS!!
YOU DID WHAT?!
YOU'VE SAVED EVERY PENNY OF YOUR MONEY SO FASTIDIOUSLY, SINCE YOU WERE A LITTLE GIRL...
I'm gonna deposit this!
I don't need a toy right now!
AND YOU'RE GOING TO USE IT FOR THAT?!
DON'T DO THIS!!
GRAB
ガッ
!!
CHECKBOOK: SAVINGS ACCOUNT (FIXED-TERM INSTALLMENT SAVINGS) BANKBOOK; MONEY: JAPAN BANK NOTE ¥10,000, BANK OF JAPAN

ENVELOPES: HAPPY NEW YEAR

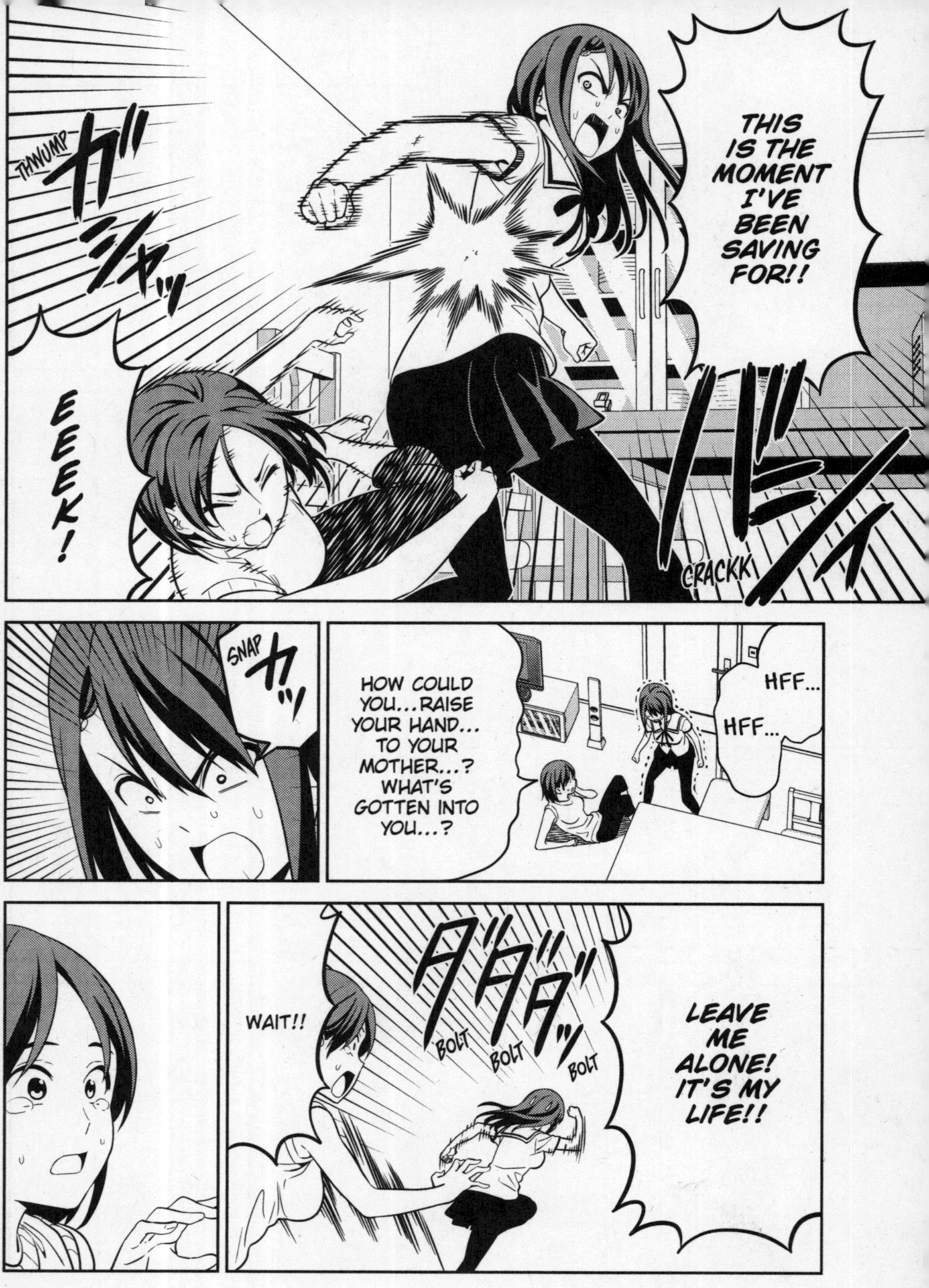
THIS IS THE MOMENT I'VE BEEN SAVING FOR!!
ドシィ
CRACKK
THWUMP
ガシャッ
EEEEK!
HFF... HFF...
HOW COULD YOU...RAISE YOUR HAND... TO YOUR MOTHER...? WHAT'S GOTTEN INTO YOU...?
SNAP
カッ
LEAVE ME ALONE! IT'S MY LIFE!!
ダダダッ
BOLT BOLT BOLT
WAIT!!

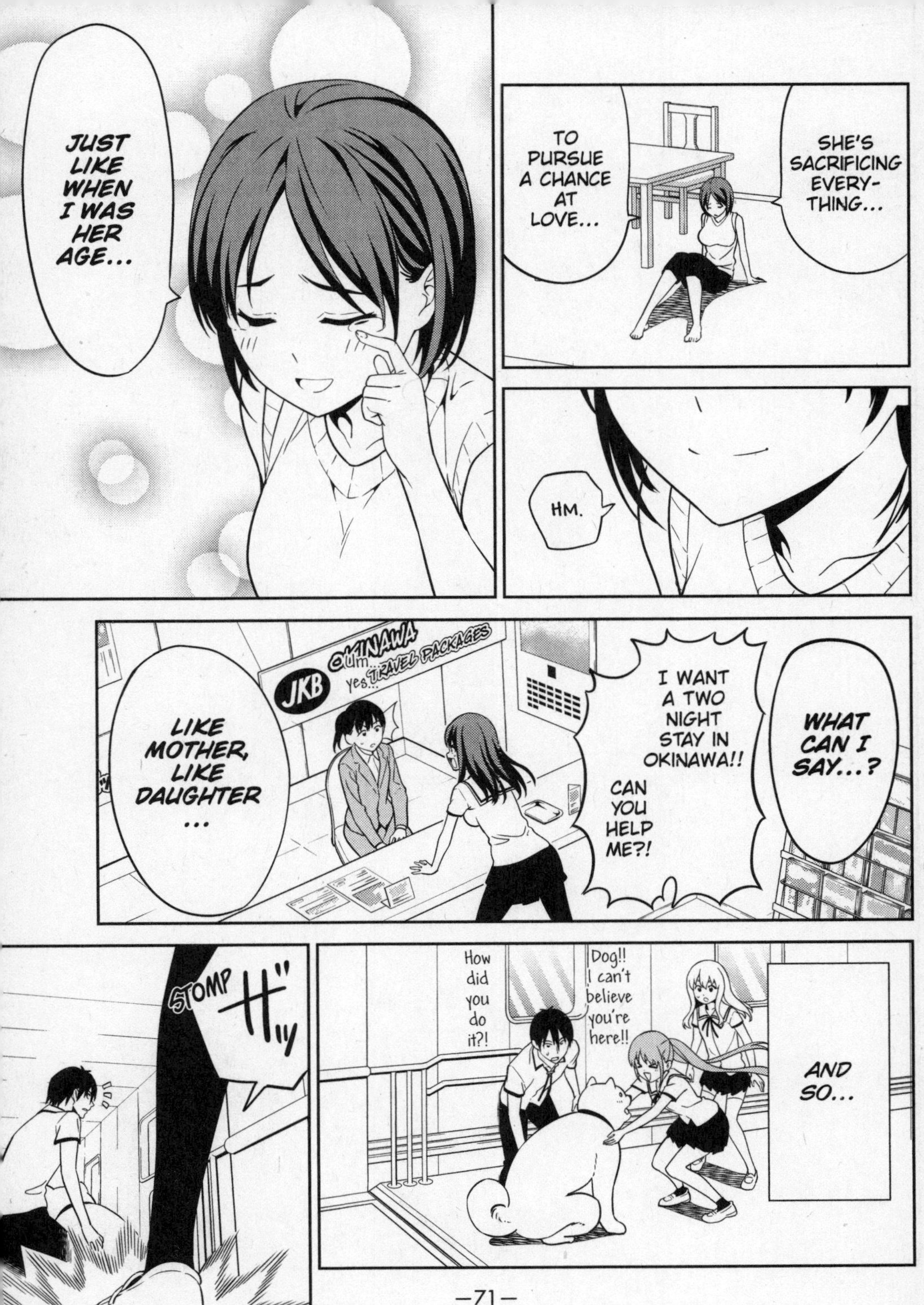
SHE'S SACRIFICING EVERYTHING...
TO PURSUE A CHANCE AT LOVE...
HM.
JUST LIKE WHEN I WAS HER AGE...
WHAT CAN I SAY...?
I WANT A TWO NIGHT STAY IN OKINAWA!!
CAN YOU HELP ME?!
OKINAWA TRAVEL PACKAGES
JKB
Um... yes...
LIKE MOTHER, LIKE DAUGHTER...
AND SO...
Dog!! I can't believe you're here!!
How did you do it?!
STOMP

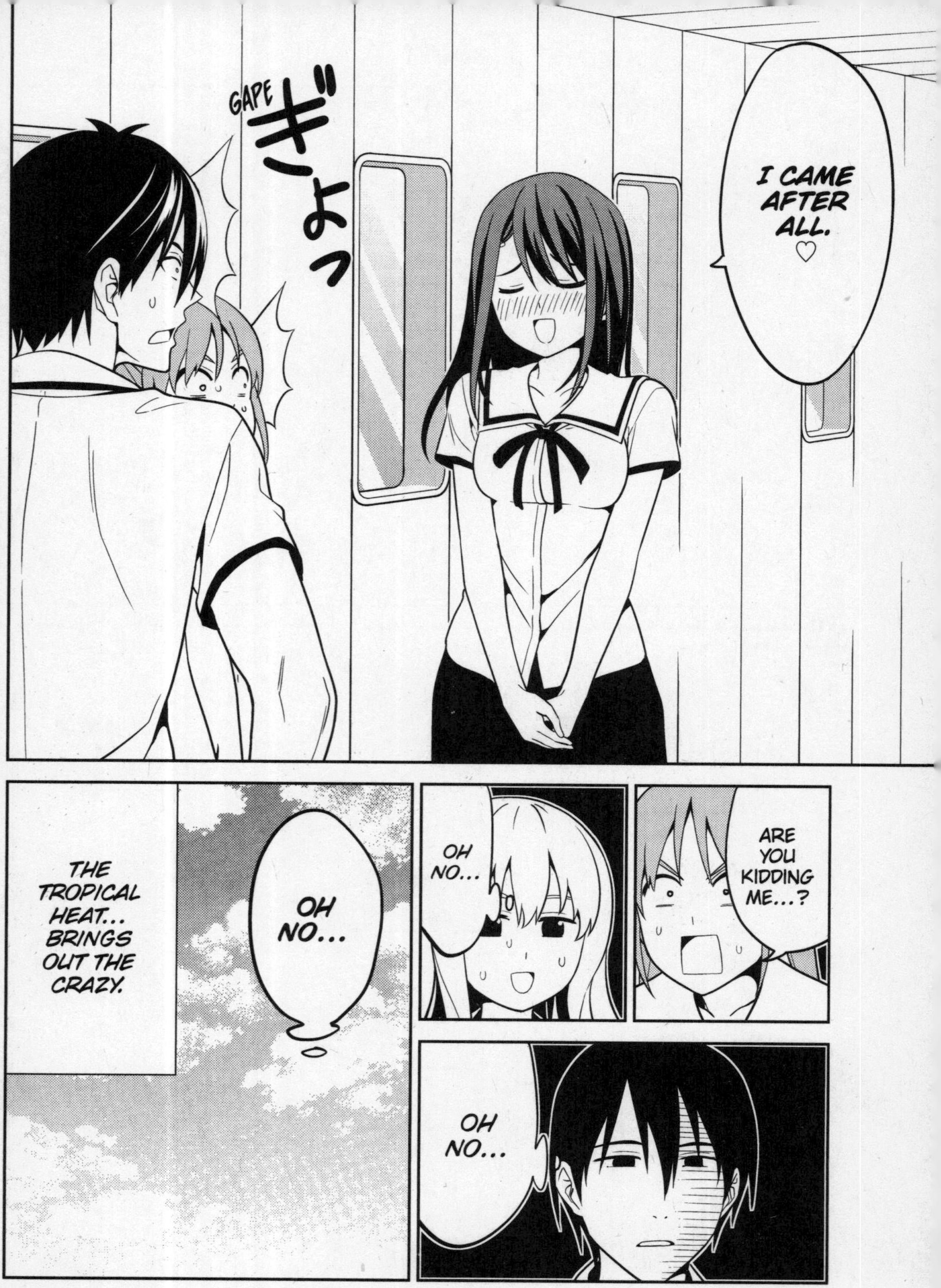
I CAME AFTER ALL. ♡
GAPE
ぎょっ
ARE YOU KIDDING ME...?
OH NO...
OH NO...
OH NO...
THE TROPICAL HEAT... BRINGS OUT THE CRAZY.

You Really Need to Come up with Something Before You Get There

UH... ABOUT THAT!!

I, UHH ...

NO, SERIOUSLY. WHAT ARE YOU DOING HERE...?

...I CAME... TO... ENFORCE THE SCHOOL'S CODE OF CONDUCT ...

WHAT AN IDIOT.

(We're messing around too much; we're children of summer)

Aho-Girl

\ˈahôˌɡərl\ *Japanese, noun.*
A clueless girl.

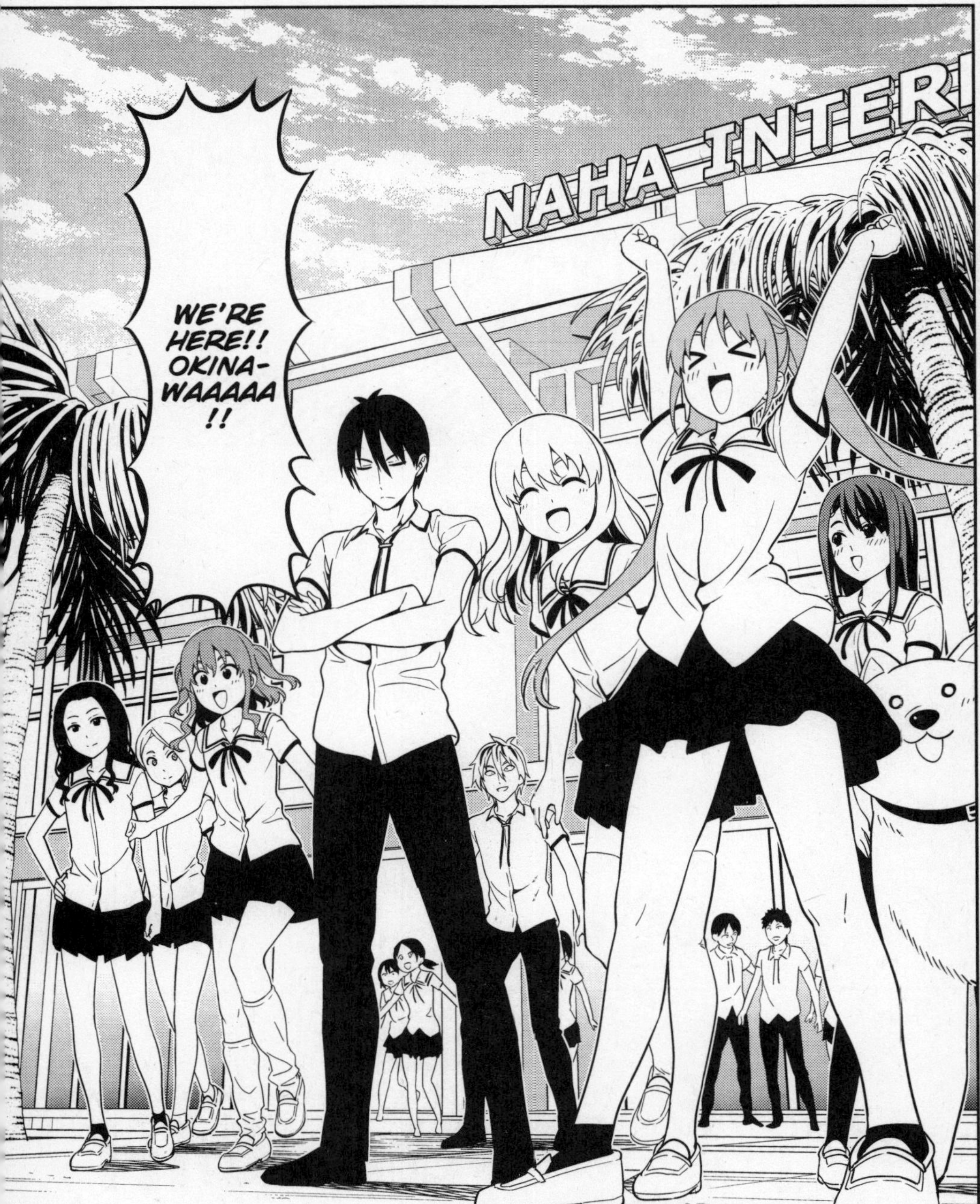
NAHA INTERI
WE'RE HERE!! OKINA-WAAAAAA!!

School Trip Chapter 6

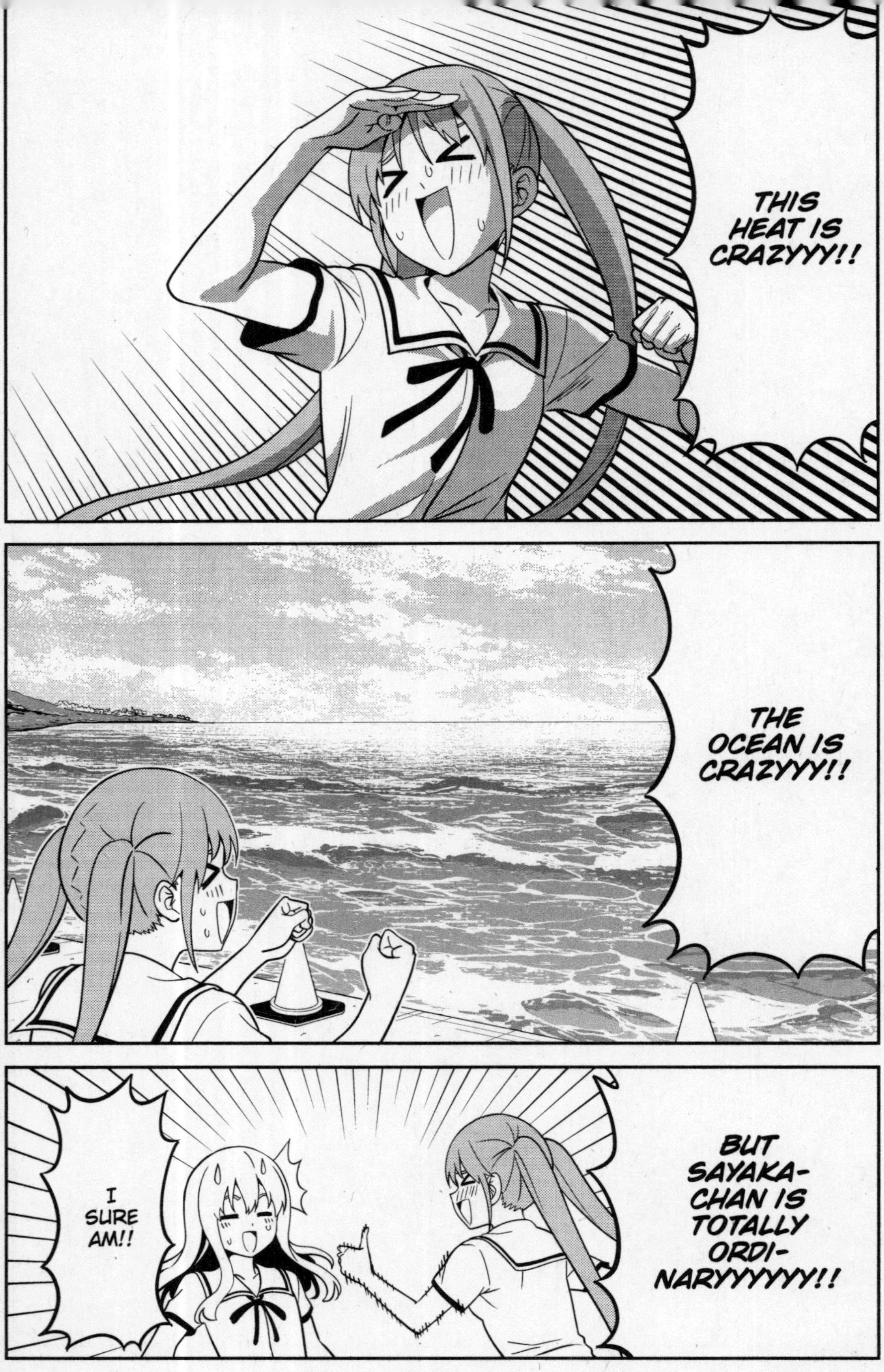
THIS HEAT IS CRAZYYY!!
THE OCEAN IS CRAZYYY!!
BUT SAYAKA-CHAN IS TOTALLY ORDI-NARYYYYYYY!!
I SURE AM!!

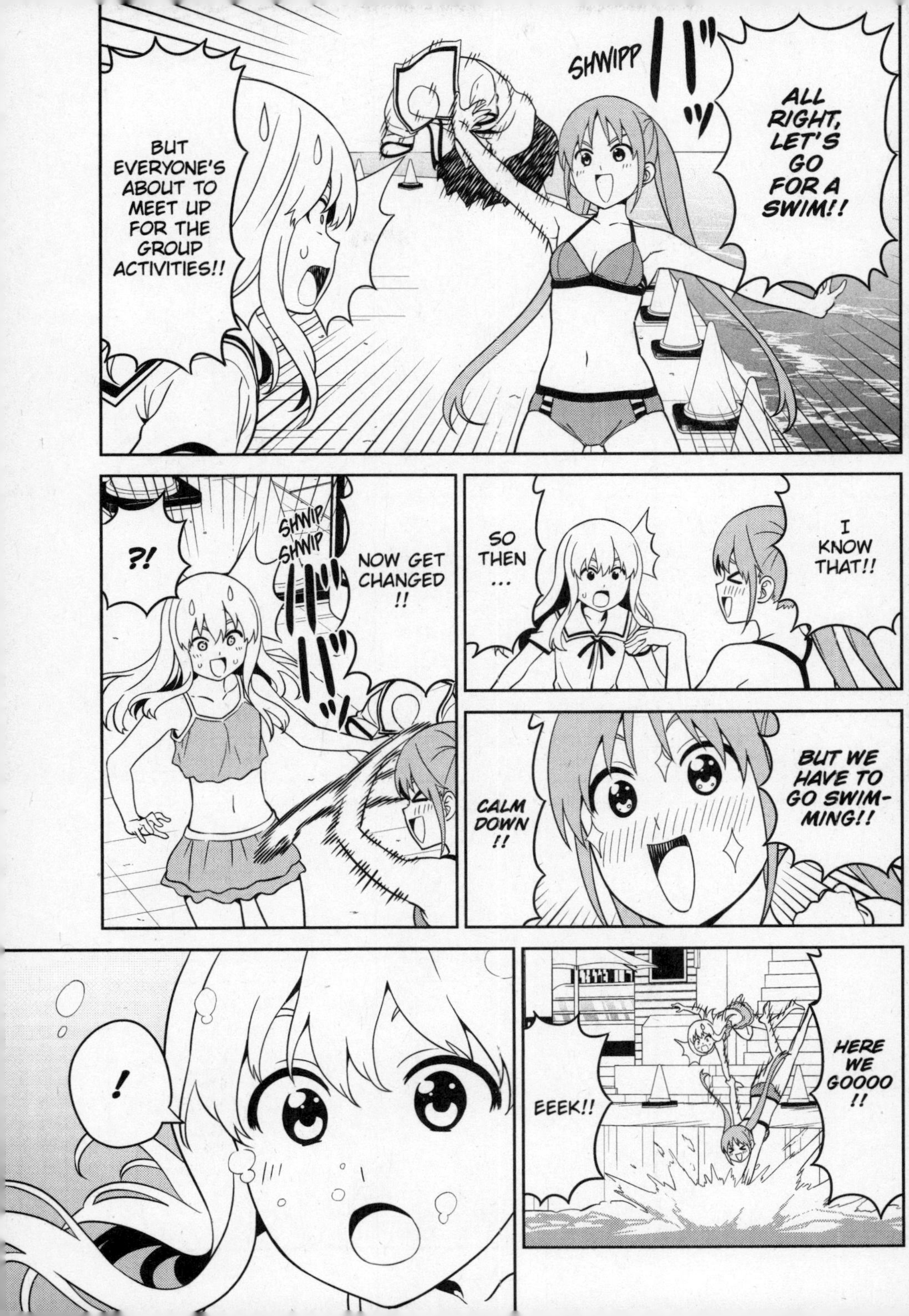
SHWIPP
ALL RIGHT, LET'S GO FOR A SWIM!!
BUT EVERYONE'S ABOUT TO MEET UP FOR THE GROUP ACTIVITIES!!
I KNOW THAT!!
SO THEN ...
BUT WE HAVE TO GO SWIMMING!!
CALM DOWN!!
SHWIP SHWIP
NOW GET CHANGED!!
?!
HERE WE GOOOO!!
EEEK!!
!

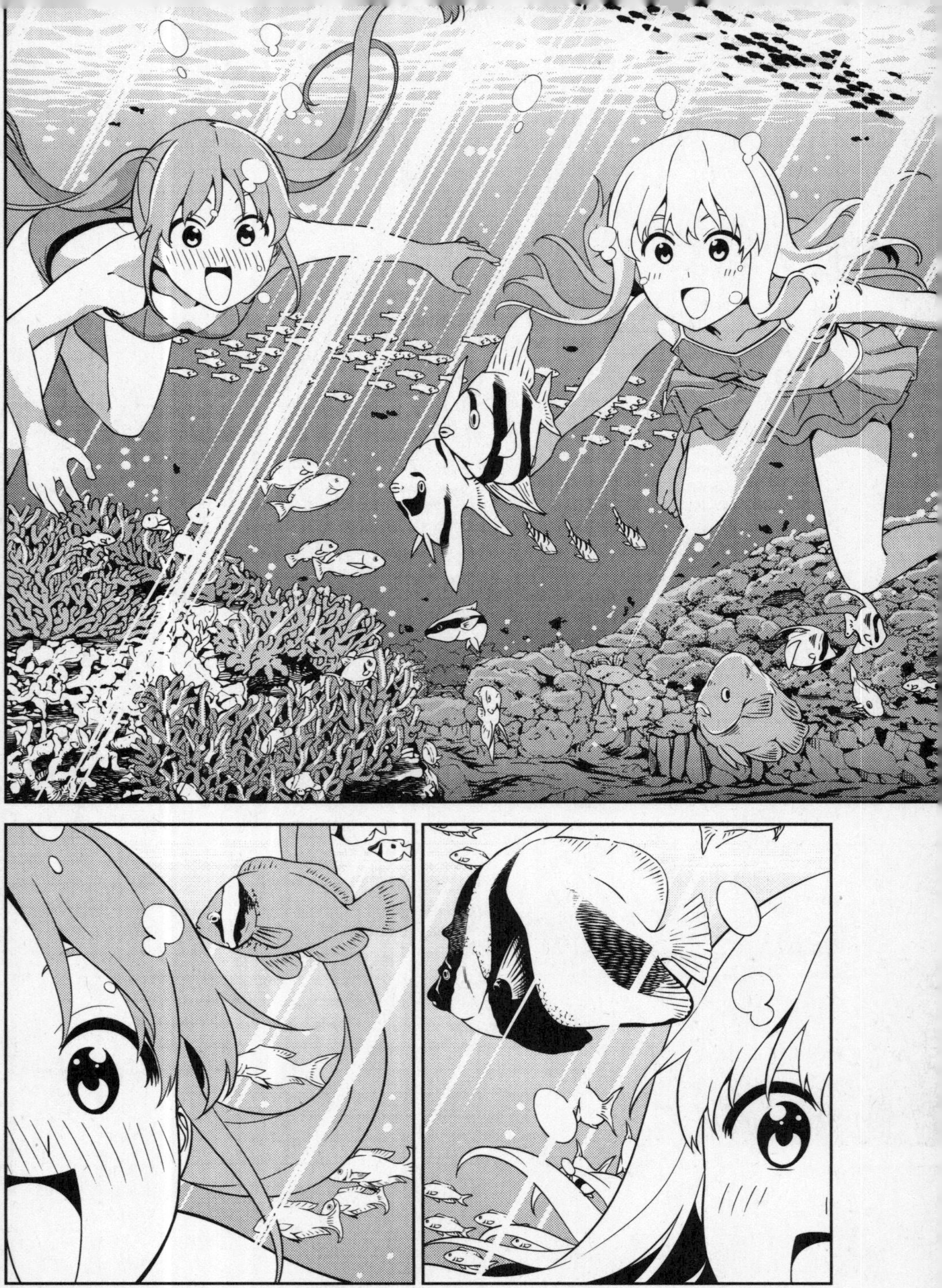

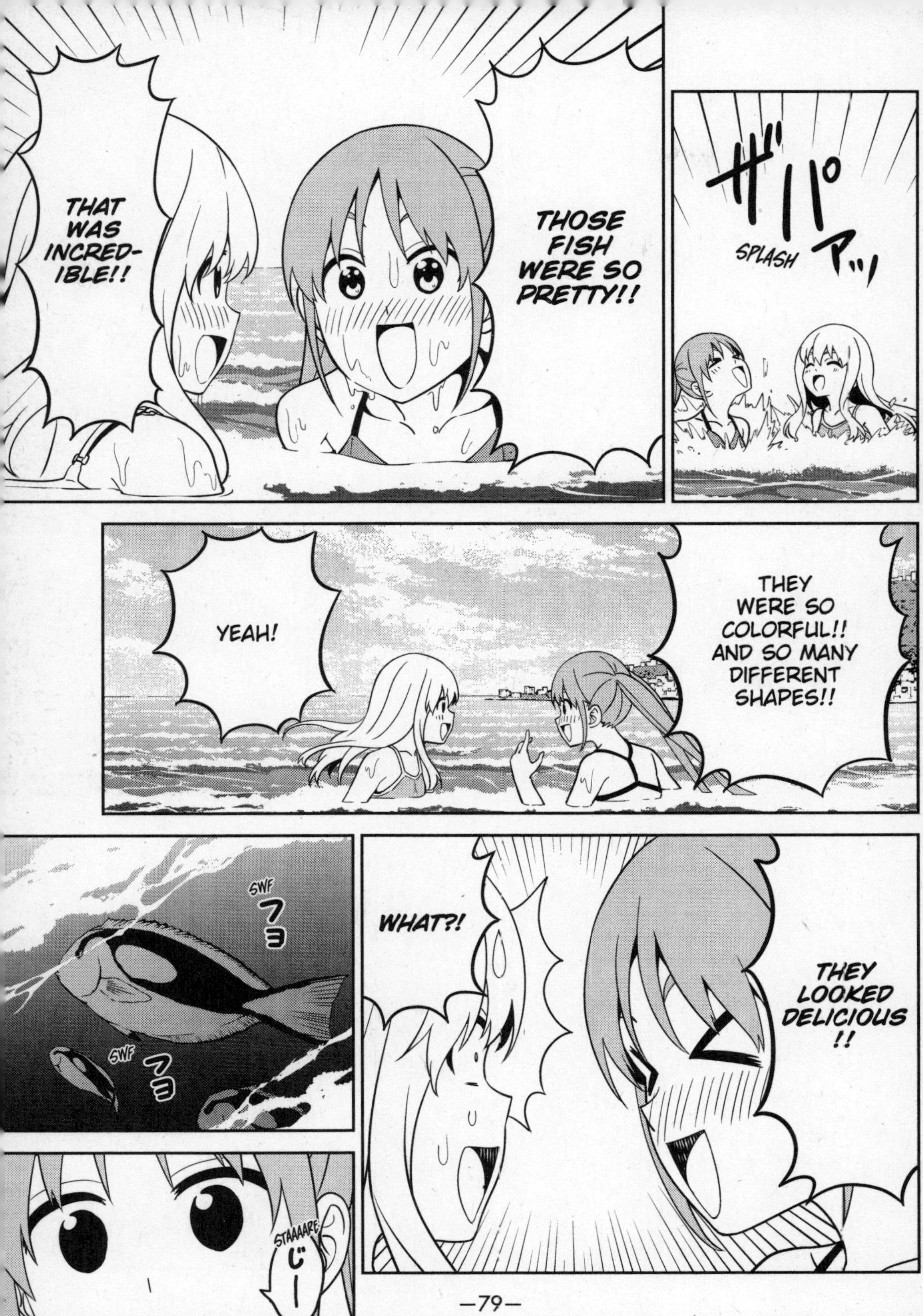
SPLASH
ザパァッ
THOSE FISH WERE SO PRETTY!!
THAT WAS INCREDIBLE!!
THEY WERE SO COLORFUL!! AND SO MANY DIFFERENT SHAPES!!
YEAH!
THEY LOOKED DELICIOUS!!
WHAT?!
SWF
フヨ
SWF
フヨ
STAAAARE
じーー

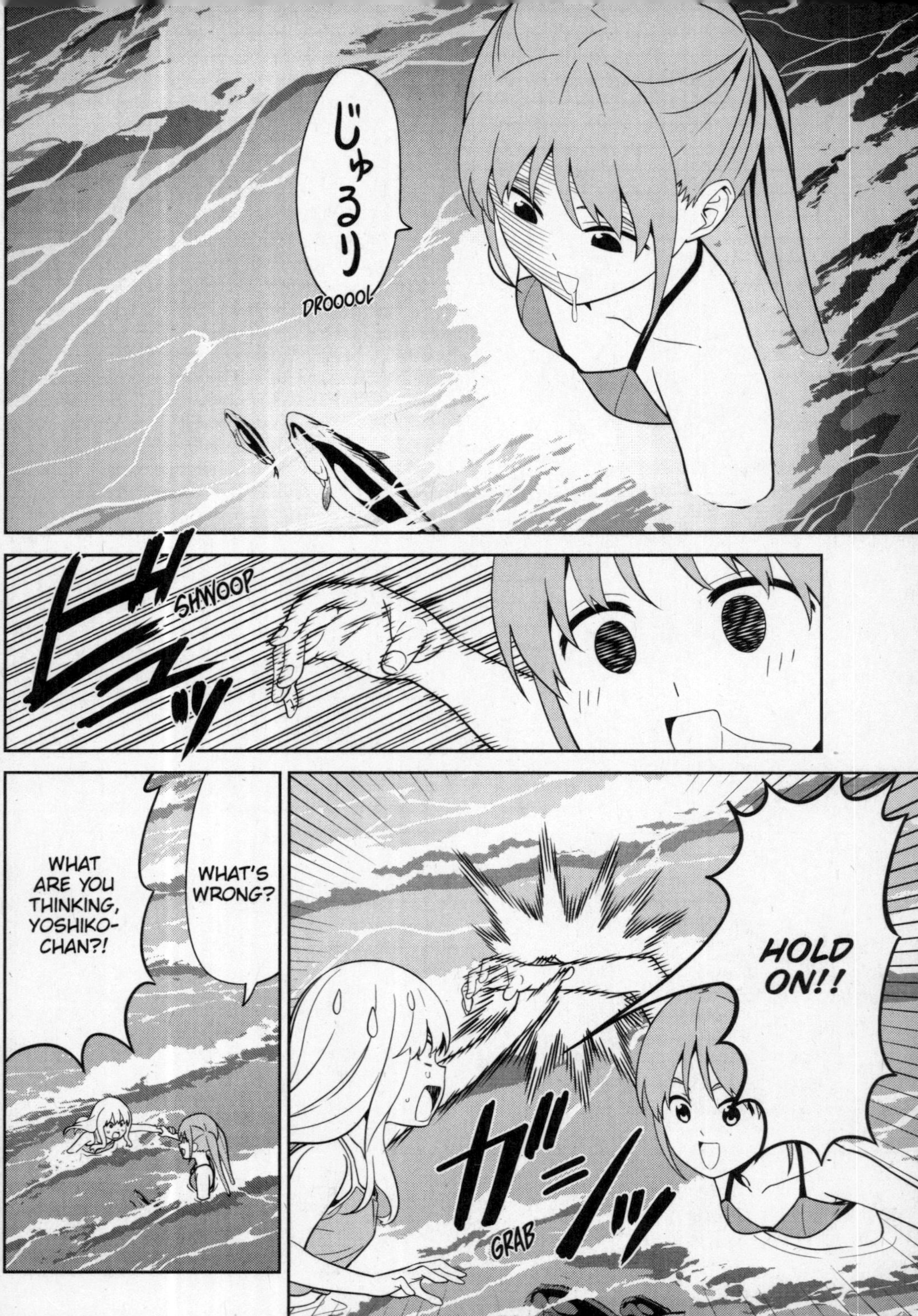
じゅるり
DROOOOL
ビュッ
SHWOOP
HOLD ON!!
ガシッ
GRAB
WHAT'S WRONG?
WHAT ARE YOU THINKING, YOSHIKO-CHAN?!

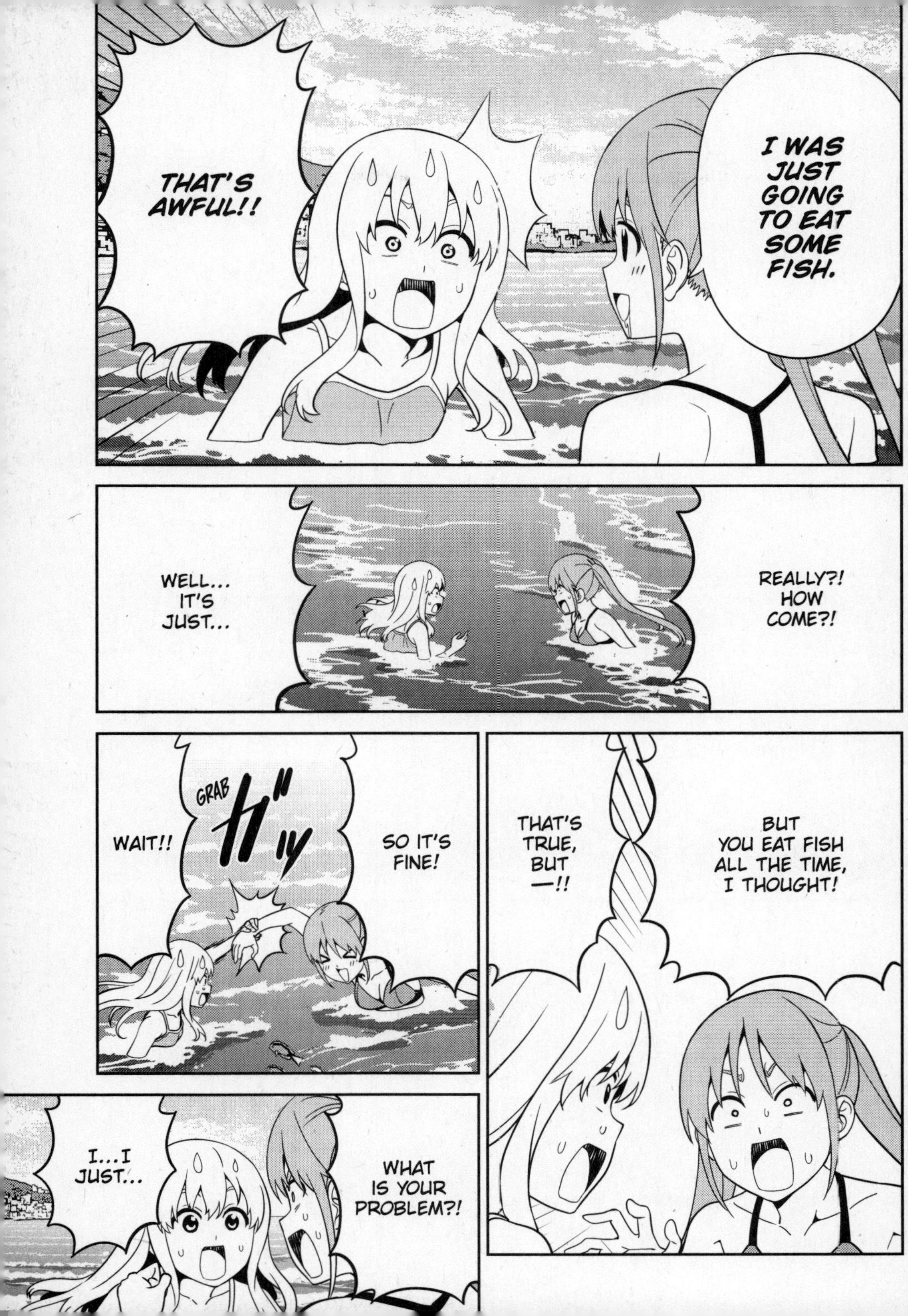

I WAS JUST GOING TO EAT SOME FISH.
THAT'S AWFUL!!
REALLY?! HOW COME?!
WELL... IT'S JUST...
BUT YOU EAT FISH ALL THE TIME, I THOUGHT!
THAT'S TRUE, BUT —!!
SO IT'S FINE!
GRAB
WAIT!!
WHAT IS YOUR PROBLEM?!
I...I JUST...

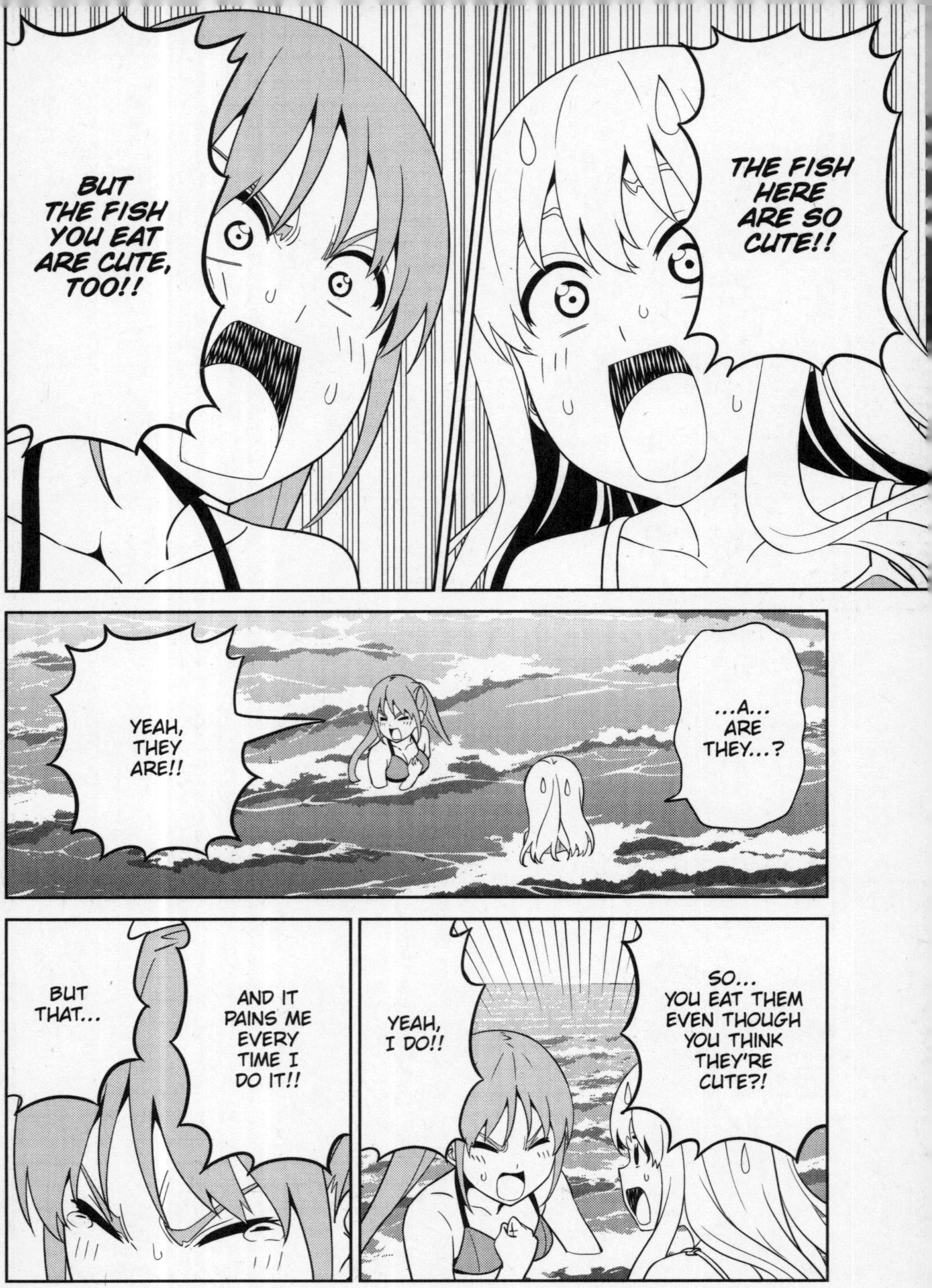
THE FISH HERE ARE SO CUTE!!
BUT THE FISH YOU EAT ARE CUTE, TOO!!
...A... ARE THEY...?
YEAH, THEY ARE!!
SO... YOU EAT THEM EVEN THOUGH YOU THINK THEY'RE CUTE?!
YEAH, I DO!!
AND IT PAINS ME EVERY TIME I DO IT!!
BUT THAT...

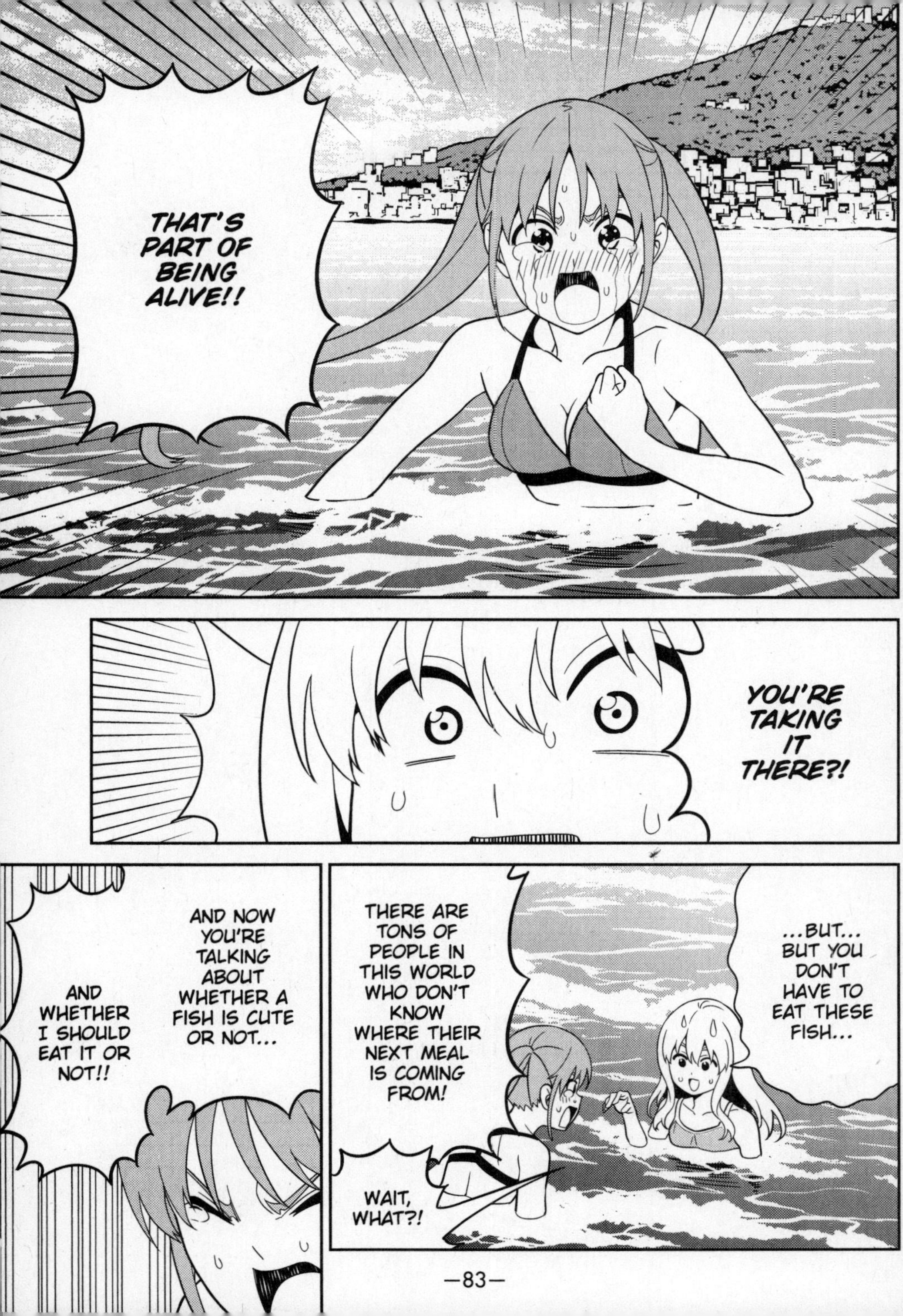
THAT'S PART OF BEING ALIVE!!
YOU'RE TAKING IT THERE?!
...BUT... BUT YOU DON'T HAVE TO EAT THESE FISH...
THERE ARE TONS OF PEOPLE IN THIS WORLD WHO DON'T KNOW WHERE THEIR NEXT MEAL IS COMING FROM!
WAIT, WHAT?!
AND NOW YOU'RE TALKING ABOUT WHETHER A FISH IS CUTE OR NOT...
AND WHETHER I SHOULD EAT IT OR NOT!!

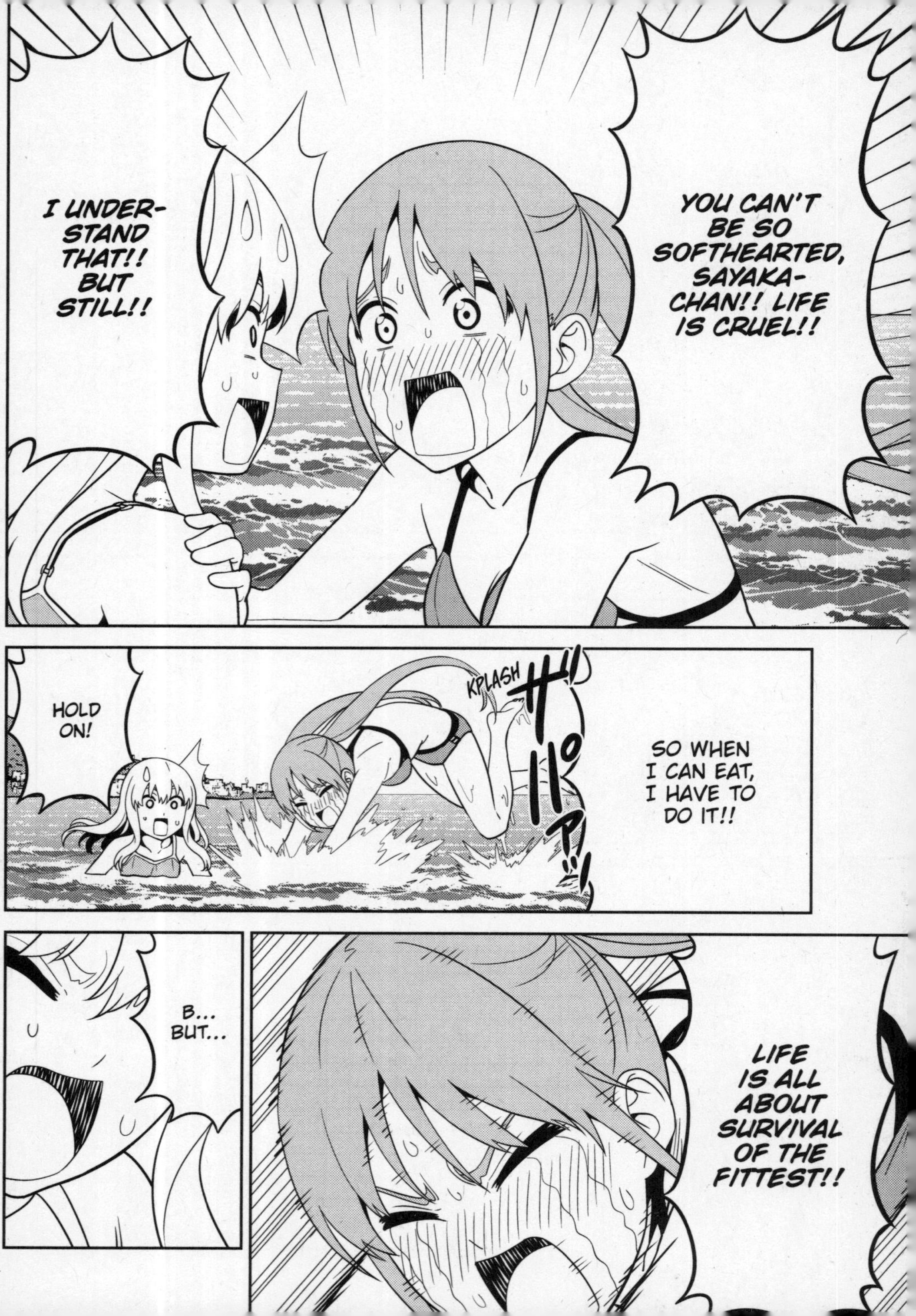
YOU CAN'T BE SO SOFTHEARTED, SAYAKA-CHAN!! LIFE IS CRUEL!!
I UNDER-STAND THAT!! BUT STILL!!
KPLASH
SO WHEN I CAN EAT, I HAVE TO DO IT!!
HOLD ON!
LIFE IS ALL ABOUT SURVIVAL OF THE FITTEST!!
B... BUT...

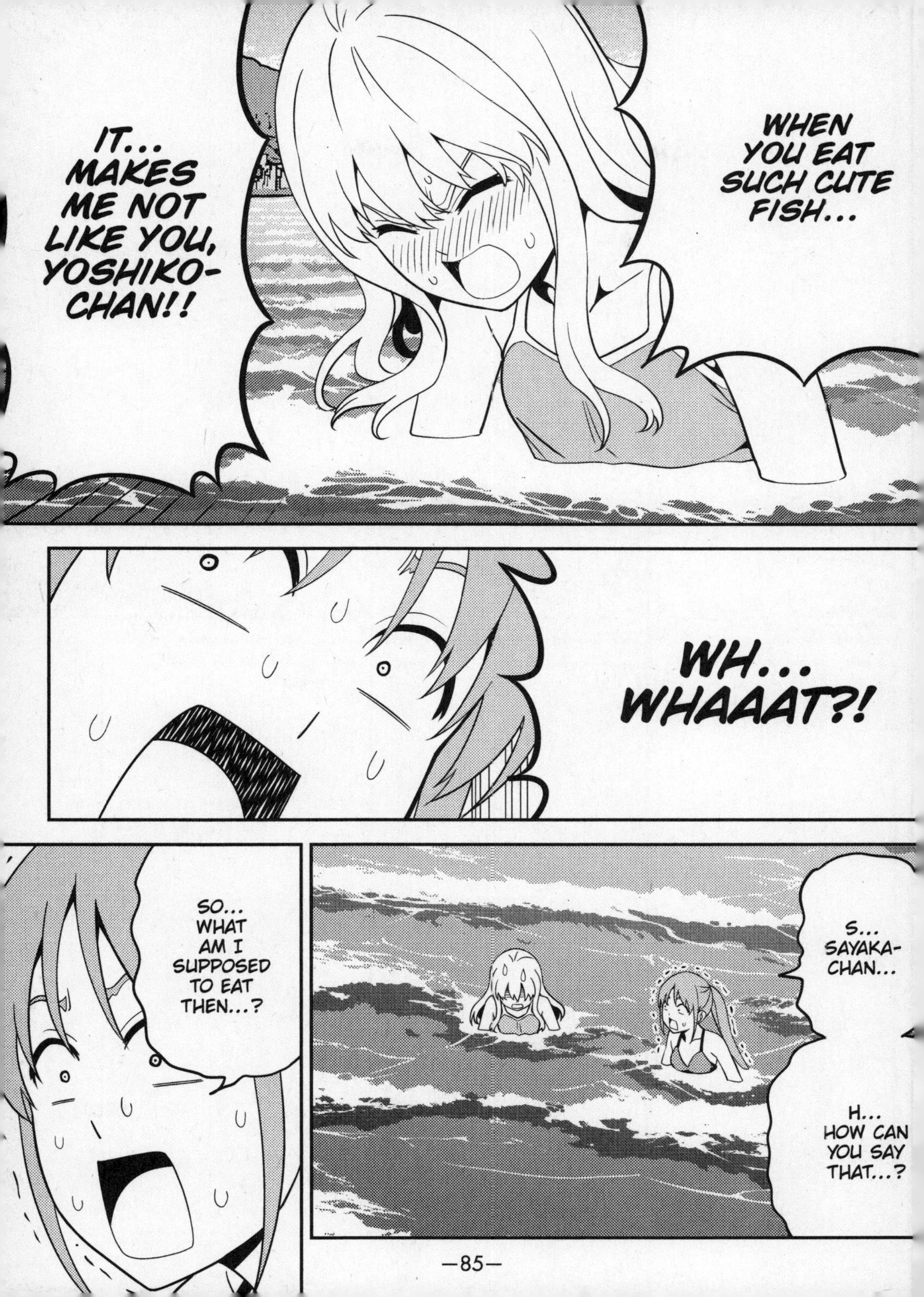
WHEN YOU EAT SUCH CUTE FISH...
IT... MAKES ME NOT LIKE YOU, YOSHIKO-CHAN!!
WH... WHAAAT?!
S... SAYAKA-CHAN...
H... HOW CAN YOU SAY THAT...?
SO... WHAT AM I SUPPOSED TO EAT THEN...?

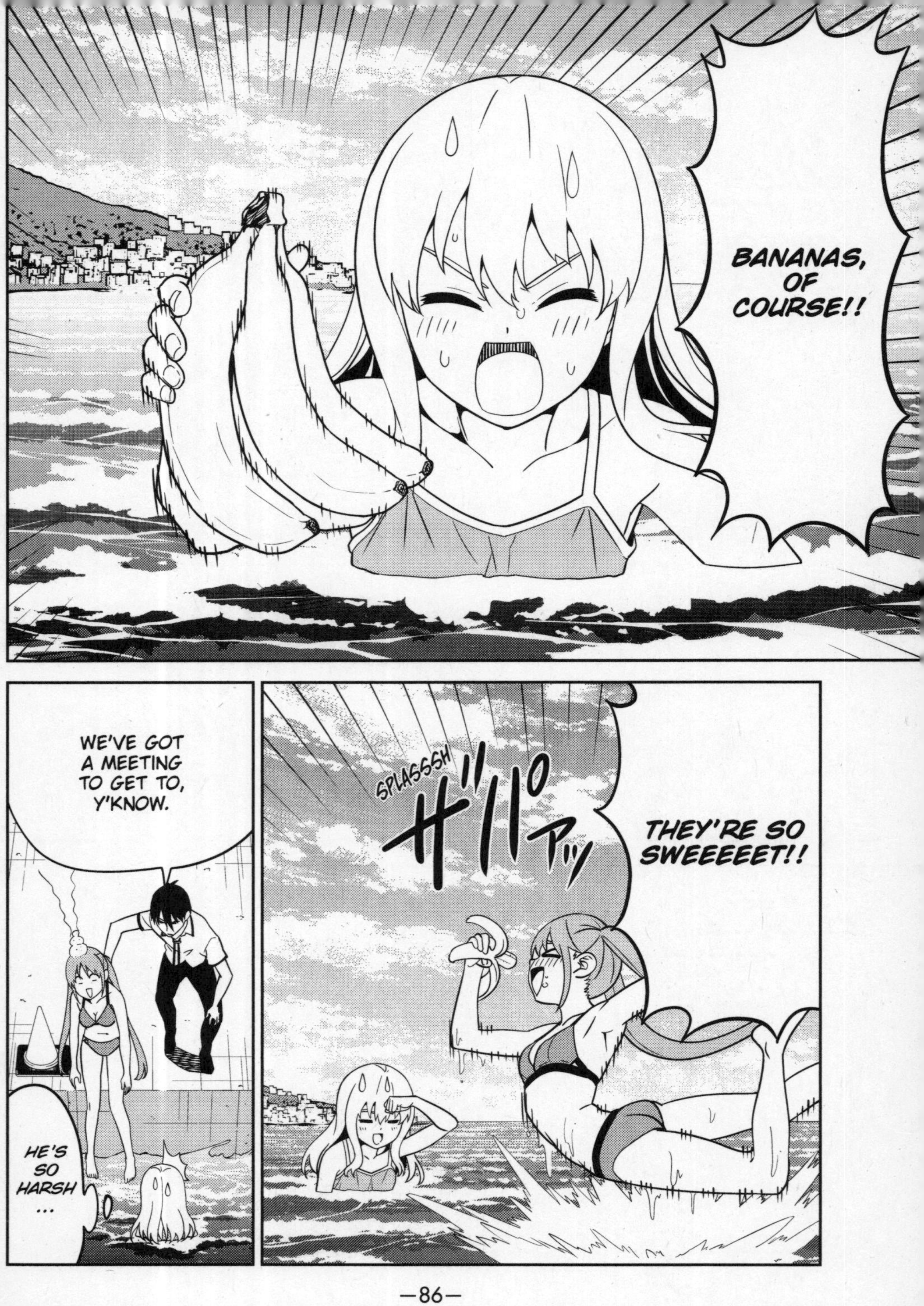
BANANAS, OF COURSE!!
SPLASSSH
ザパァッ
THEY'RE SO SWEEEEET!!
WE'VE GOT A MEETING TO GET TO, Y'KNOW.
HE'S SO HARSH ...

You Can Eat the Yummy Ones

OH, FISH... I REALLY ENJOYED EATING YOU...
I DON'T MIND IF YOU EAT REGULAR FISH.
YESSSS!!

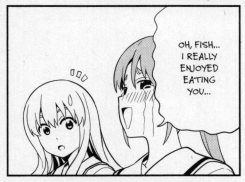

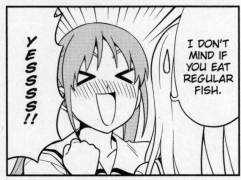

(You ever notice all those June)

Aho-Girl
\ˈahô͜ˌɡərl \ *Japanese, noun.*
A clueless girl.

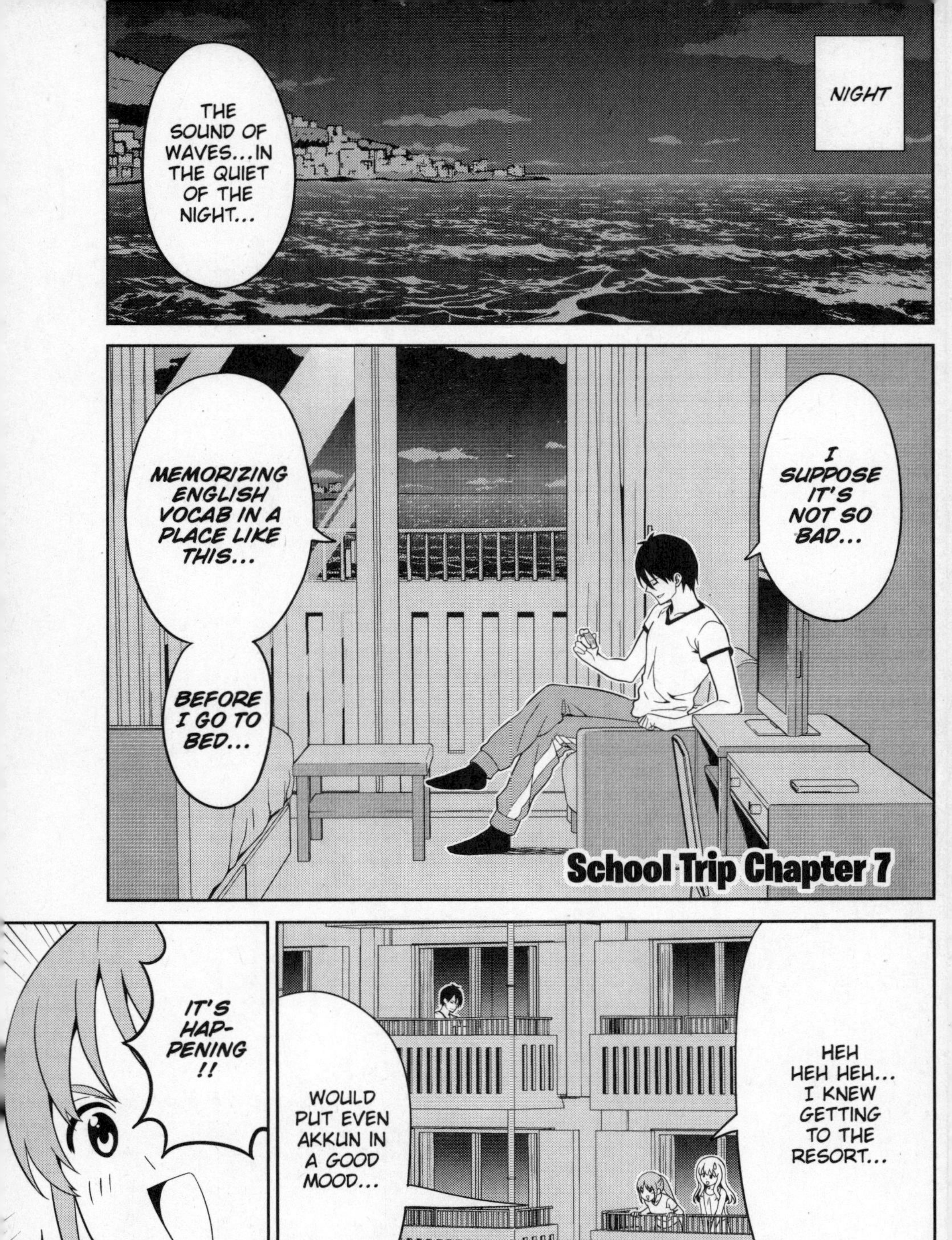
NIGHT
THE SOUND OF WAVES...IN THE QUIET OF THE NIGHT...
I SUPPOSE IT'S NOT SO BAD...
MEMORIZING ENGLISH VOCAB IN A PLACE LIKE THIS...
BEFORE I GO TO BED...
School Trip Chapter 7
HEH HEH HEH... I KNEW GETTING TO THE RESORT...
WOULD PUT EVEN AKKUN IN A GOOD MOOD...
IT'S HAP-PENING!!

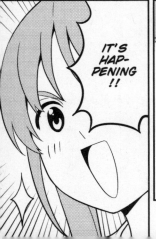

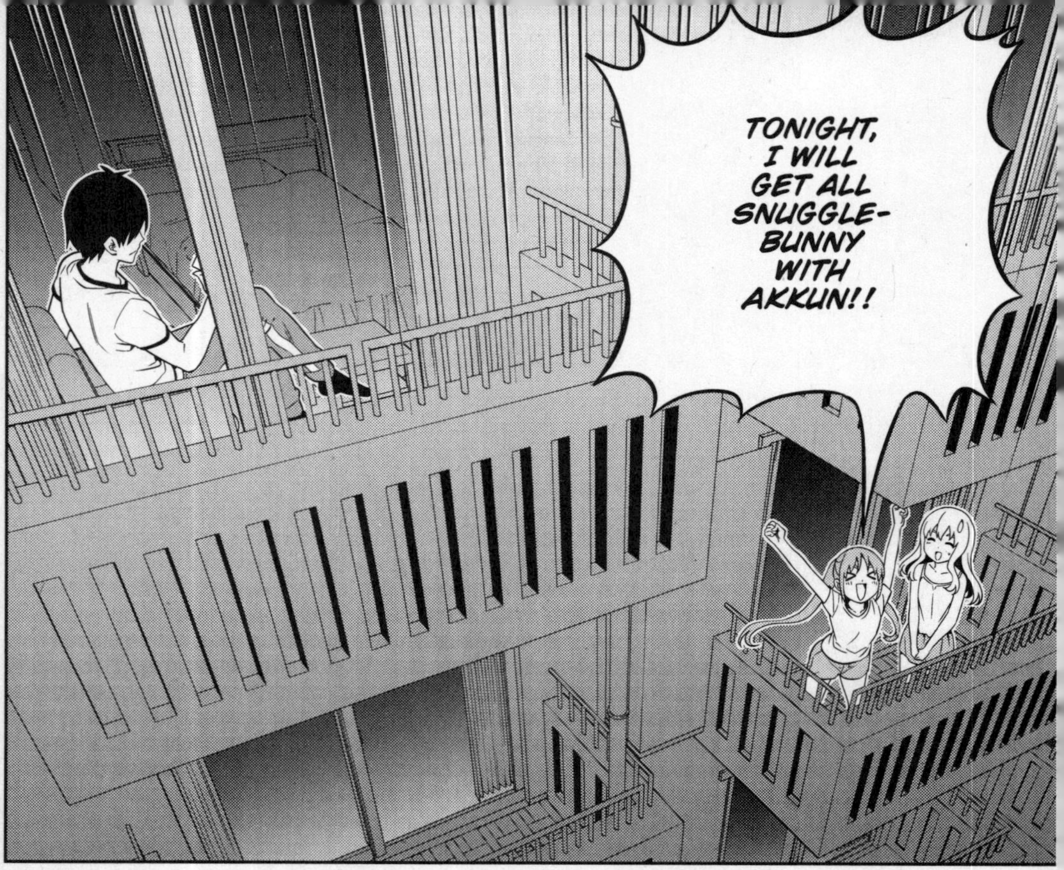
TONIGHT, I WILL GET ALL SNUGGLE-BUNNY WITH AKKUN!!

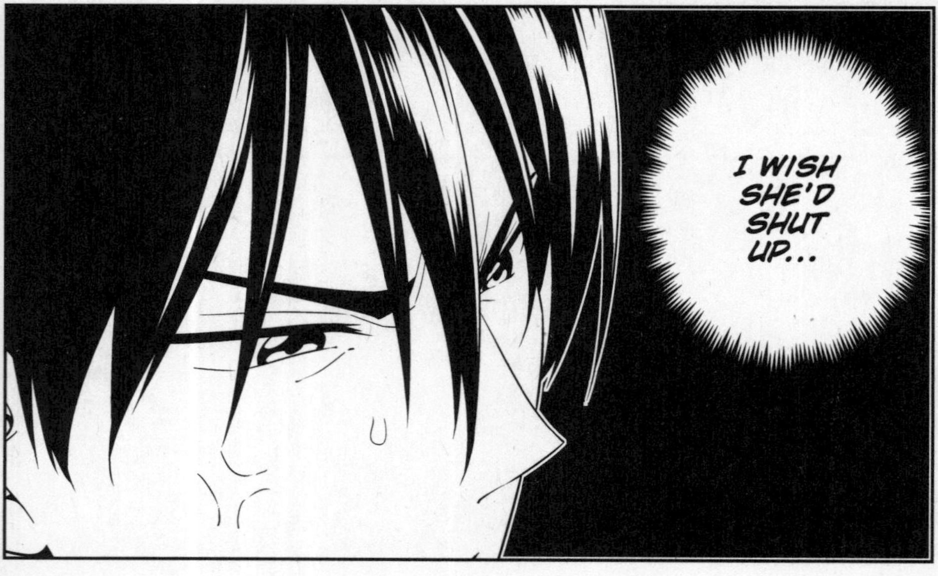
I WISH SHE'D SHUT UP...

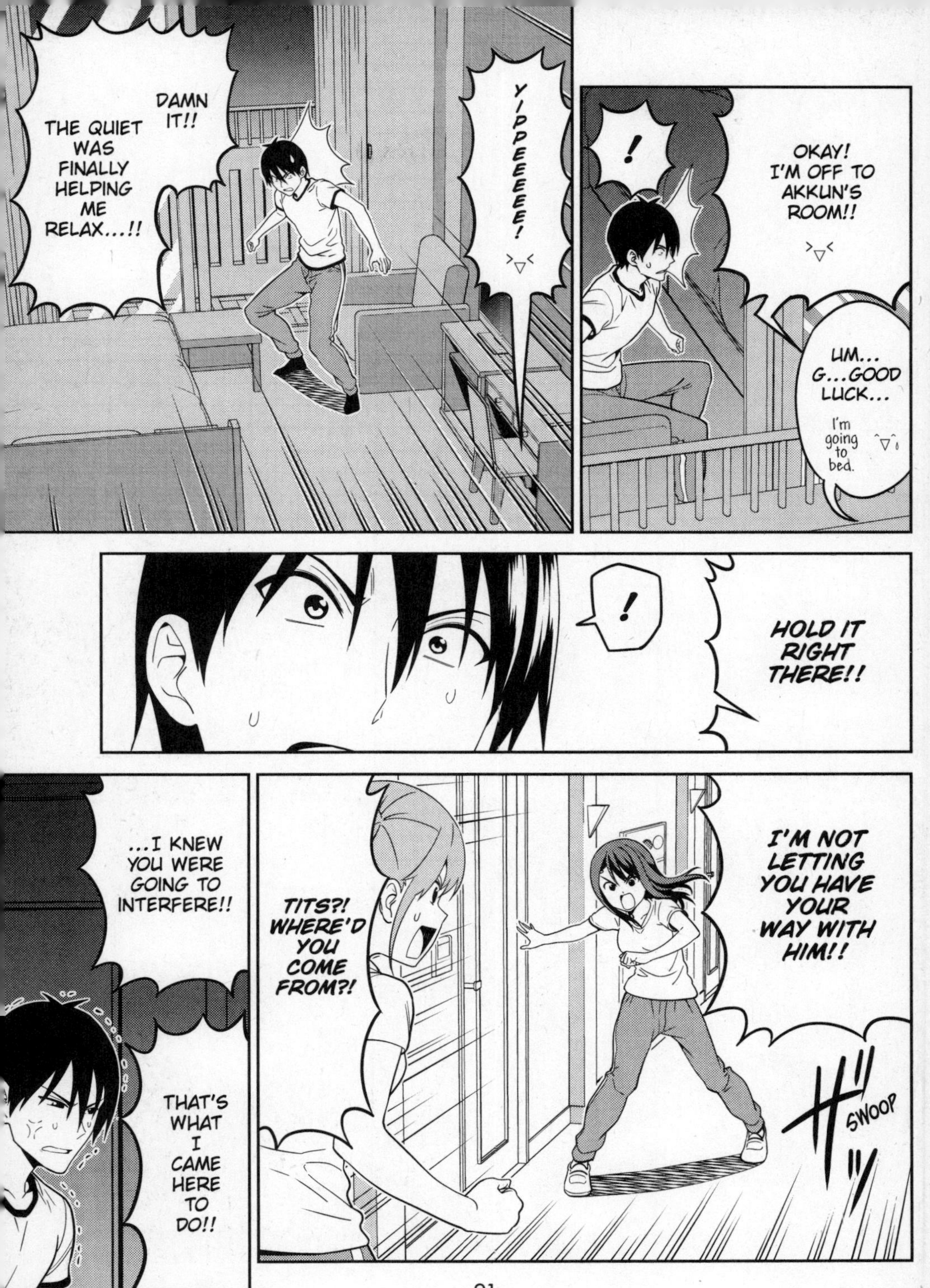
OKAY! I'M OFF TO AKKUN'S ROOM!!
!
UM... G...GOOD LUCK...
I'm going to bed.
YIPPEEEEEE!
DAMN IT!!
THE QUIET WAS FINALLY HELPING ME RELAX...!!
HOLD IT RIGHT THERE!!
!
I'M NOT LETTING YOU HAVE YOUR WAY WITH HIM!!
SWOOP
TITS?! WHERE'D YOU COME FROM?!
...I KNEW YOU WERE GOING TO INTERFERE!!
THAT'S WHAT I CAME HERE TO DO!!

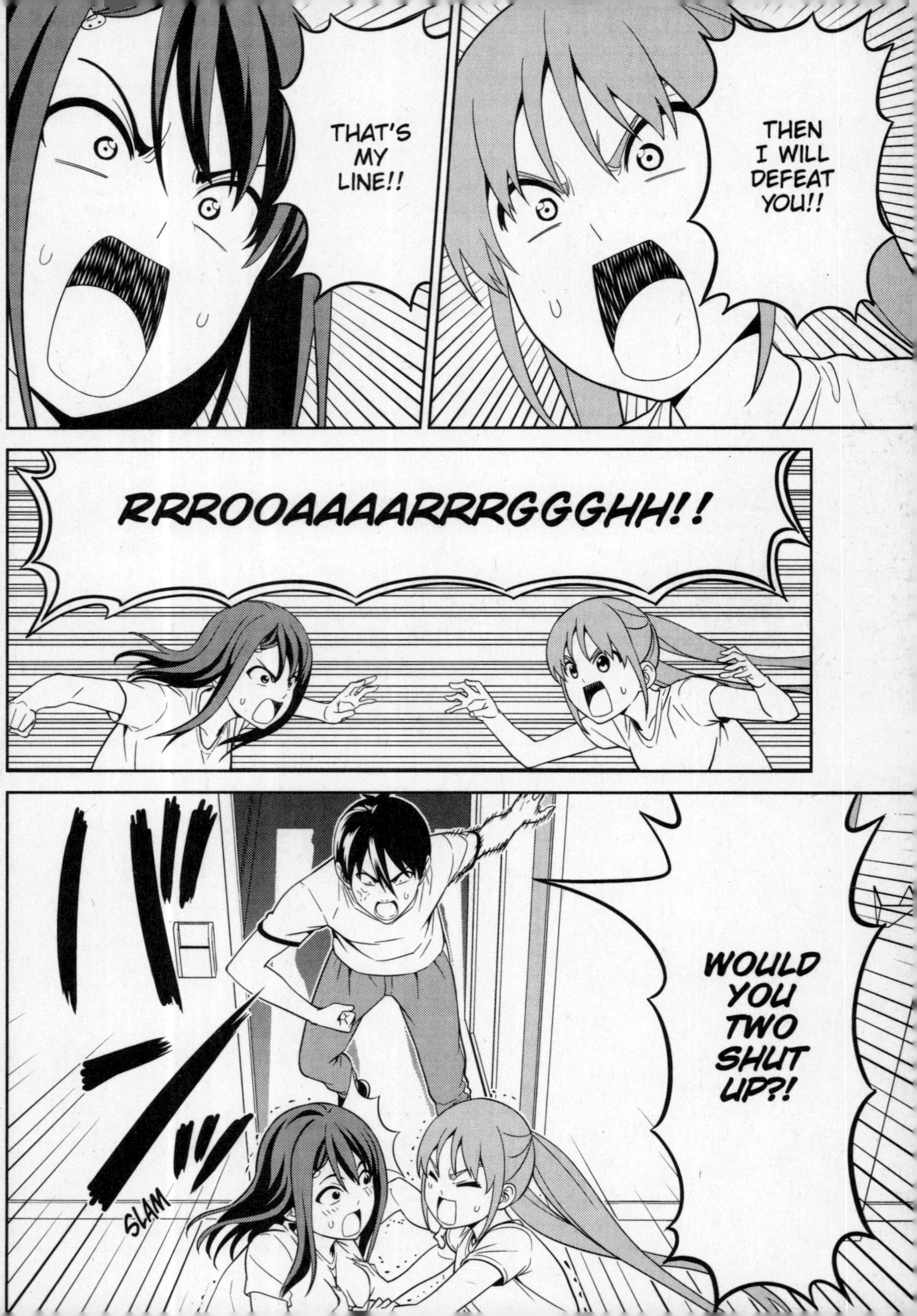
THEN I WILL DEFEAT YOU!!
THAT'S MY LINE!!
RRROOAAAARRRGGGHH!!
WOULD YOU TWO SHUT UP?!
SLAM

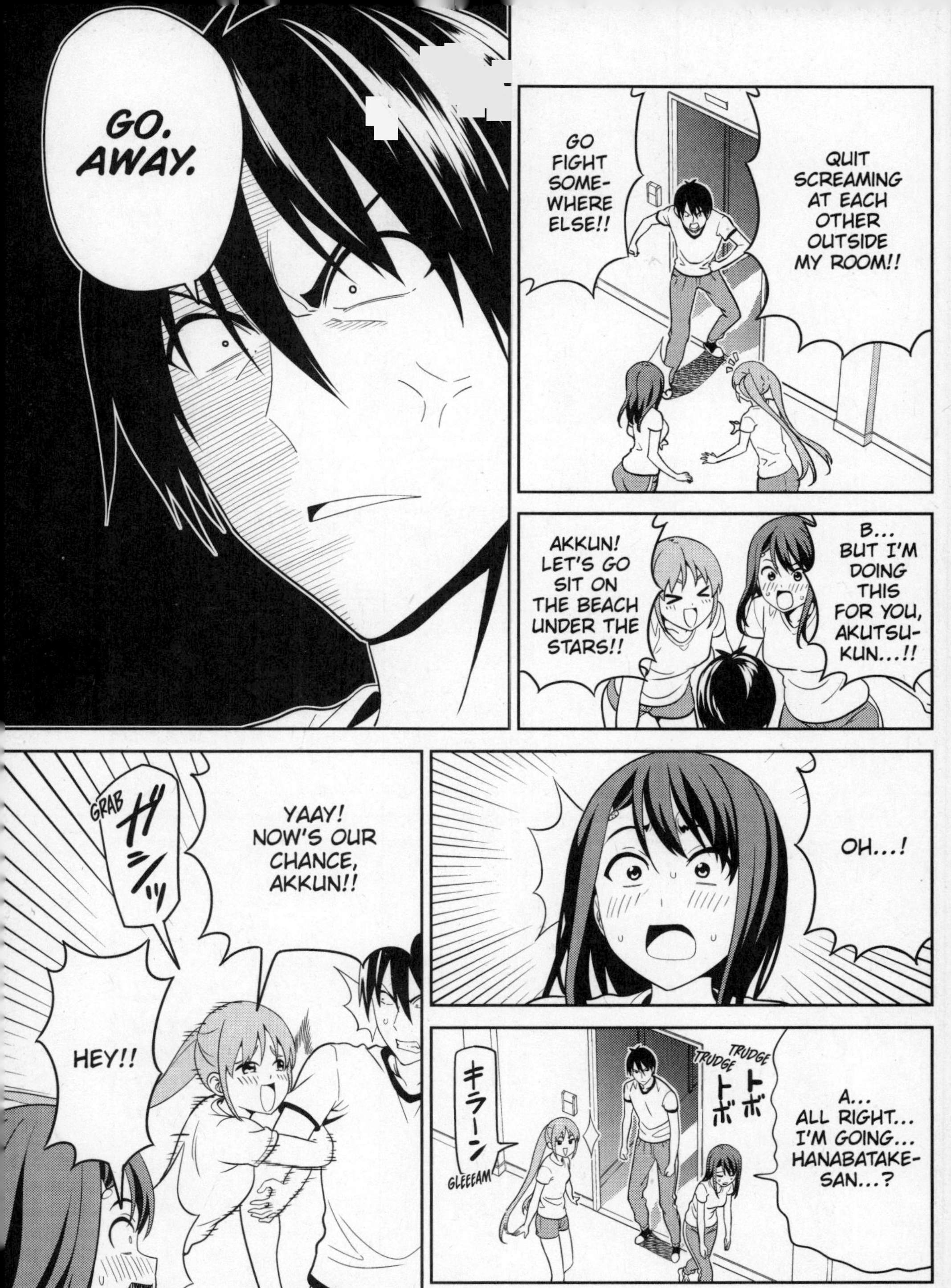
QUIT SCREAMING AT EACH OTHER OUTSIDE MY ROOM!!
GO FIGHT SOME-WHERE ELSE!!
B... BUT I'M DOING THIS FOR YOU, AKUTSU-KUN...!!
AKKUN! LET'S GO SIT ON THE BEACH UNDER THE STARS!!
GO. AWAY.
OH...!
A... ALL RIGHT... I'M GOING... HANABATAKE-SAN...?
TRUDGE TRUDGE
トボトボ
キラーン
GLEEEAM
YAAY! NOW'S OUR CHANCE, AKKUN!!
GRAB
ガシッ
HEY!!

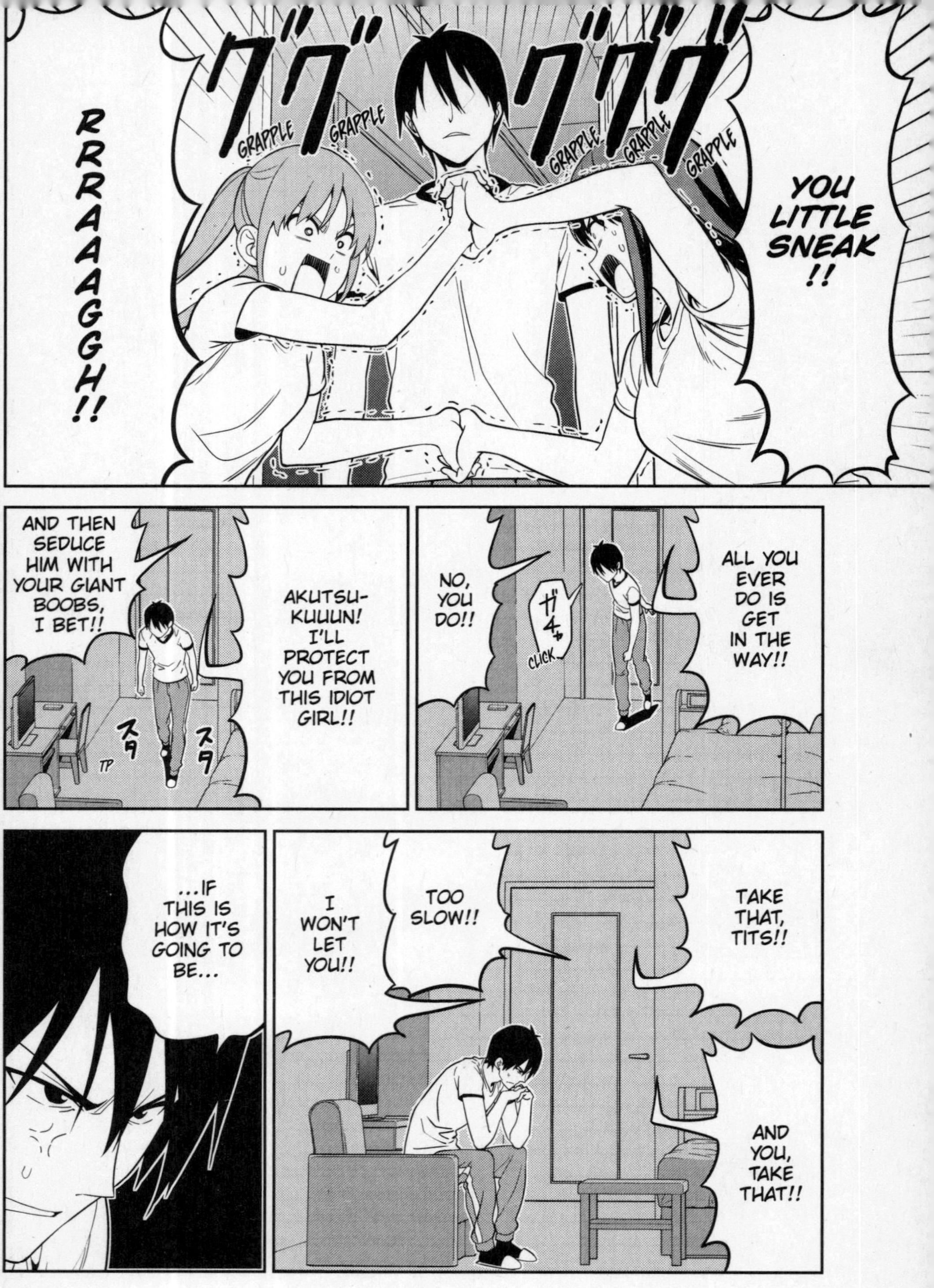
YOU LITTLE SNEAK!!
グググ
GRAPPLE GRAPPLE GRAPPLE
ググ
GRAPPLE GRAPPLE
RRRAAAAGGGH!!
ALL YOU EVER DO IS GET IN THE WAY!!
NO, YOU DO!!
ガチャ
CLICK
AKUTSU-KUUUN! I'LL PROTECT YOU FROM THIS IDIOT GIRL!!
AND THEN SEDUCE HIM WITH YOUR GIANT BOOBS, I BET!!
スタ スタ
TP
TAKE THAT, TITS!!
TOO SLOW!!
I WON'T LET YOU!!
AND YOU, TAKE THAT!!
...IF THIS IS HOW IT'S GOING TO BE...

ザザーーー...
KSHKSSSH

ZZZ...
スヤ...

ZZZ...
スヤ...

HM...?

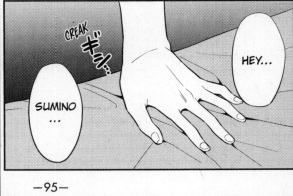

CREAK
ギシ...

SUMINO
...

HEY...

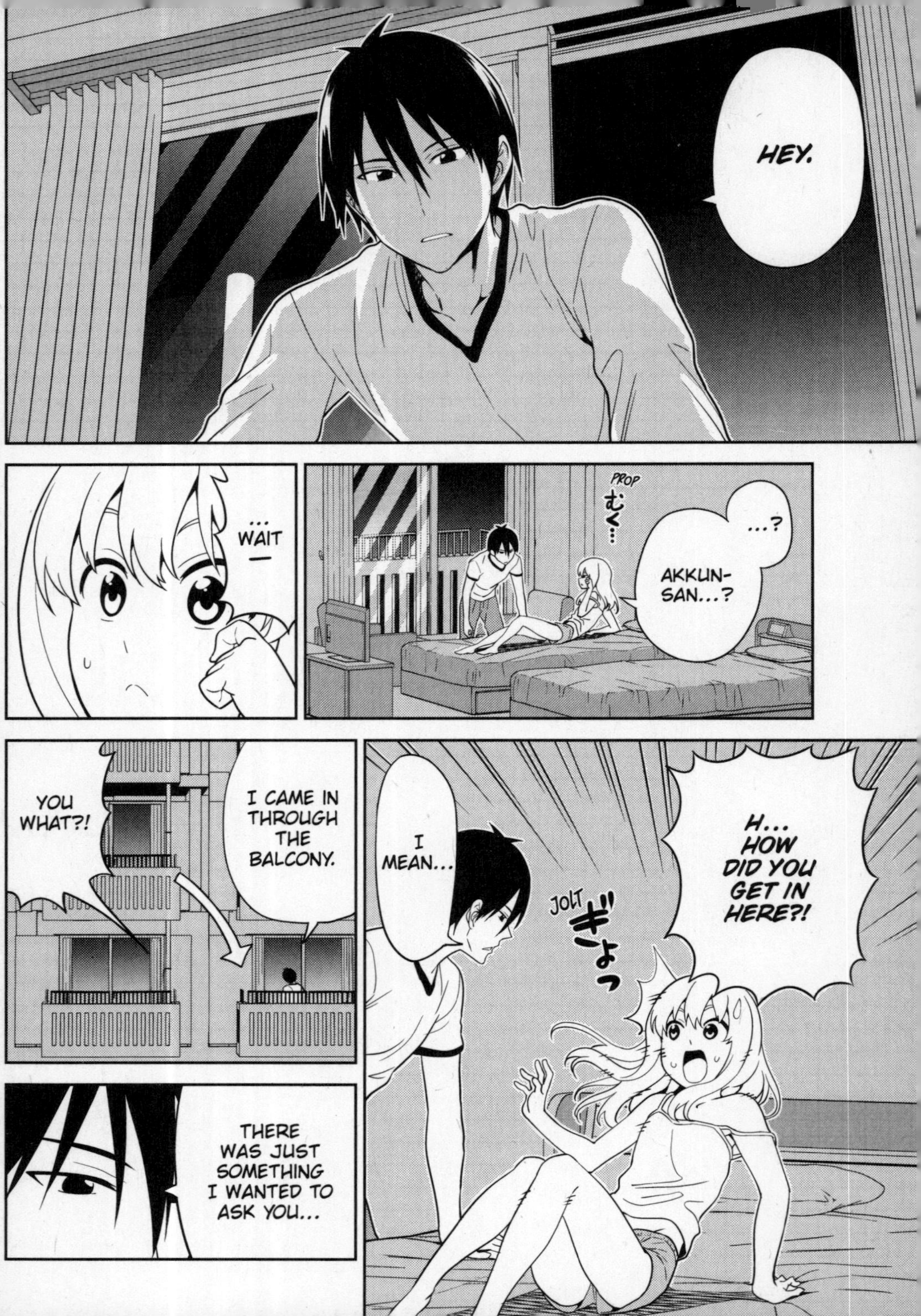
HEY.
PROP
むく…
...?
AKKUN-SAN...?
... WAIT —
H... HOW DID YOU GET IN HERE?!
JOLT
ギョっ
I MEAN...
I CAME IN THROUGH THE BALCONY.
YOU WHAT?!
THERE WAS JUST SOMETHING I WANTED TO ASK YOU...

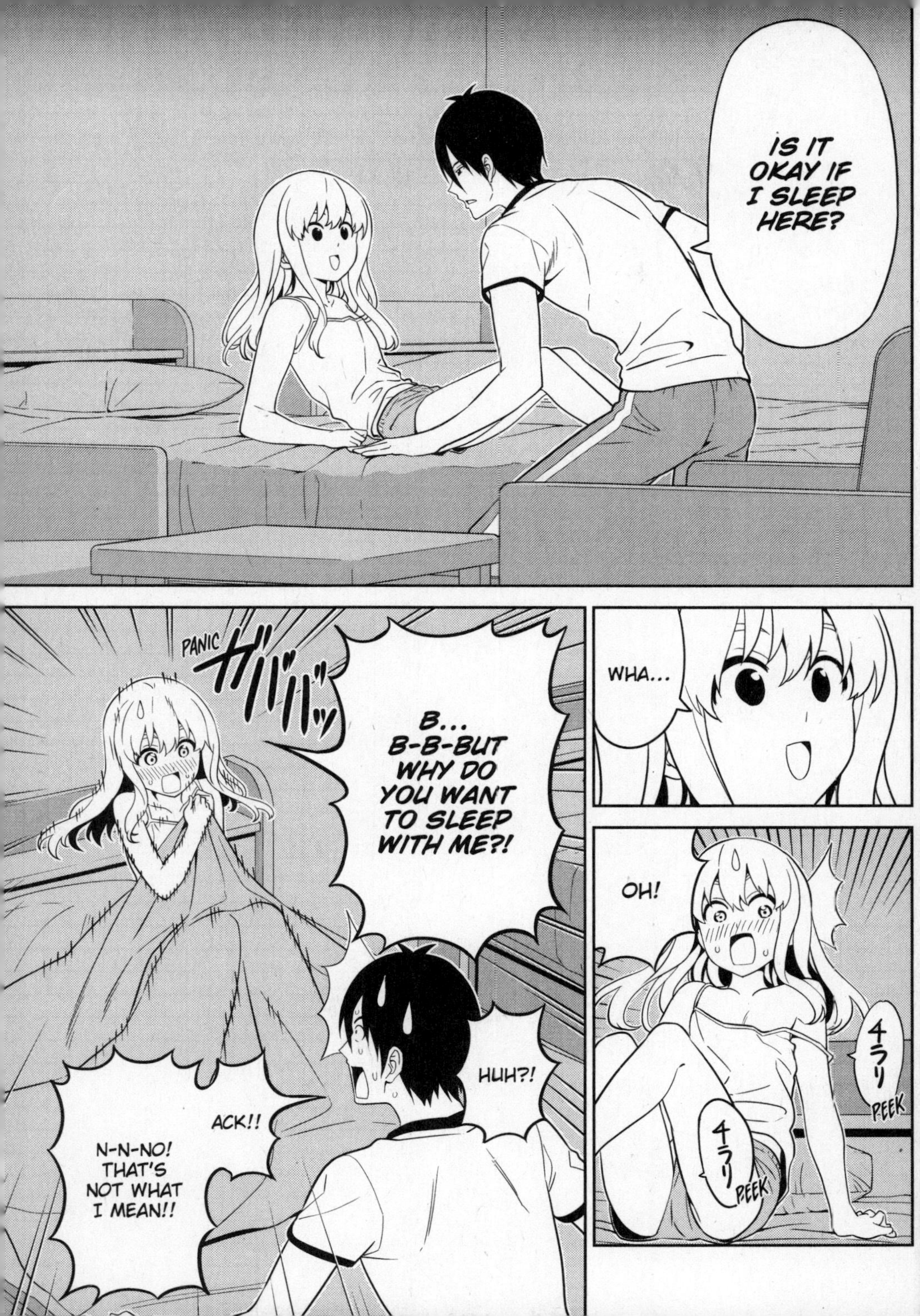
IS IT OKAY IF I SLEEP HERE?
WHA...
OH!
チラリ
PEEK
チラリ
PEEK
PANIC
ガバッ
B... B-B-BUT WHY DO YOU WANT TO SLEEP WITH ME?!
HUH?!
ACK!!
N-N-NO! THAT'S NOT WHAT I MEAN!!

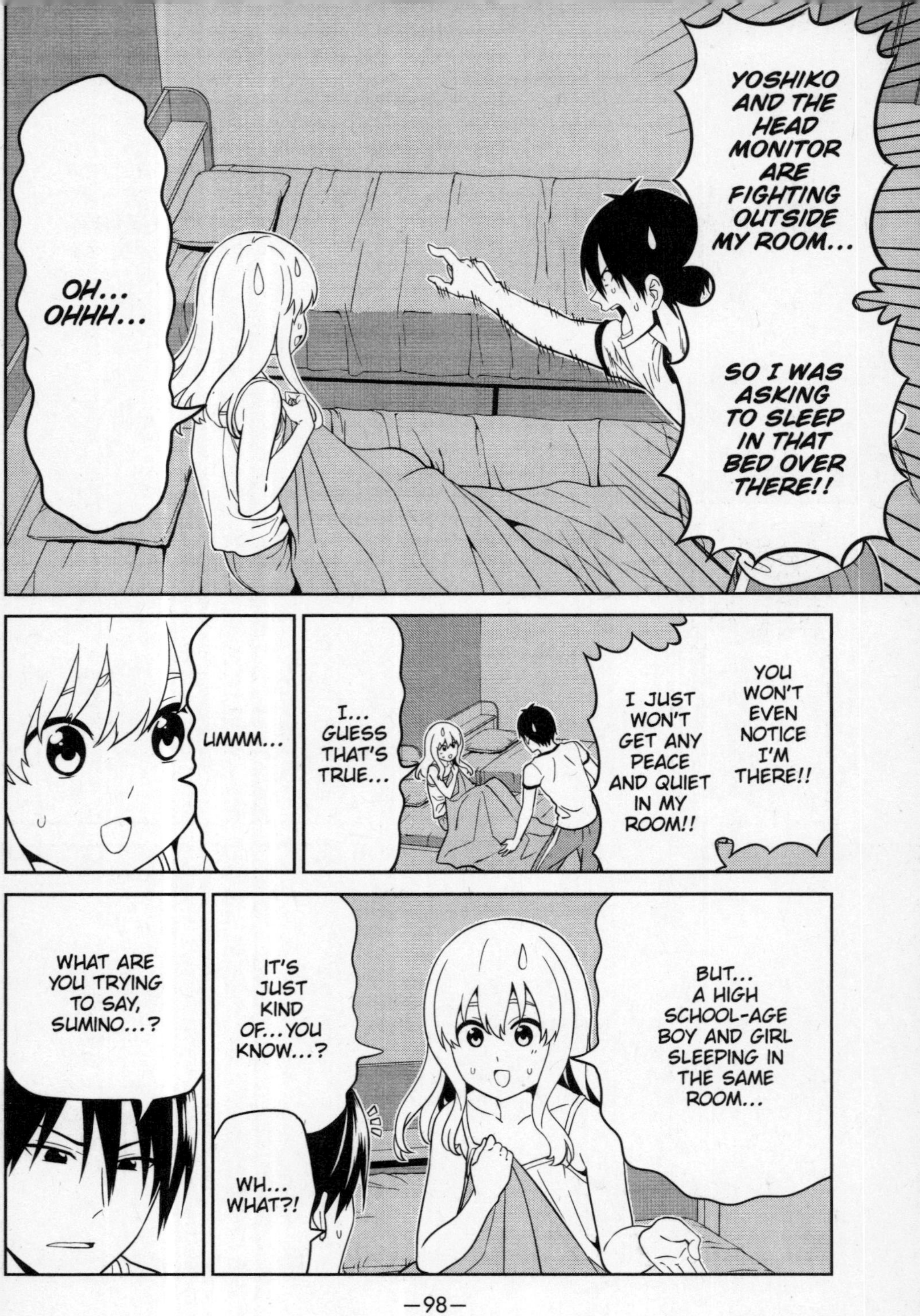
YOSHIKO AND THE HEAD MONITOR ARE FIGHTING OUTSIDE MY ROOM...
SO I WAS ASKING TO SLEEP IN THAT BED OVER THERE!!
OH... OHHH...
YOU WON'T EVEN NOTICE I'M THERE!!
I JUST WON'T GET ANY PEACE AND QUIET IN MY ROOM!!
I... GUESS THAT'S TRUE...
UMMM...
BUT... A HIGH SCHOOL-AGE BOY AND GIRL SLEEPING IN THE SAME ROOM...
IT'S JUST KIND OF...YOU KNOW...?
WH... WHAT?!
WHAT ARE YOU TRYING TO SAY, SUMINO...?

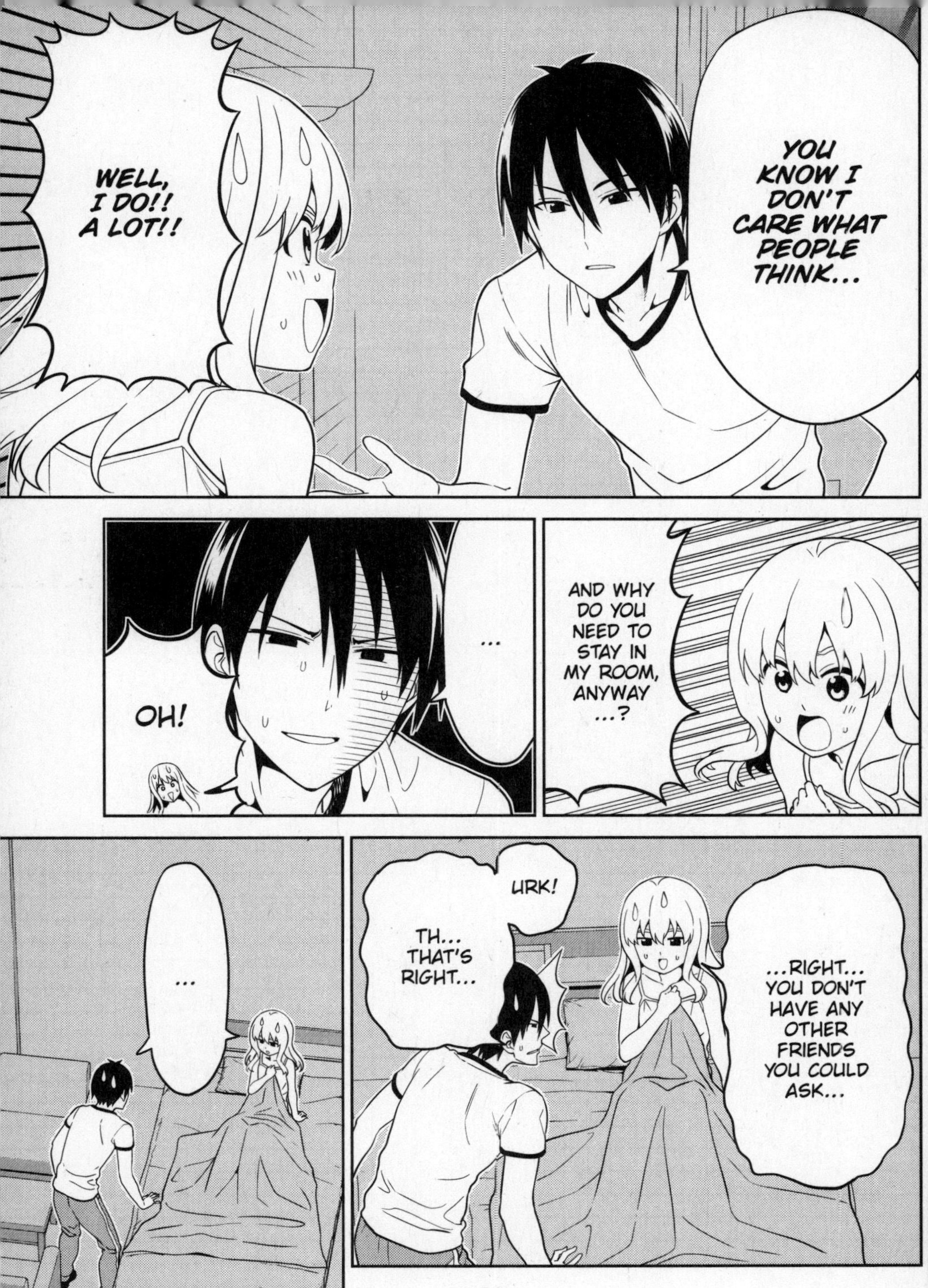
YOU KNOW I DON'T CARE WHAT PEOPLE THINK...
WELL, I DO!! A LOT!!
AND WHY DO YOU NEED TO STAY IN MY ROOM, ANYWAY ...?
...
OH!
...RIGHT... YOU DON'T HAVE ANY OTHER FRIENDS YOU COULD ASK...
URK!
TH... THAT'S RIGHT...
...

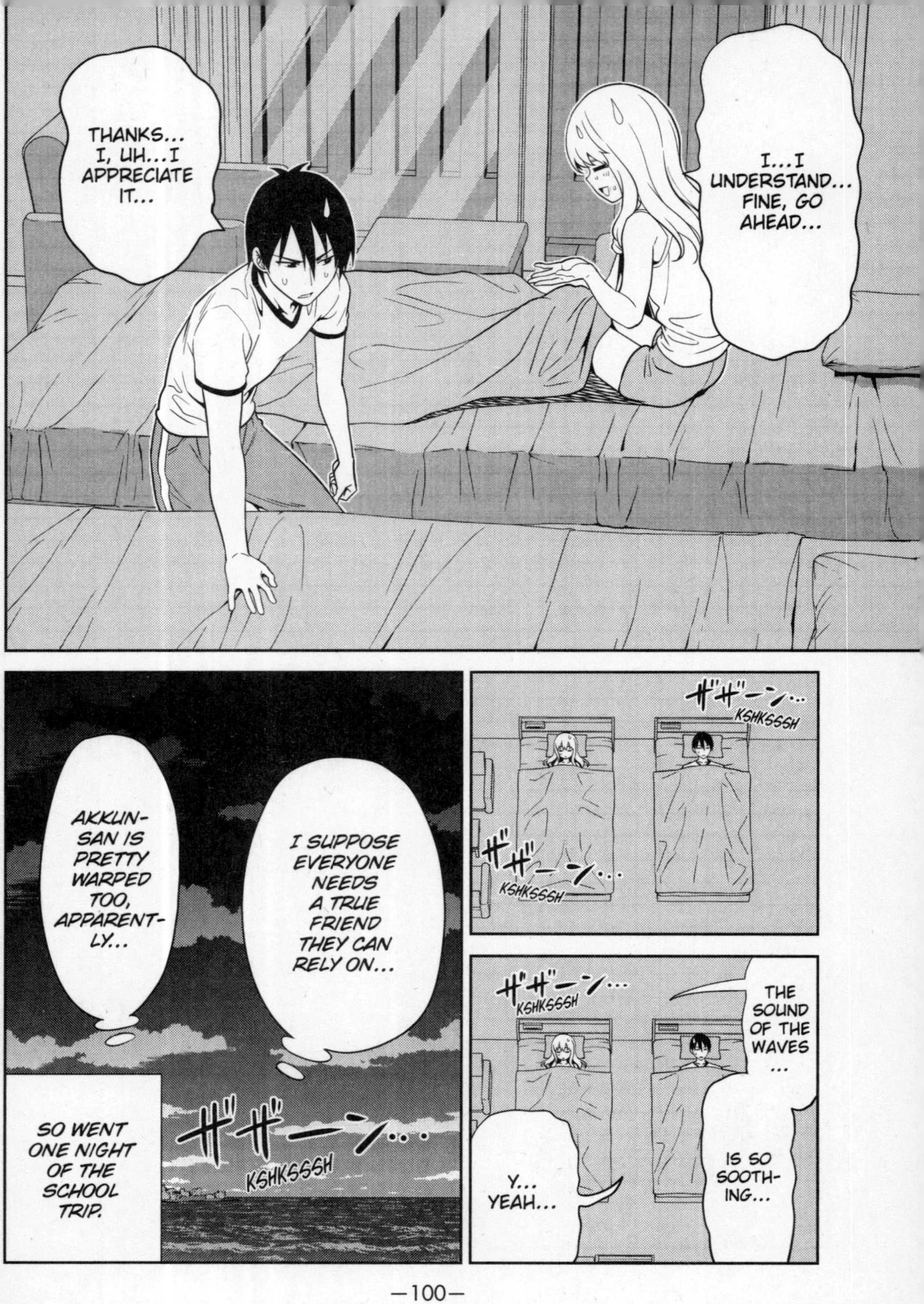
I...I UNDERSTAND... FINE, GO AHEAD...
THANKS... I, UH...I APPRECIATE IT...
ザザーン…
KSHKSSSH
ザザーン…
KSHKSSSH
ザザーン…
KSHKSSSH
THE SOUND OF THE WAVES... IS SO SOOTHING...
Y... YEAH...
I SUPPOSE EVERYONE NEEDS A TRUE FRIEND THEY CAN RELY ON...
AKKUN-SAN IS PRETTY WARPED TOO, APPARENTLY...
ザザーン…
KSHKSSSH
SO WENT ONE NIGHT OF THE SCHOOL TRIP.

Free Activity Time!!

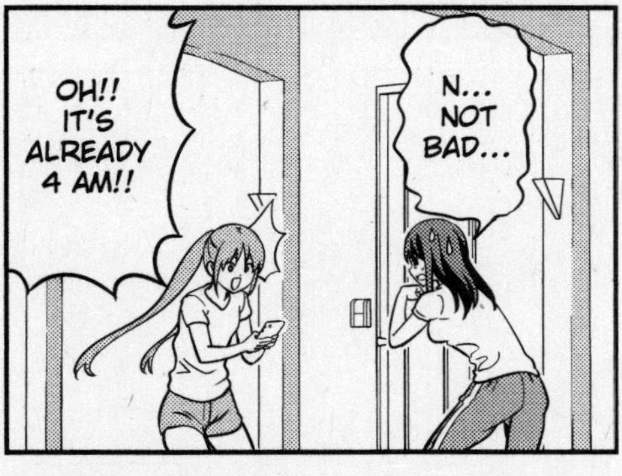
N... NOT BAD...
OH!! IT'S ALREADY 4 AM!!

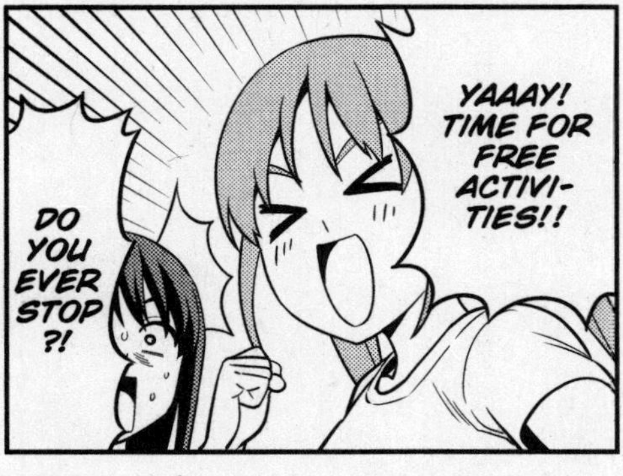
YAAAY! TIME FOR FREE ACTIVI-TIES!!
DO YOU EVER STOP?!

(Barefoot, bewitching)

Aho-Girl

\ˈahô͵gərl\ *Japanese, noun*.
A clueless girl.

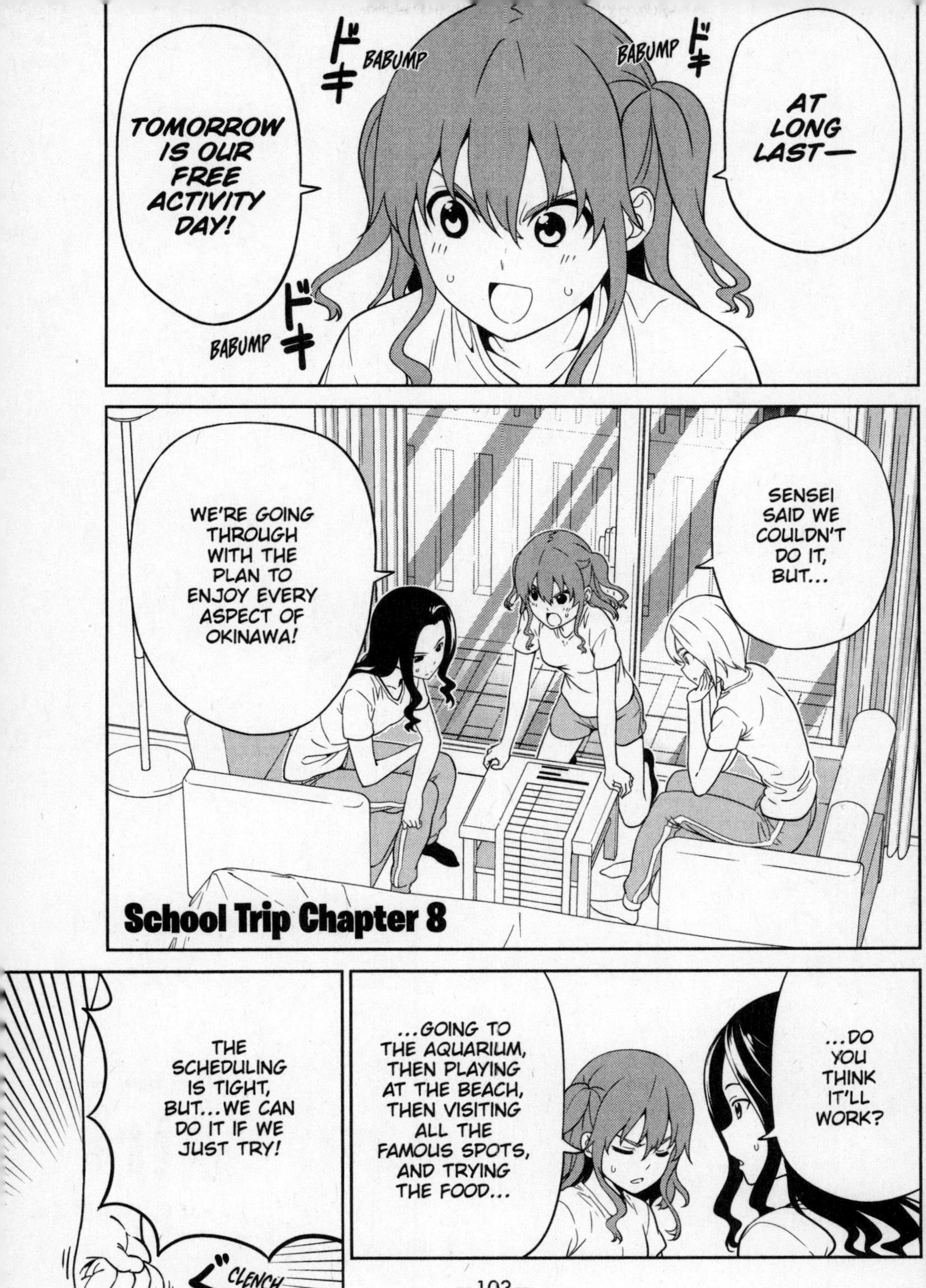
BABUMP ドキ
AT LONG LAST—
ドキ BABUMP
TOMORROW IS OUR FREE ACTIVITY DAY!
ドキ BABUMP
SENSEI SAID WE COULDN'T DO IT, BUT...
WE'RE GOING THROUGH WITH THE PLAN TO ENJOY EVERY ASPECT OF OKINAWA!
School Trip Chapter 8
...DO YOU THINK IT'LL WORK?
...GOING TO THE AQUARIUM, THEN PLAYING AT THE BEACH, THEN VISITING ALL THE FAMOUS SPOTS, AND TRYING THE FOOD...
THE SCHEDULING IS TIGHT, BUT...WE CAN DO IT IF WE JUST TRY!
ぐっ CLENCH

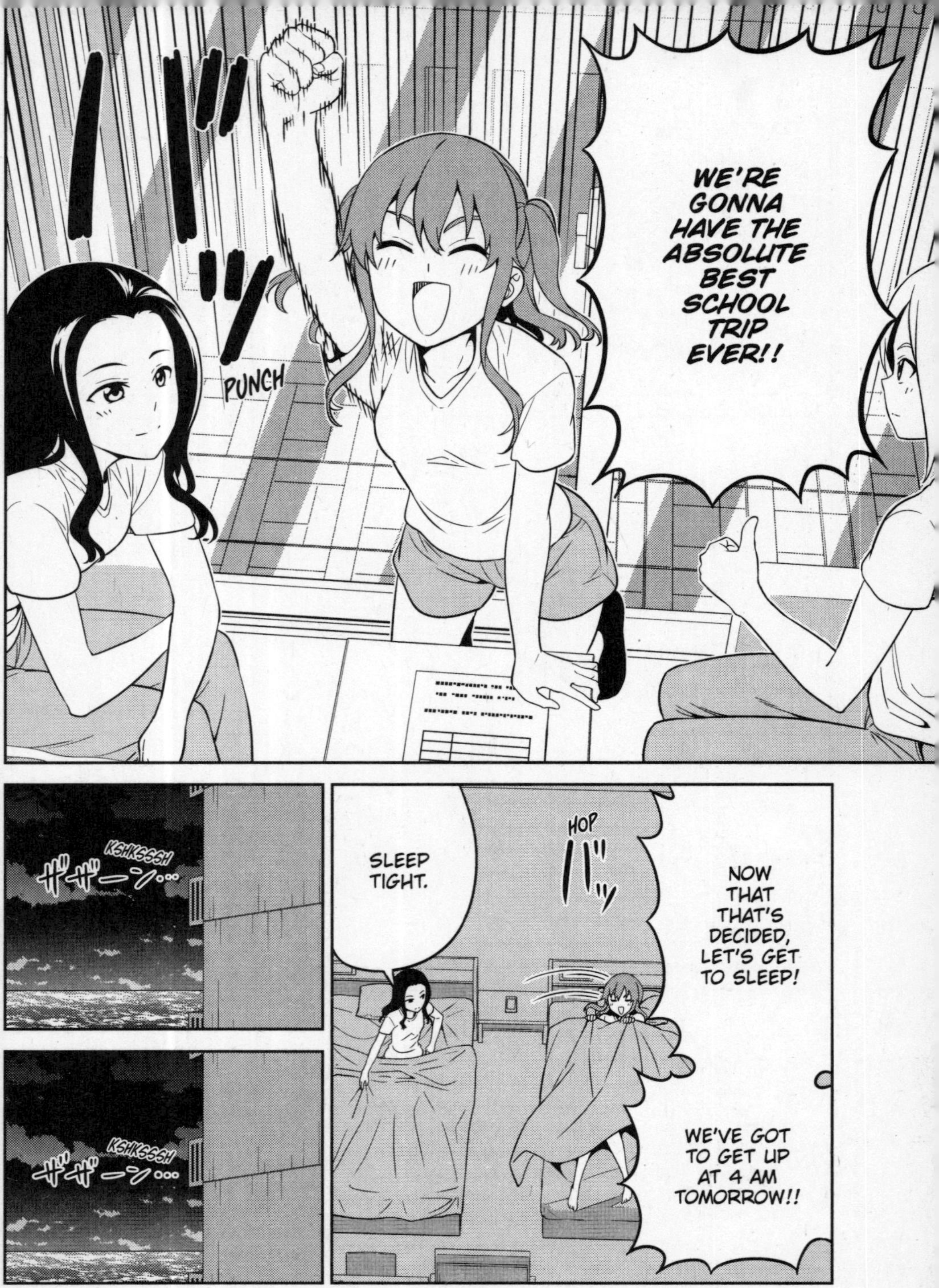

WE'RE GONNA HAVE THE ABSOLUTE BEST SCHOOL TRIP EVER!!
PUNCH
NOW THAT THAT'S DECIDED, LET'S GET TO SLEEP!
WE'VE GOT TO GET UP AT 4 AM TOMORROW!!
HOP
バッ
SLEEP TIGHT.
KSHKSSSH
ザザーン…
KSHKSSSH
ザザーン…

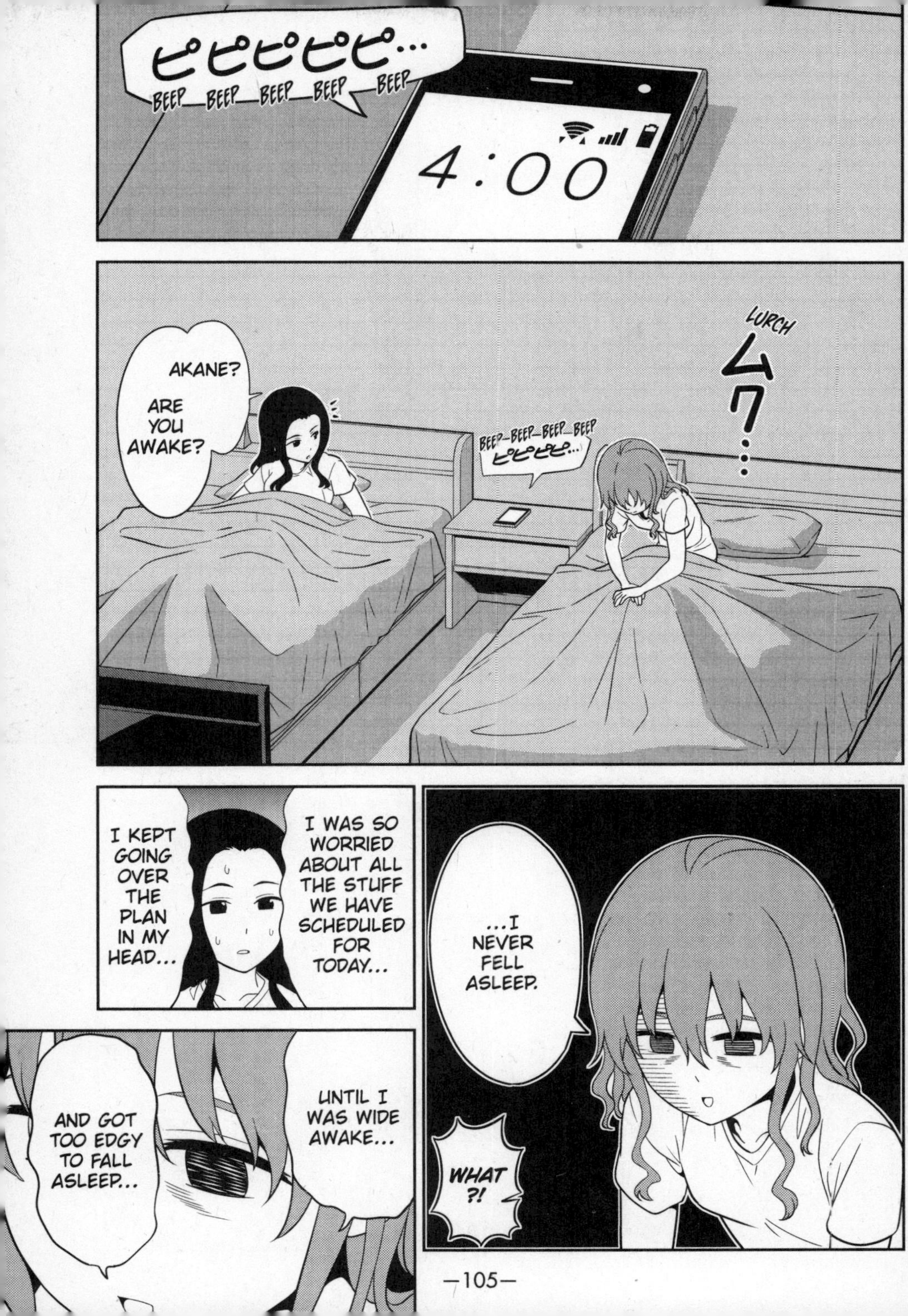
ピピピピピ…
BEEP BEEP BEEP BEEP BEEP
4:00
LURCH
ムク…
BEEP BEEP BEEP BEEP
ピピピピ…
AKANE? ARE YOU AWAKE?
…I NEVER FELL ASLEEP.
WHAT ?!
I WAS SO WORRIED ABOUT ALL THE STUFF WE HAVE SCHEDULED FOR TODAY…
I KEPT GOING OVER THE PLAN IN MY HEAD…
UNTIL I WAS WIDE AWAKE…
AND GOT TOO EDGY TO FALL ASLEEP…

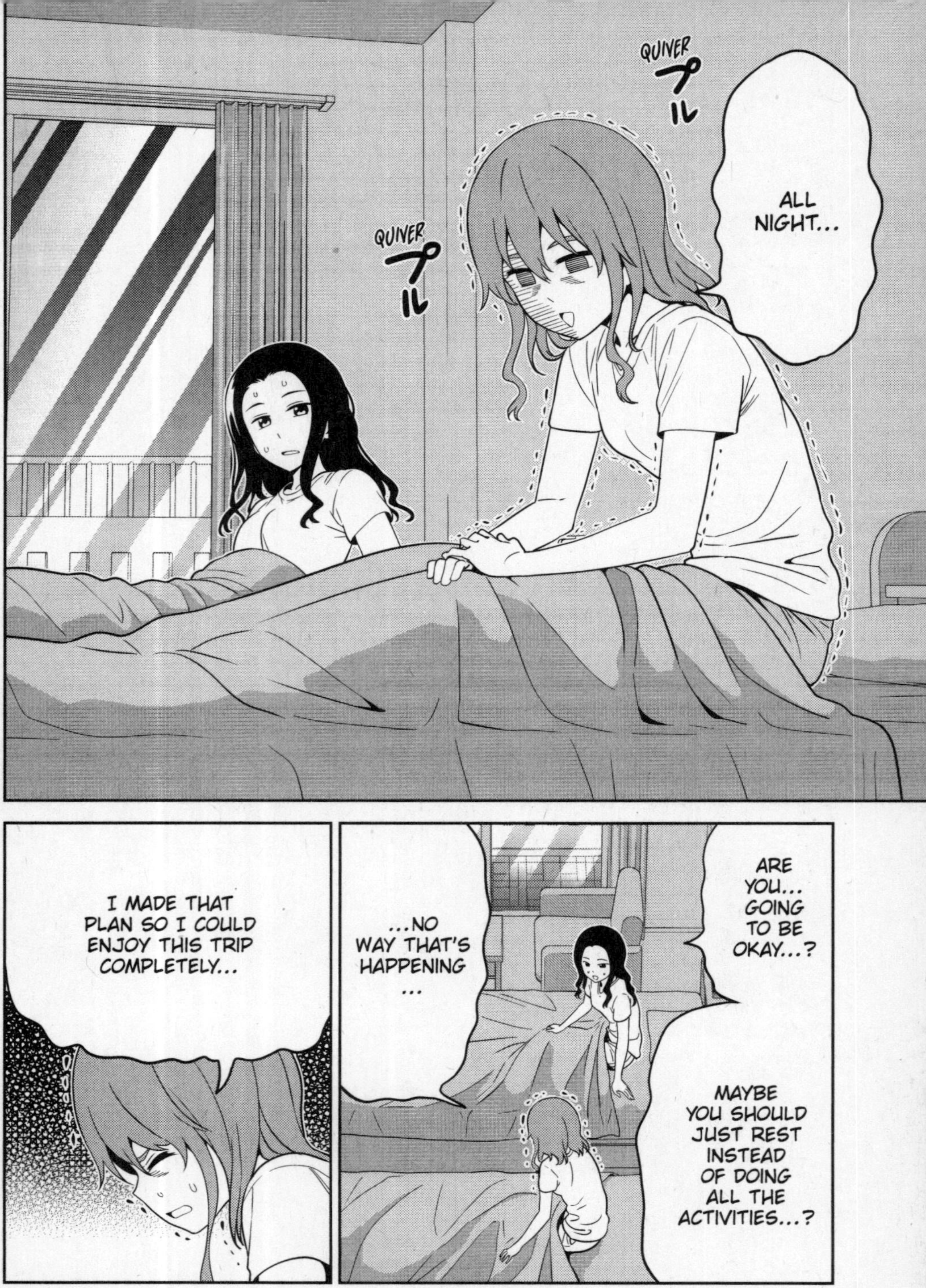
QUIVER プル
ALL NIGHT...
QUIVER プル
ARE YOU... GOING TO BE OKAY...?
MAYBE YOU SHOULD JUST REST INSTEAD OF DOING ALL THE ACTIVITIES...?
...NO WAY THAT'S HAPPENING...
I MADE THAT PLAN SO I COULD ENJOY THIS TRIP COMPLETELY...

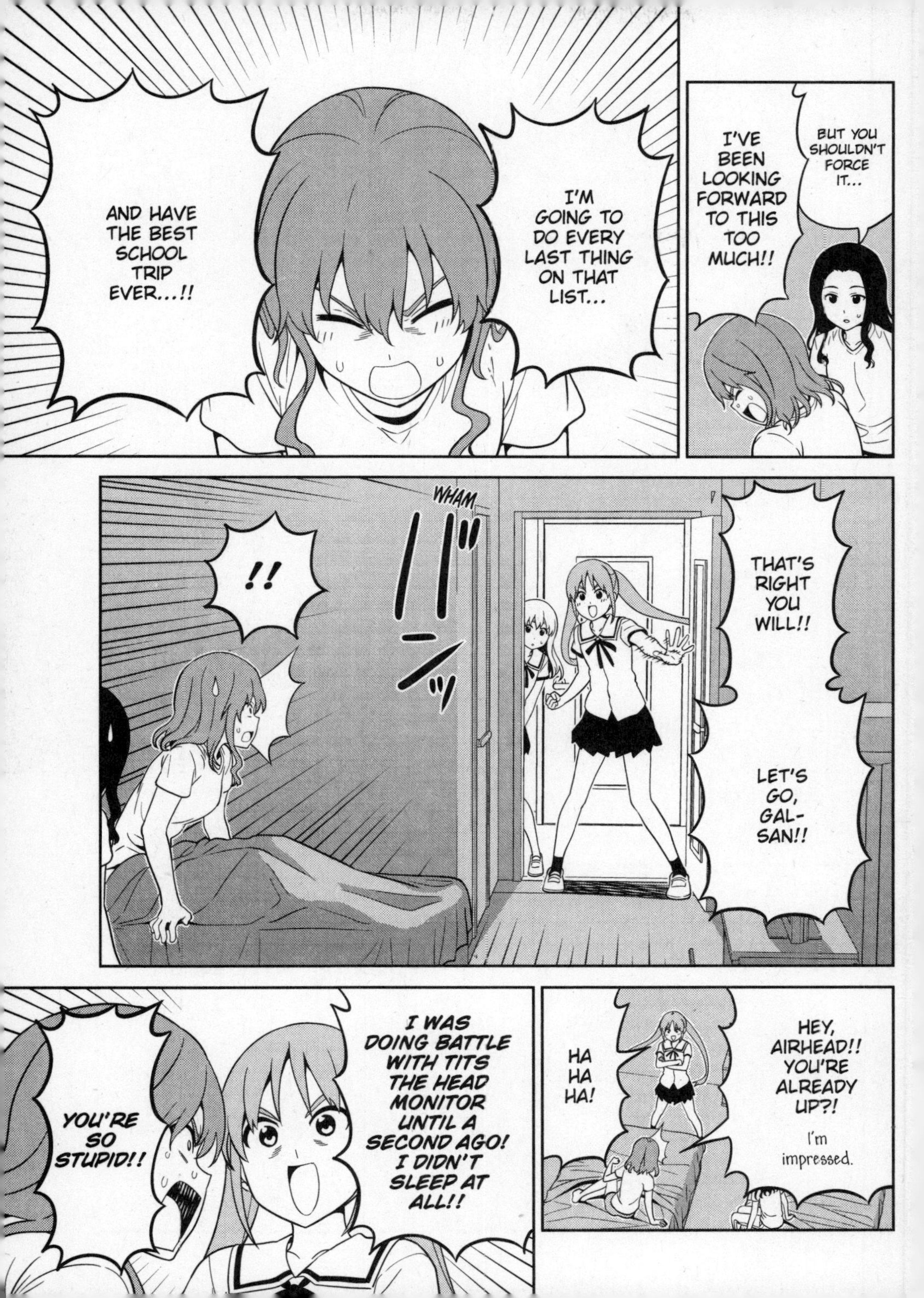
BUT YOU SHOULDN'T FORCE IT...
I'VE BEEN LOOKING FORWARD TO THIS TOO MUCH!!
I'M GOING TO DO EVERY LAST THING ON THAT LIST...
AND HAVE THE BEST SCHOOL TRIP EVER...!!
THAT'S RIGHT YOU WILL!!
WHAM
!!
LET'S GO, GAL-SAN!!
HEY, AIRHEAD!! YOU'RE ALREADY UP?!
I'm impressed.
HA HA HA!
I WAS DOING BATTLE WITH TITS THE HEAD MONITOR UNTIL A SECOND AGO! I DIDN'T SLEEP AT ALL!!
YOU'RE SO STUPID!!

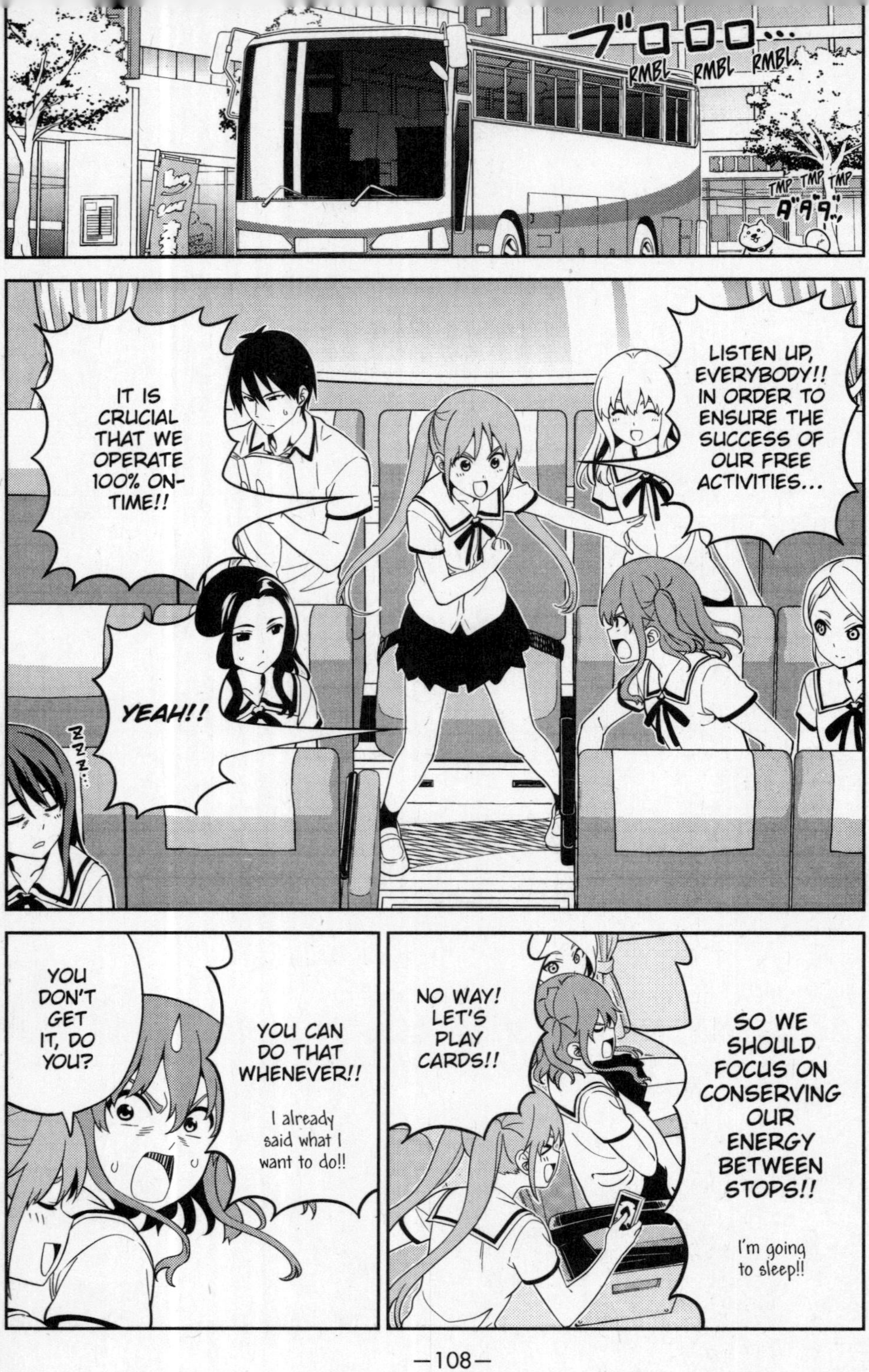
ブロロロ…
RMBL RMBL RMBL
TMP TMP TMP
ダダダ…
LISTEN UP, EVERYBODY!! IN ORDER TO ENSURE THE SUCCESS OF OUR FREE ACTIVITIES...
IT IS CRUCIAL THAT WE OPERATE 100% ON-TIME!!
YEAH!!
ZZZ...
SO WE SHOULD FOCUS ON CONSERVING OUR ENERGY BETWEEN STOPS!!
I'm going to sleep!!
NO WAY! LET'S PLAY CARDS!!
YOU CAN DO THAT WHENEVER!!
I already said what I want to do!!
YOU DON'T GET IT, DO YOU?

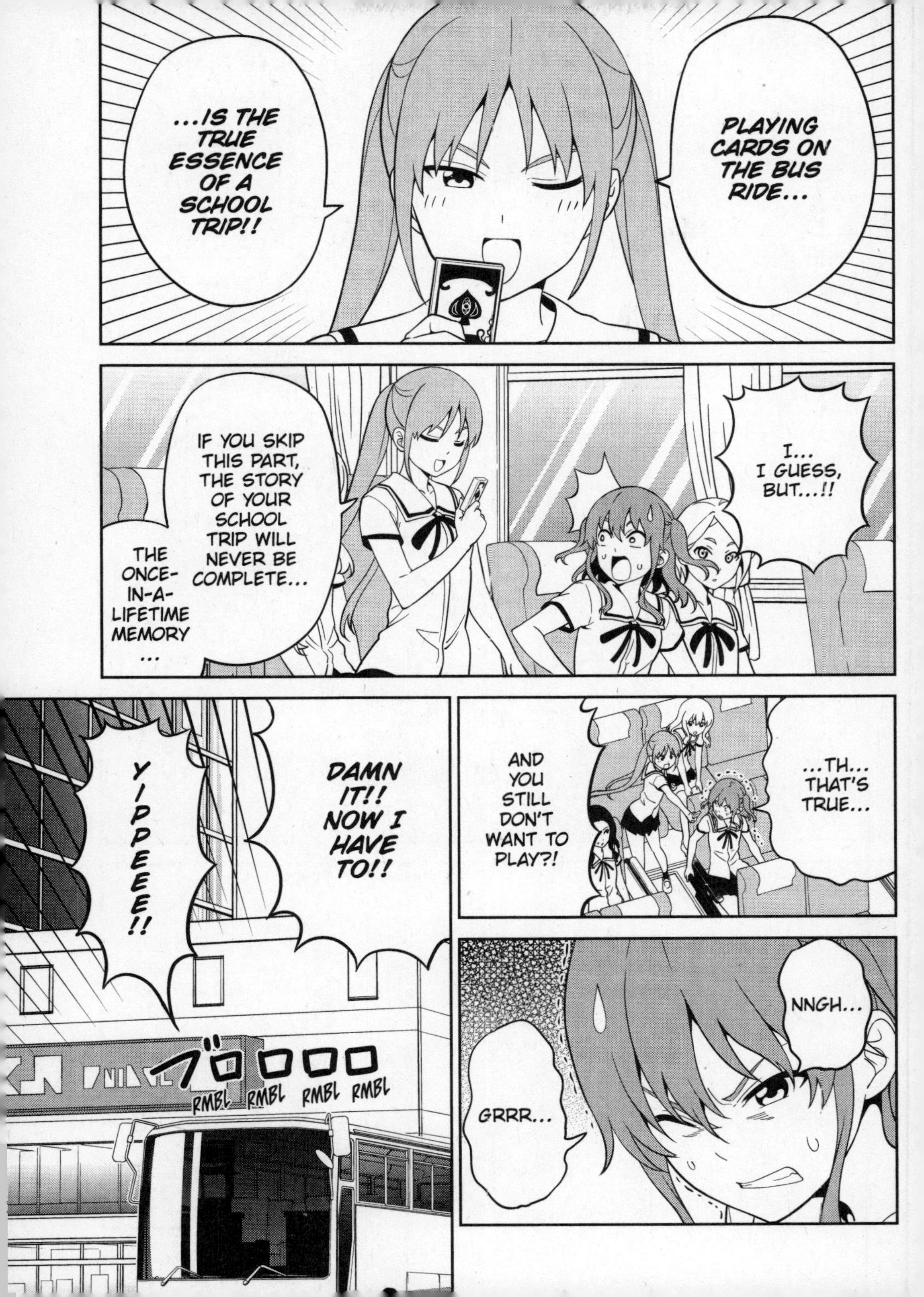
PLAYING CARDS ON THE BUS RIDE...
...IS THE TRUE ESSENCE OF A SCHOOL TRIP!!
I... I GUESS, BUT...!!
IF YOU SKIP THIS PART, THE STORY OF YOUR SCHOOL TRIP WILL NEVER BE COMPLETE...
THE ONCE-IN-A-LIFETIME MEMORY...
...TH... THAT'S TRUE...
AND YOU STILL DON'T WANT TO PLAY?!
NNGH...
GRRR...
DAMN IT!! NOW I HAVE TO!!
YIPPEEE!!
ブロロロロ
RMBL RMBL RMBL RMBL

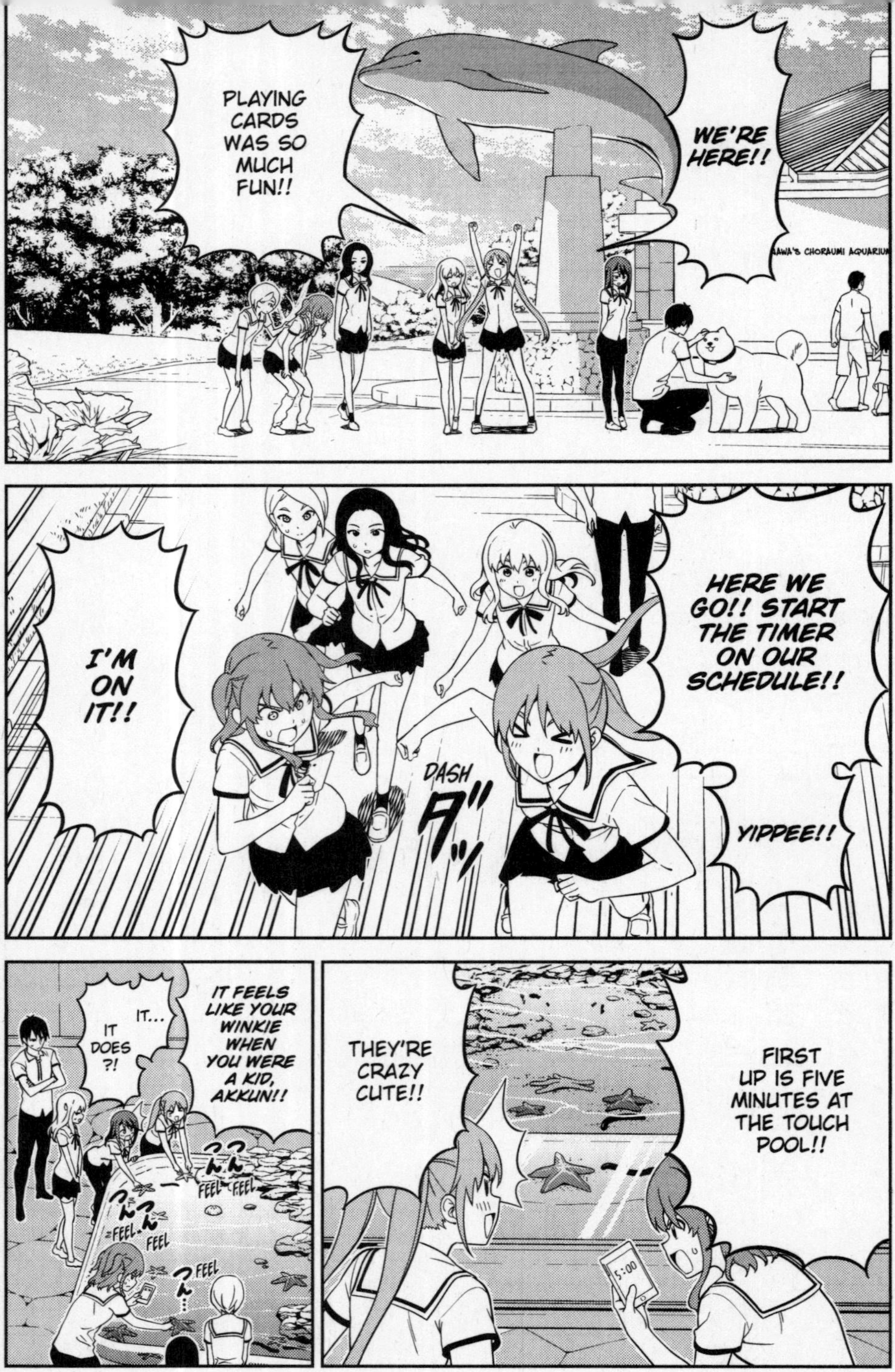
WE'RE HERE!!
AAWA'S CHORAUMI AQUARIUM
PLAYING CARDS WAS SO MUCH FUN!!
HERE WE GO!! START THE TIMER ON OUR SCHEDULE!!
YIPPEE!!
DASH
I'M ON IT!!
FIRST UP IS FIVE MINUTES AT THE TOUCH POOL!!
5:00
THEY'RE CRAZY CUTE!!
IT FEELS LIKE YOUR WINKIE WHEN YOU WERE A KID, AKKUN!!
IT...
IT DOES?!
FEEL FEEL
FEEL
FEEL
FEEL

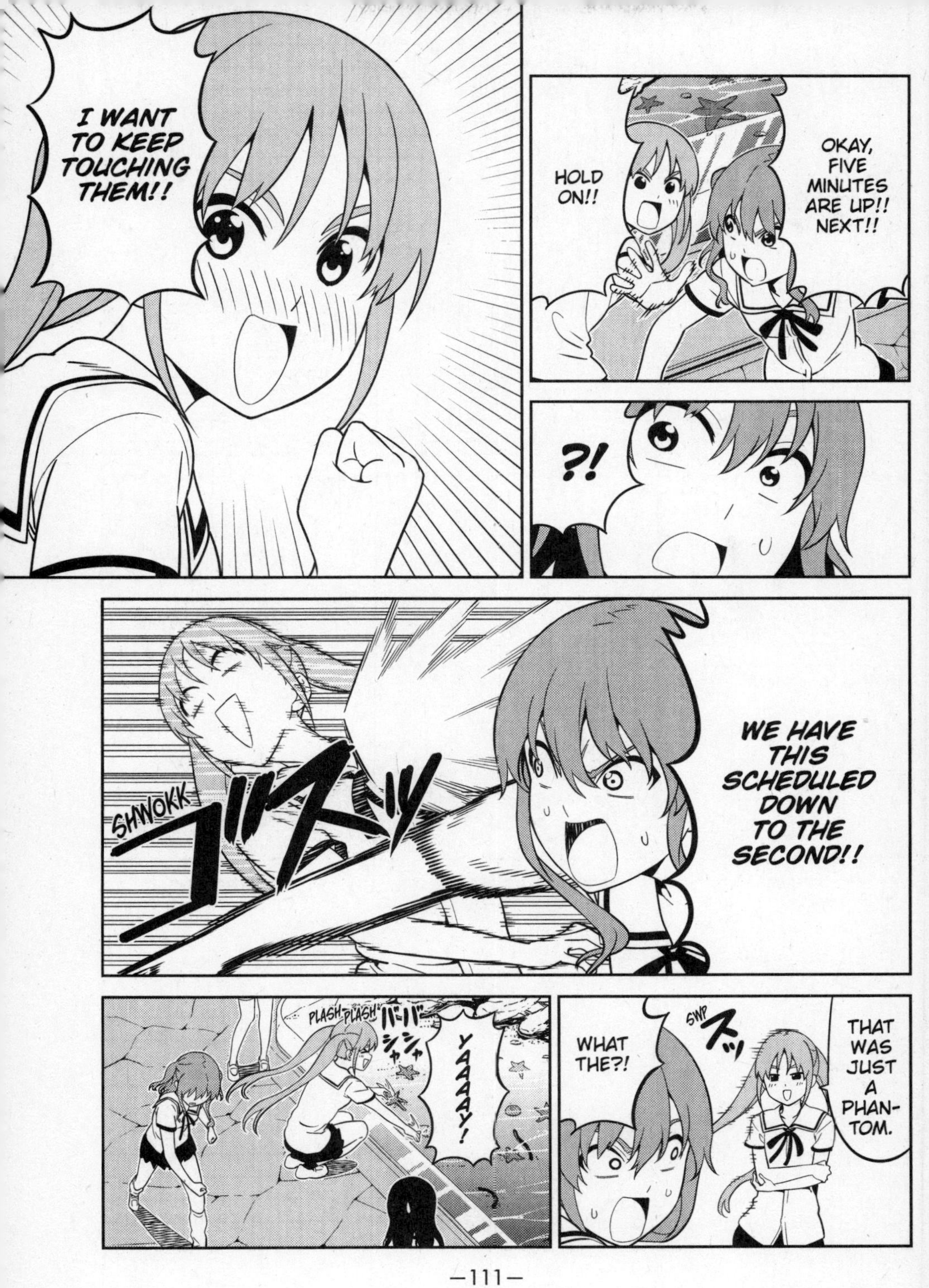
OKAY, FIVE MINUTES ARE UP!! NEXT!!
HOLD ON!!
?!
I WANT TO KEEP TOUCHING THEM!!
WE HAVE THIS SCHEDULED DOWN TO THE SECOND!!
SHWOKK
THAT WAS JUST A PHAN-TOM.
SWP
WHAT THE?!
YAAAAY!
PLASH PLASH
シャシャ

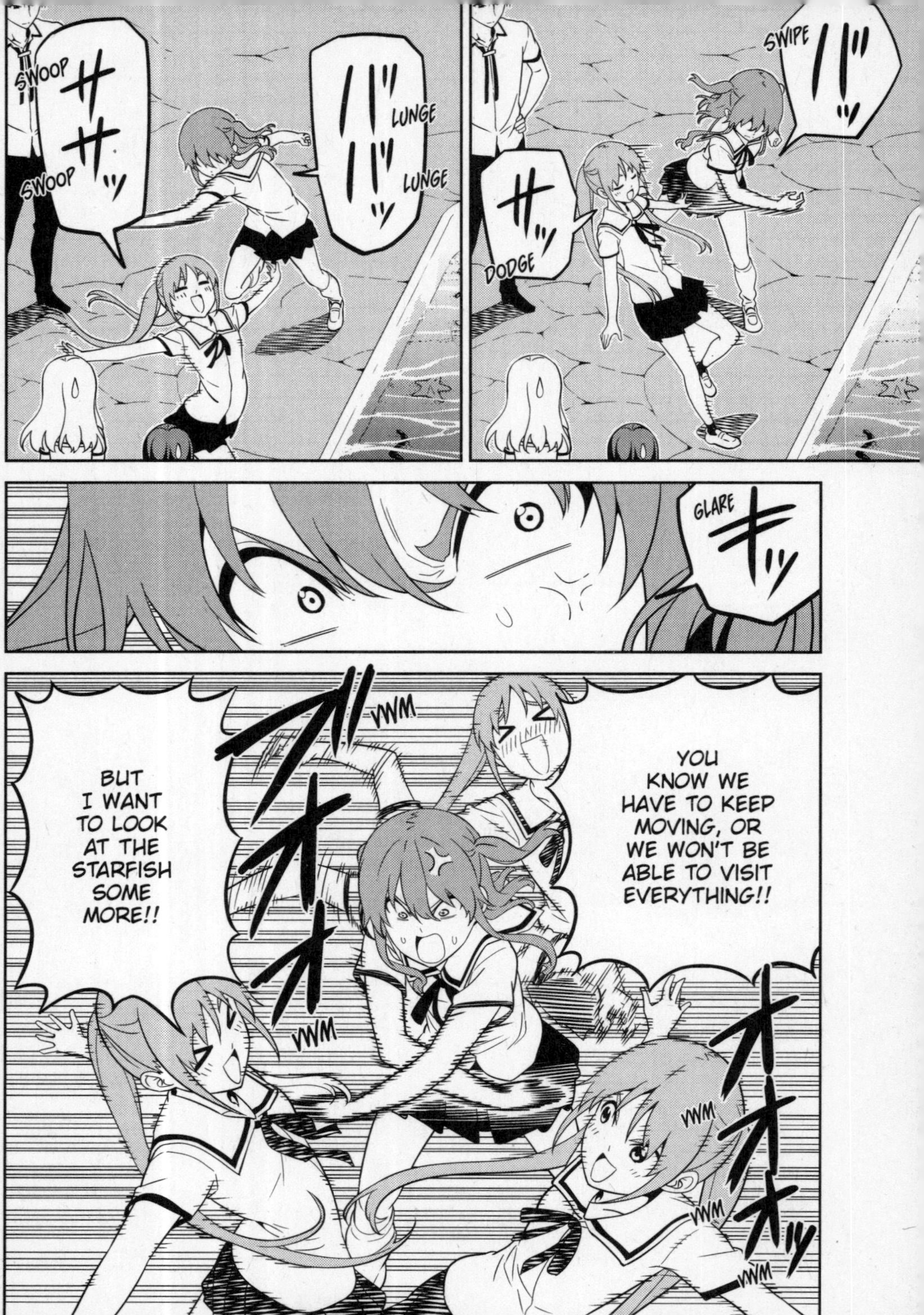
SWIPE
DODGE
SWOOP
SWOOP
LUNGE
LUNGE
GLARE
VWM
YOU KNOW WE HAVE TO KEEP MOVING, OR WE WON'T BE ABLE TO VISIT EVERYTHING!!
BUT I WANT TO LOOK AT THE STARFISH SOME MORE!!
VWM
VWM
VWM
VWM

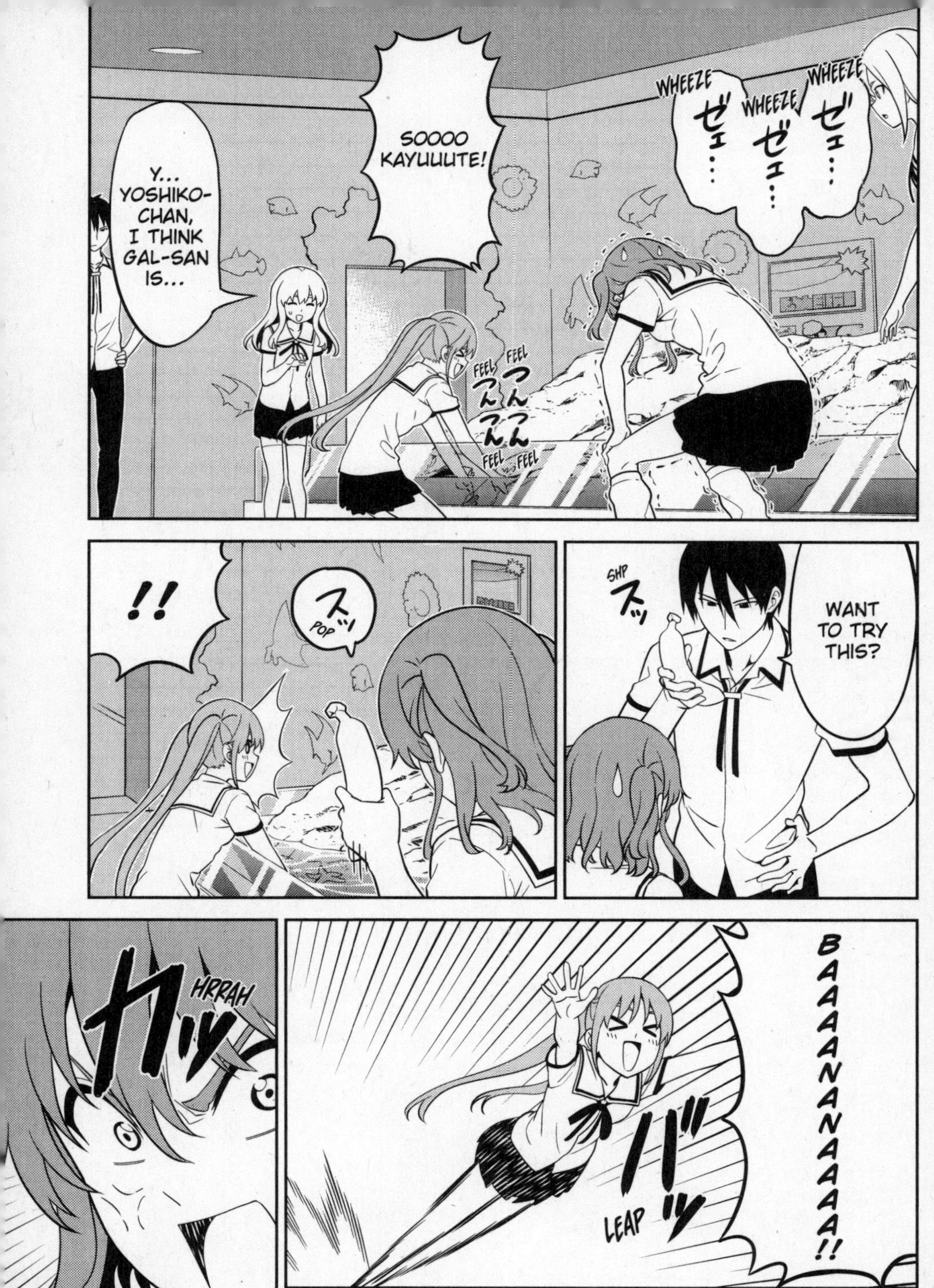
WHEEZE
ゼェ…
WHEEZE
ゼェ…
WHEEZE
ゼェ…
SOOOO KAYUUUTE!
Y... YOSHIKO-CHAN, I THINK GAL-SAN IS...
FEEL FEEL
つんつん
つんつん
FEEL FEEL
SHP
スッ
WANT TO TRY THIS?
!!
スッ
POP
BAAAANAAAAAA!!
バッ
LEAP
カッ
HRRAH

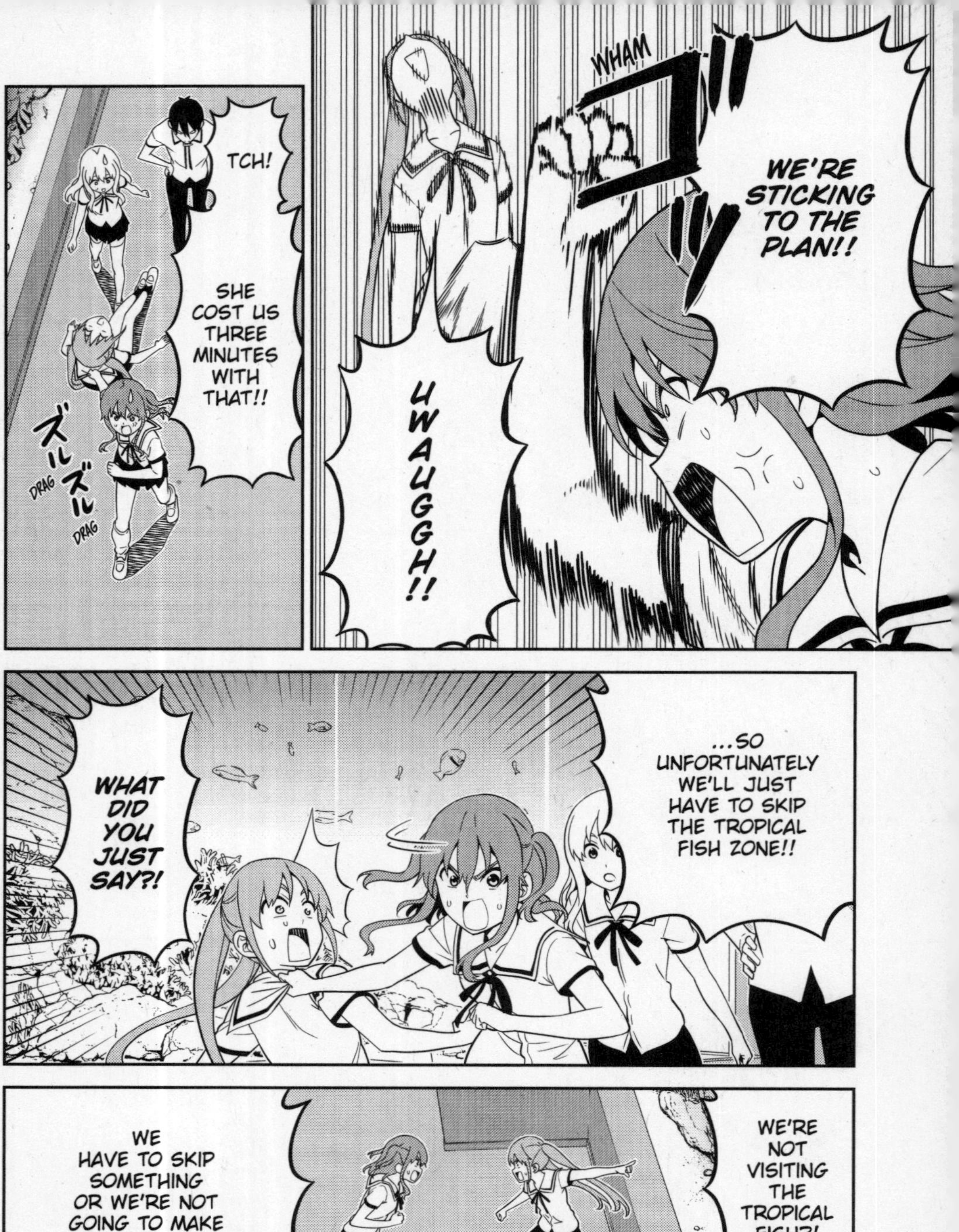
WHAM
ゴ
WE'RE STICKING TO THE PLAN!!
UWAUGGH!!
TCH!
SHE COST US THREE MINUTES WITH THAT!!
ズルズル
DRAG DRAG
...SO UNFORTUNATELY WE'LL JUST HAVE TO SKIP THE TROPICAL FISH ZONE!!
WHAT DID YOU JUST SAY?!
WE'RE NOT VISITING THE TROPICAL FISH?!
WE HAVE TO SKIP SOMETHING OR WE'RE NOT GOING TO MAKE THE BUS BACK TO TOWN!!

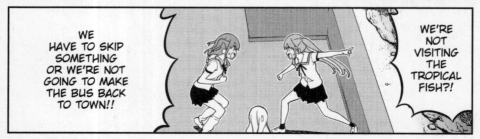

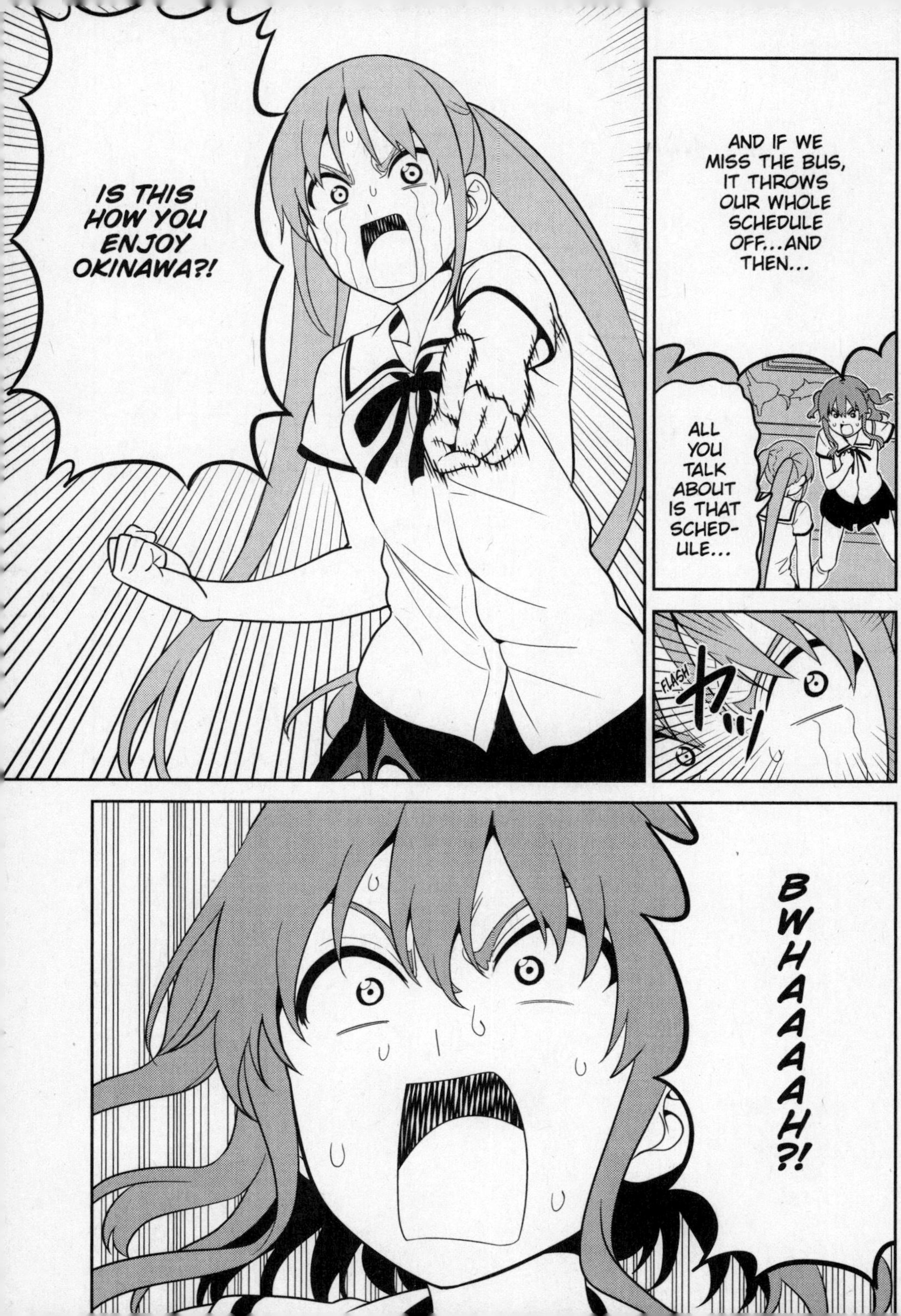
AND IF WE MISS THE BUS, IT THROWS OUR WHOLE SCHEDULE OFF...AND THEN...
ALL YOU TALK ABOUT IS THAT SCHED-ULE...
FLASH
IS THIS HOW YOU ENJOY OKINAWA?!
BWHAAAAAAH?!

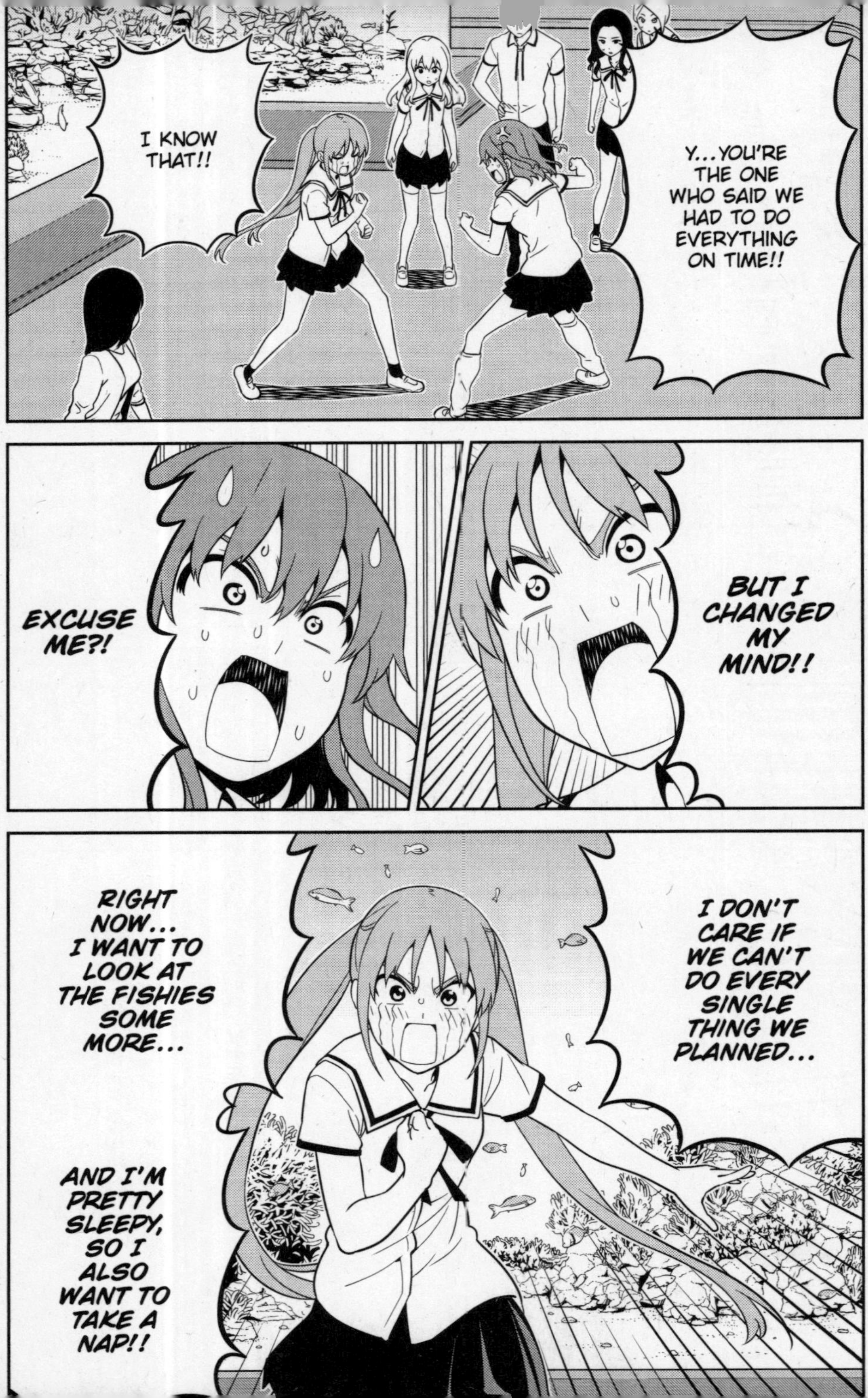
Y...YOU'RE THE ONE WHO SAID WE HAD TO DO EVERYTHING ON TIME!!
I KNOW THAT!!
BUT I CHANGED MY MIND!!
EXCUSE ME?!
I DON'T CARE IF WE CAN'T DO EVERY SINGLE THING WE PLANNED...
RIGHT NOW... I WANT TO LOOK AT THE FISHIES SOME MORE...
AND I'M PRETTY SLEEPY, SO I ALSO WANT TO TAKE A NAP!!

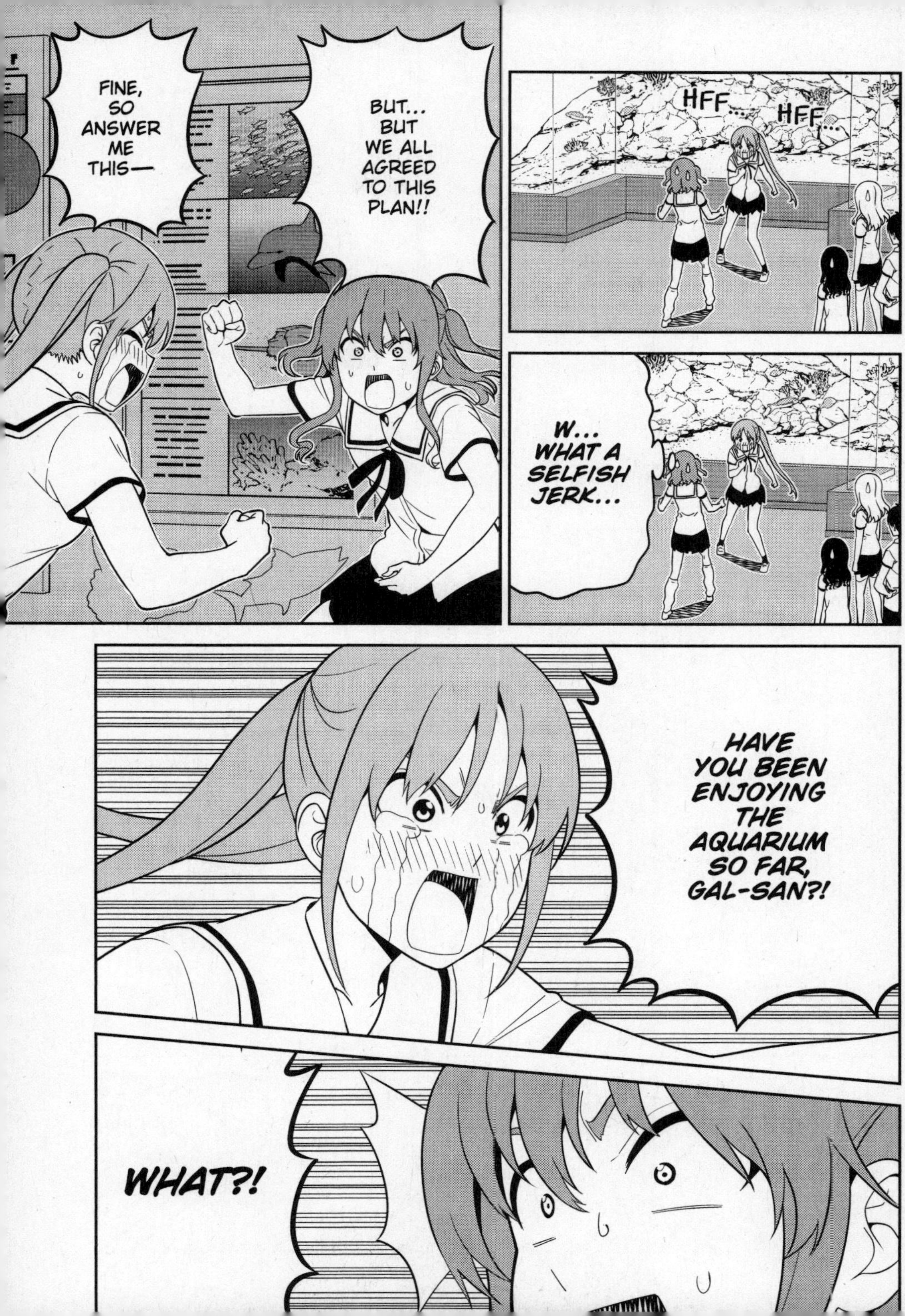
HFF... HFF...
W... WHAT A SELFISH JERK...
BUT... BUT WE ALL AGREED TO THIS PLAN!!
FINE, SO ANSWER ME THIS—
HAVE YOU BEEN ENJOYING THE AQUARIUM SO FAR, GAL-SAN?!
WHAT?!

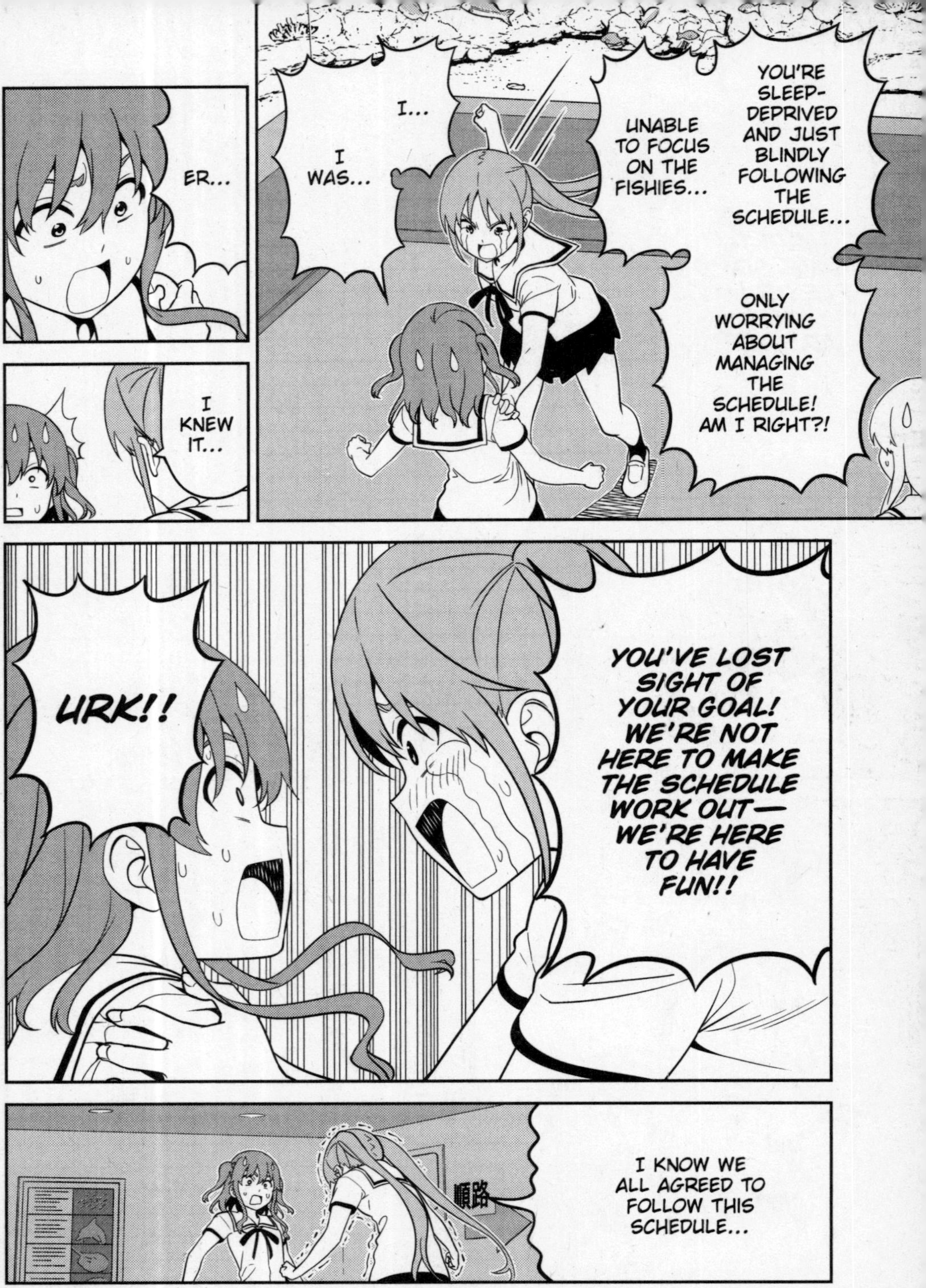

YOU'RE SLEEP-DEPRIVED AND JUST BLINDLY FOLLOWING THE SCHEDULE...
UNABLE TO FOCUS ON THE FISHIES...
ONLY WORRYING ABOUT MANAGING THE SCHEDULE! AM I RIGHT?!
I...
I WAS...
ER...
I KNEW IT...
YOU'VE LOST SIGHT OF YOUR GOAL! WE'RE NOT HERE TO MAKE THE SCHEDULE WORK OUT— WE'RE HERE TO HAVE FUN!!
URK!!
I KNOW WE ALL AGREED TO FOLLOW THIS SCHEDULE...
順路

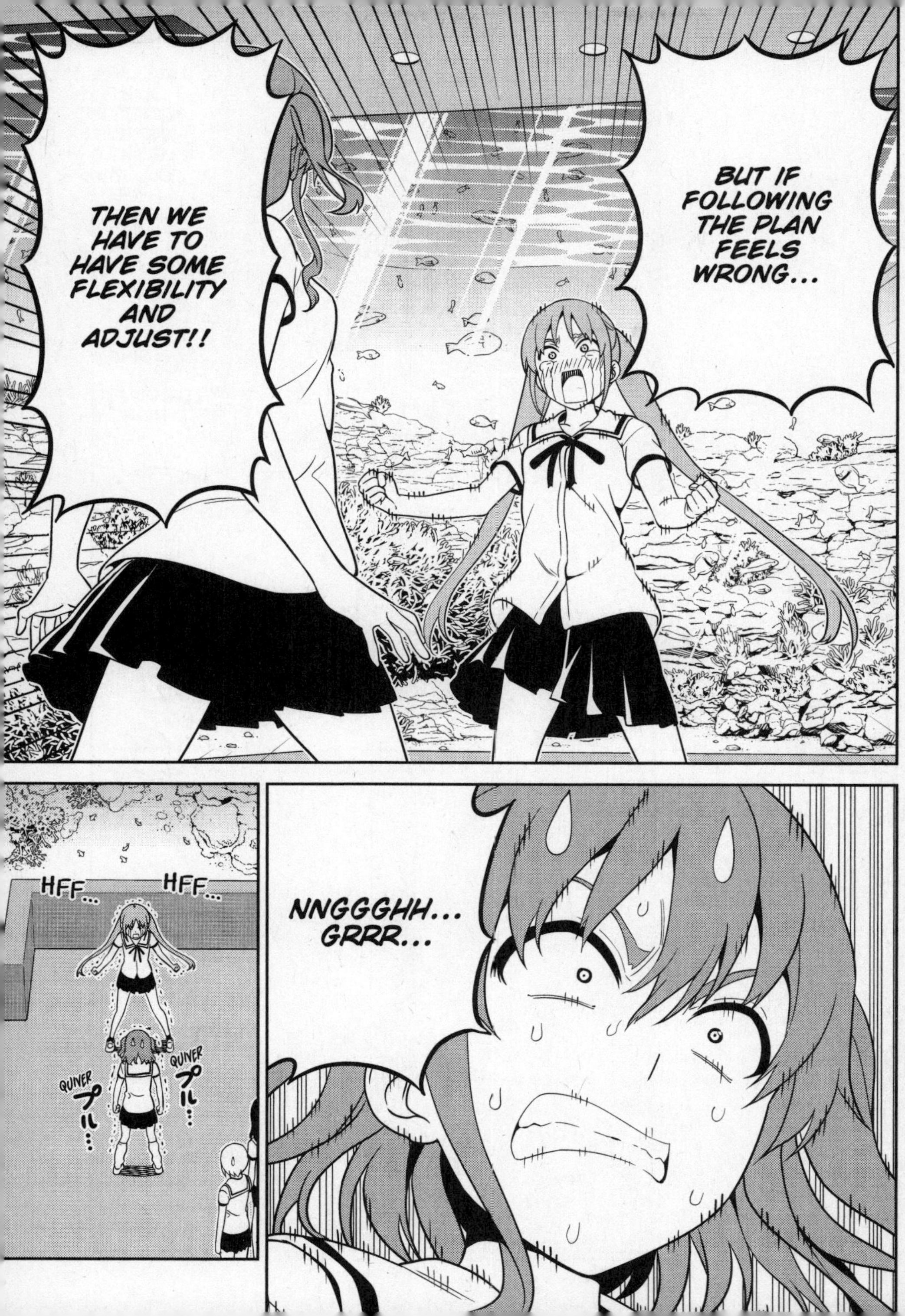
BUT IF FOLLOWING THE PLAN FEELS WRONG...
THEN WE HAVE TO HAVE SOME FLEXIBILITY AND ADJUST!!
NNGGGHH... GRRR...
HFF... HFF...
QUIVER プル...
QUIVER プル...

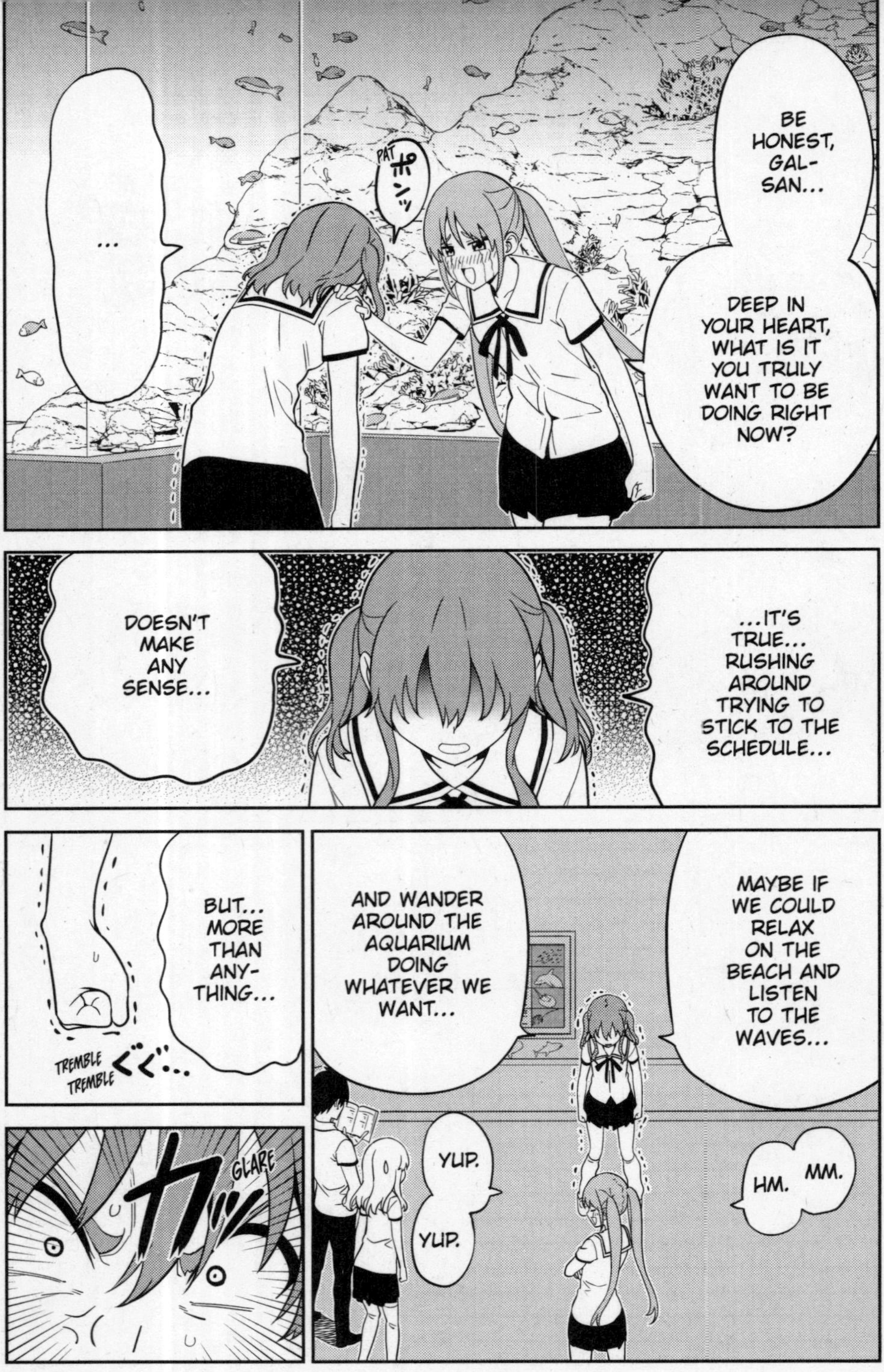
BE HONEST, GAL-SAN...
DEEP IN YOUR HEART, WHAT IS IT YOU TRULY WANT TO BE DOING RIGHT NOW?
PAT ポンッ
...
...IT'S TRUE... RUSHING AROUND TRYING TO STICK TO THE SCHEDULE...
DOESN'T MAKE ANY SENSE...
MAYBE IF WE COULD RELAX ON THE BEACH AND LISTEN TO THE WAVES...
AND WANDER AROUND THE AQUARIUM DOING WHATEVER WE WANT...
MM.
HM.
YUP.
YUP.
BUT... MORE THAN ANY-THING...
TREMBLE TREMBLE ぐぐ...
GLARE カッ

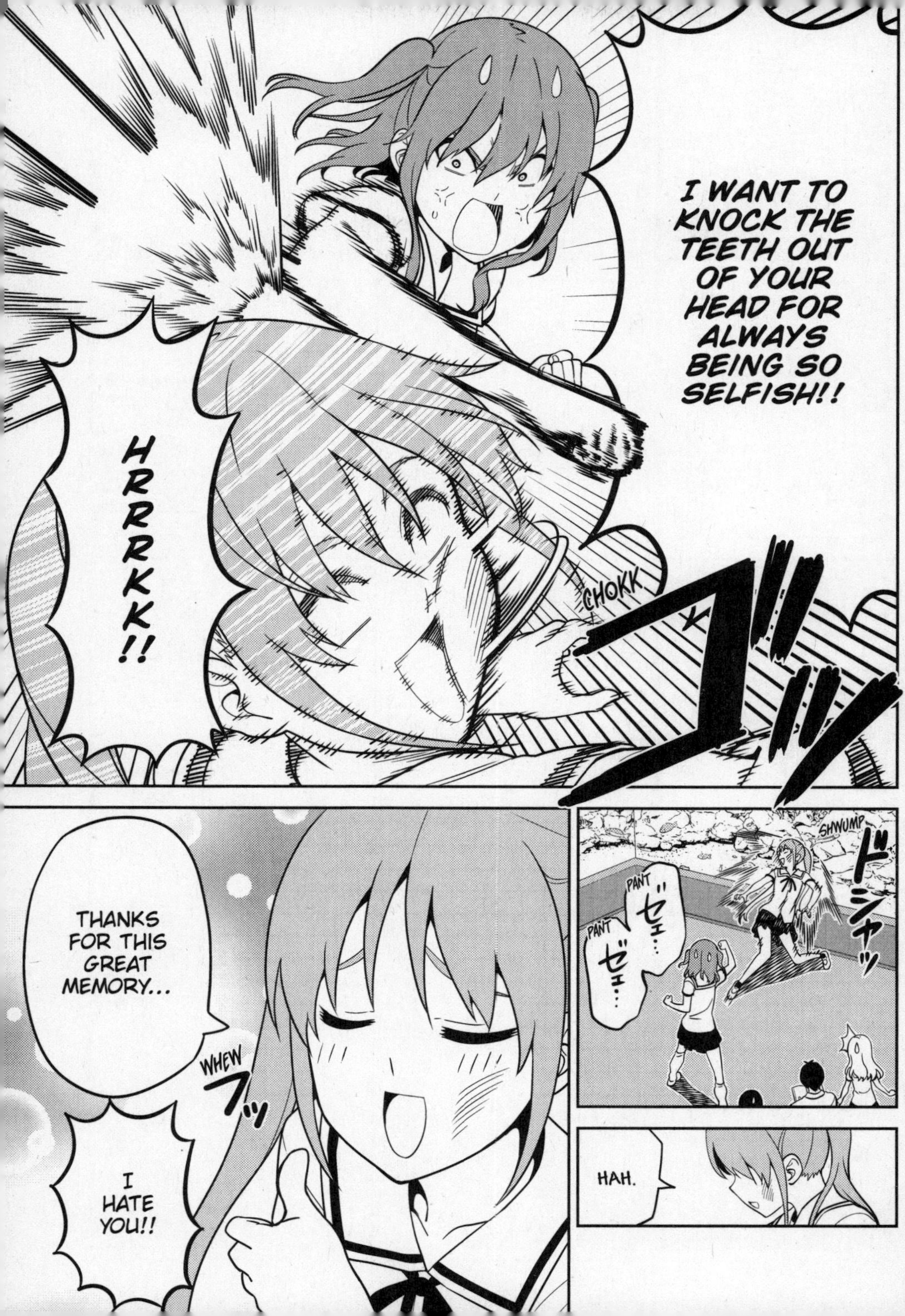
I WANT TO KNOCK THE TEETH OUT OF YOUR HEAD FOR ALWAYS BEING SO SELFISH!!
HRRRKK!!
CHOKK
ゴッ
SHWUMP
ドシャッ
PANT
ゼェ…
PANT
ゼェ…
HAH.
THANKS FOR THIS GREAT MEMORY…
WHEW
フッ
I HATE YOU!!

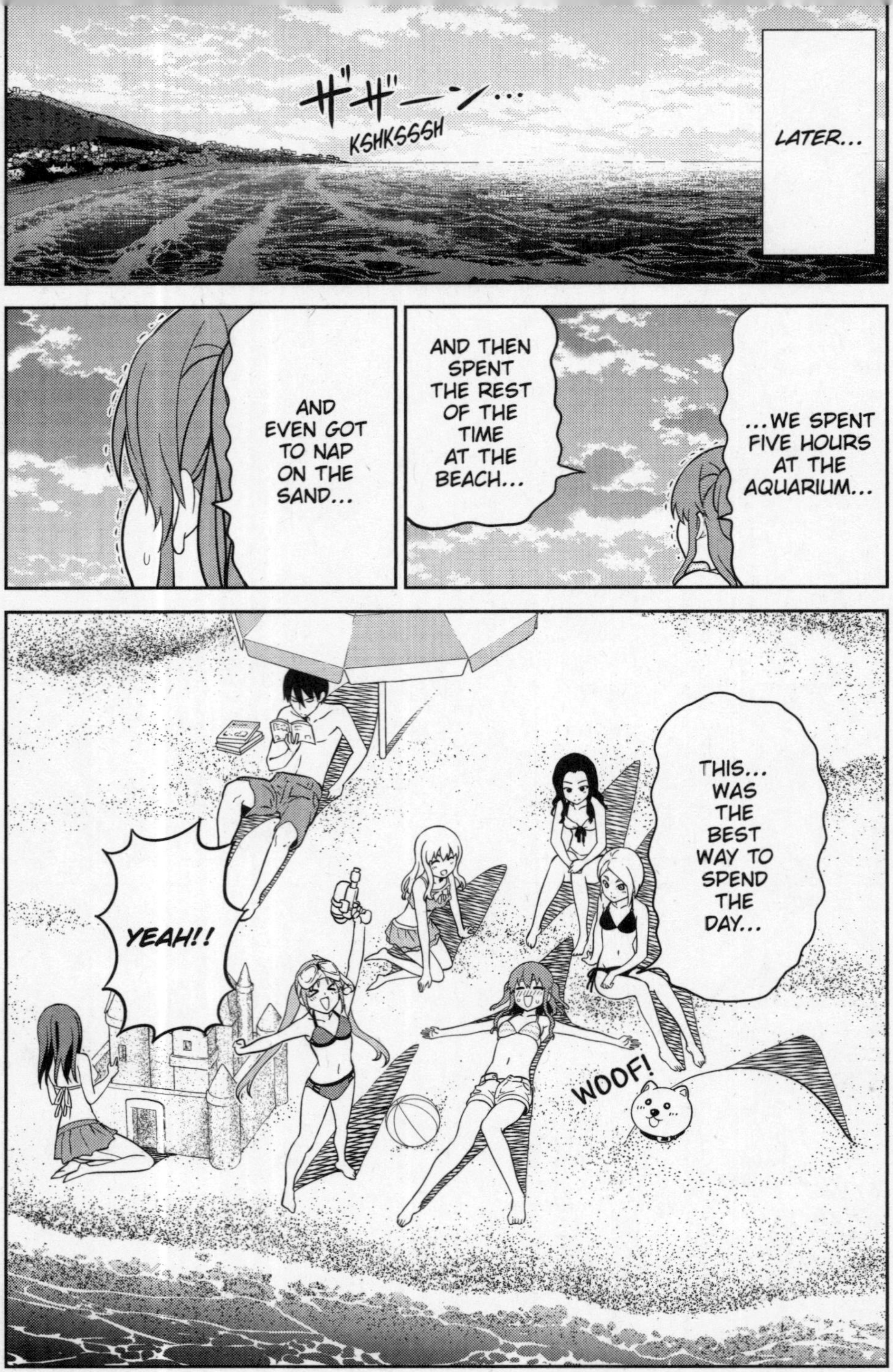
LATER...
ザザーン…
KSHKSSSH
...WE SPENT FIVE HOURS AT THE AQUARIUM...
AND THEN SPENT THE REST OF THE TIME AT THE BEACH...
AND EVEN GOT TO NAP ON THE SAND...
THIS... WAS THE BEST WAY TO SPEND THE DAY...
WOOF!
YEAH!!

I'll Never Surrender This Desire

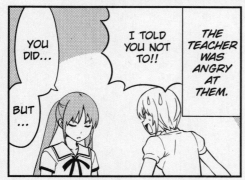

THE TEACHER WAS ANGRY AT THEM.
I TOLD YOU NOT TO!!
YOU DID...
BUT ...
THERE ARE TIMES... WHEN A PERSON SIMPLY CAN'T BE STOPPED...
DON'T GIVE ME THAT!!

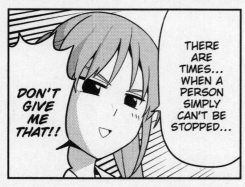

(Your sexy pheromones got me)

Aho-Girl

\ˈahô͵gərl\ *Japanese, noun.*
A clueless girl.

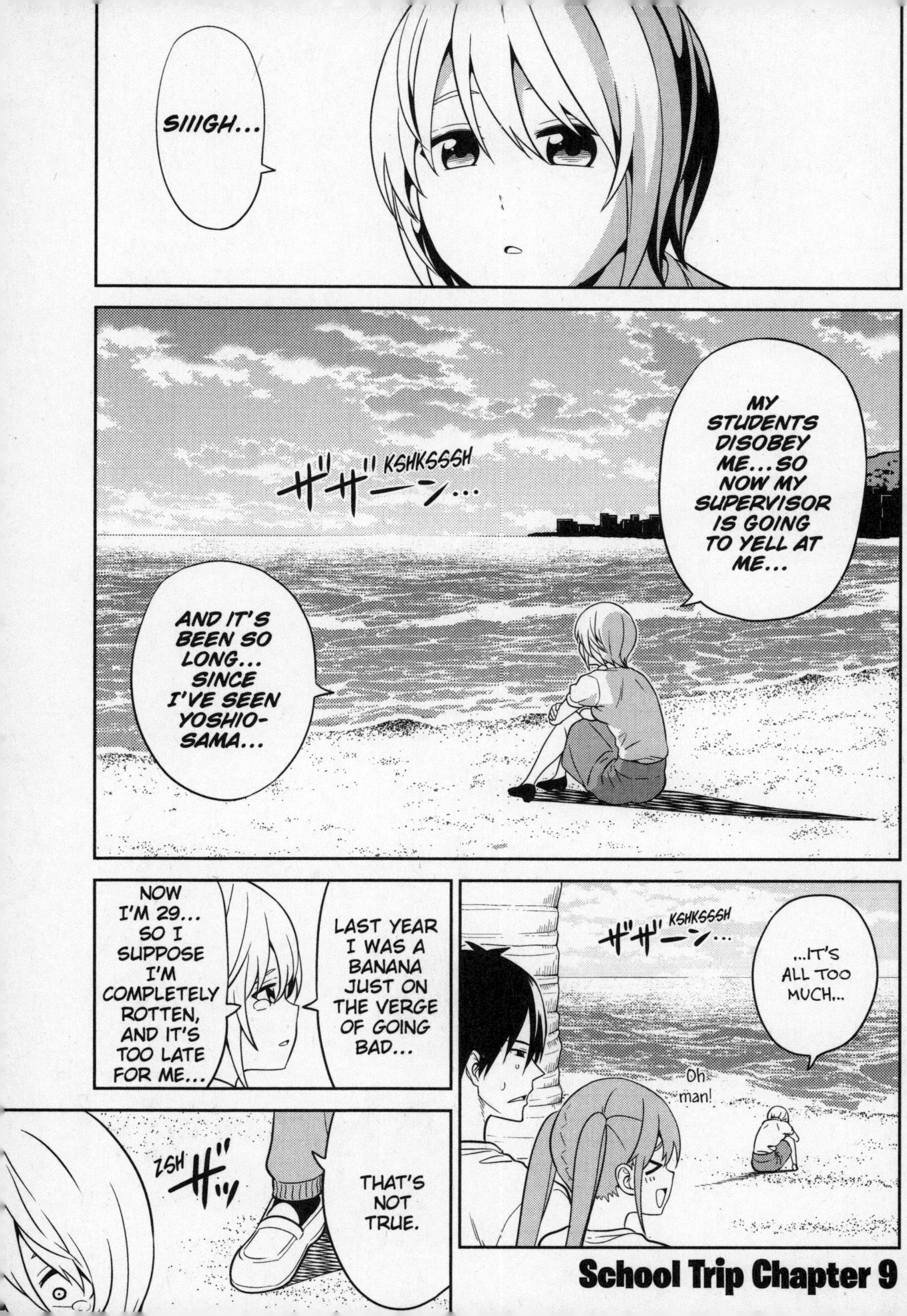
SIIIGH...
MY STUDENTS DISOBEY ME...SO NOW MY SUPERVISOR IS GOING TO YELL AT ME...
ザザーン... KSHKSSSH
AND IT'S BEEN SO LONG... SINCE I'VE SEEN YOSHIO-SAMA...
ザザーン... KSHKSSSH
...IT'S ALL TOO MUCH...
Oh man!
LAST YEAR I WAS A BANANA JUST ON THE VERGE OF GOING BAD...
NOW I'M 29... SO I SUPPOSE I'M COMPLETELY ROTTEN, AND IT'S TOO LATE FOR ME...
ザッ ZSH
THAT'S NOT TRUE.

School Trip Chapter 9

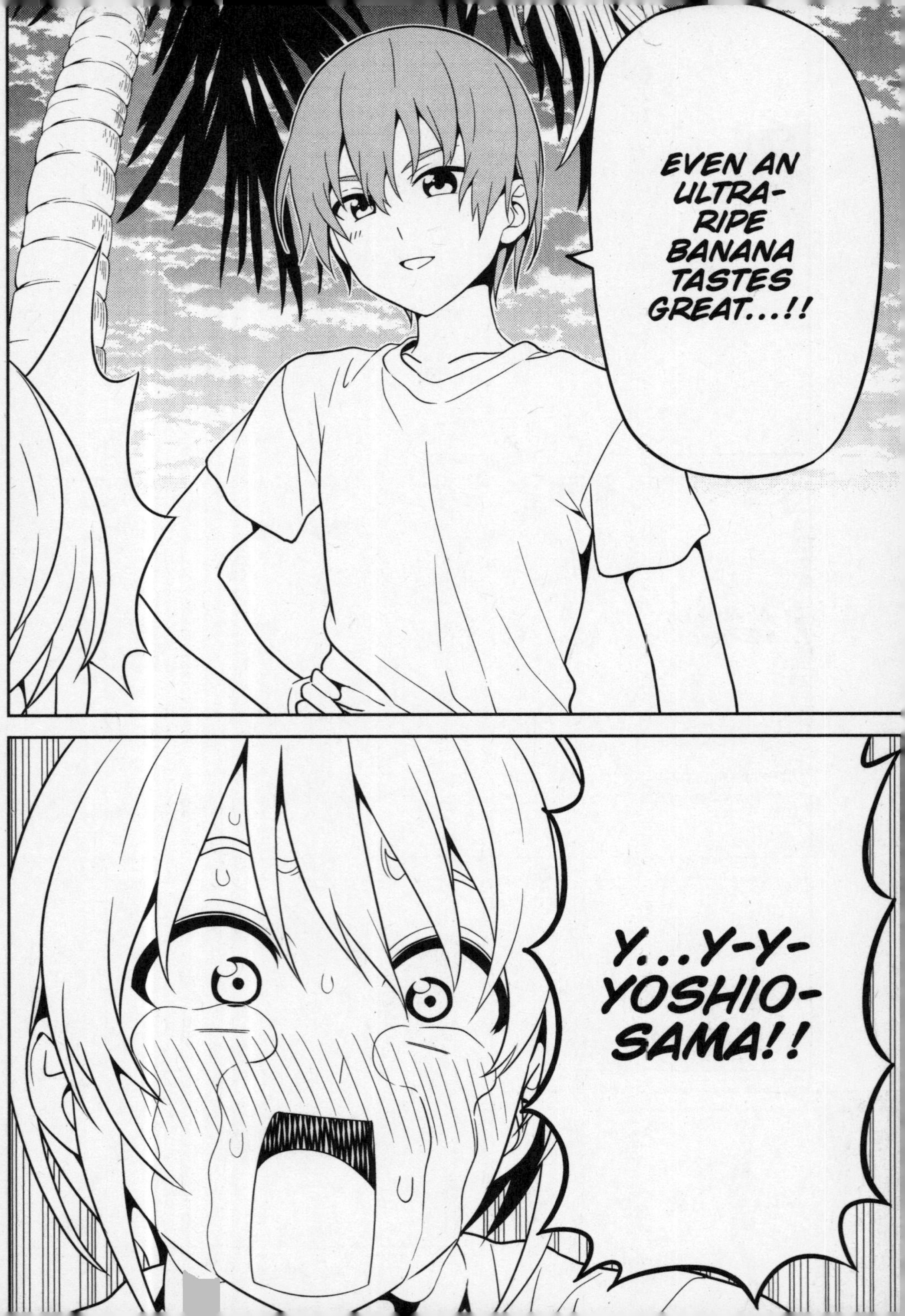
EVEN AN ULTRA-RIPE BANANA TASTES GREAT...!!
Y...Y-Y-YOSHIO-SAMA!!

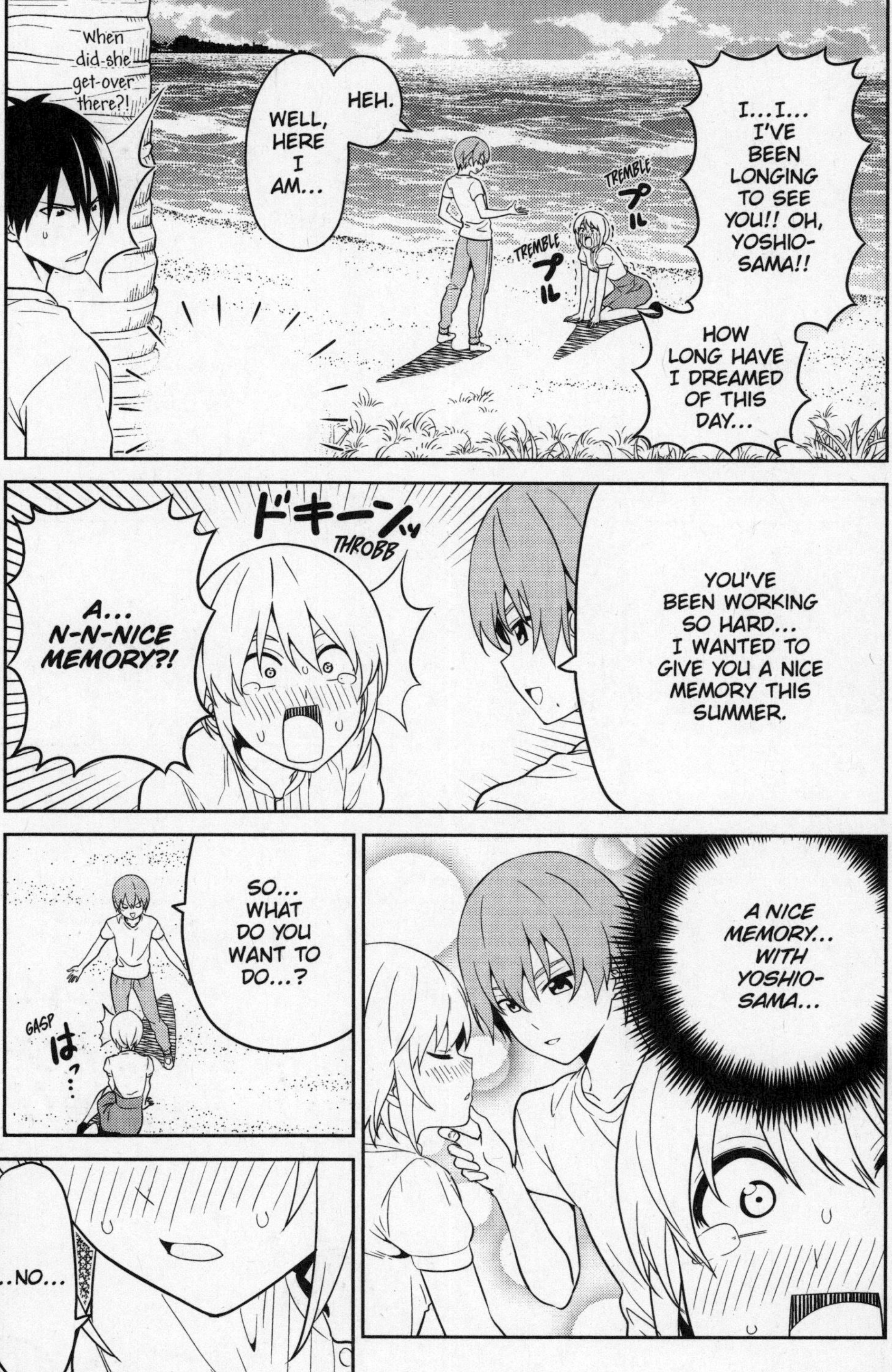
I...I... I'VE BEEN LONGING TO SEE YOU!! OH, YOSHIO-SAMA!!
HOW LONG HAVE I DREAMED OF THIS DAY...
TREMBLE
プル
TREMBLE
プル
HEH.
WELL, HERE I AM...
When did she get over there?!
YOU'VE BEEN WORKING SO HARD... I WANTED TO GIVE YOU A NICE MEMORY THIS SUMMER.
ドキーンッ
THROBB
A... N-N-NICE MEMORY?!
A NICE MEMORY... WITH YOSHIO-SAMA...
SO... WHAT DO YOU WANT TO DO...?
GASP
はっ...
...NO...

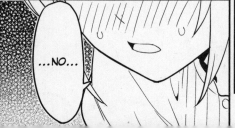

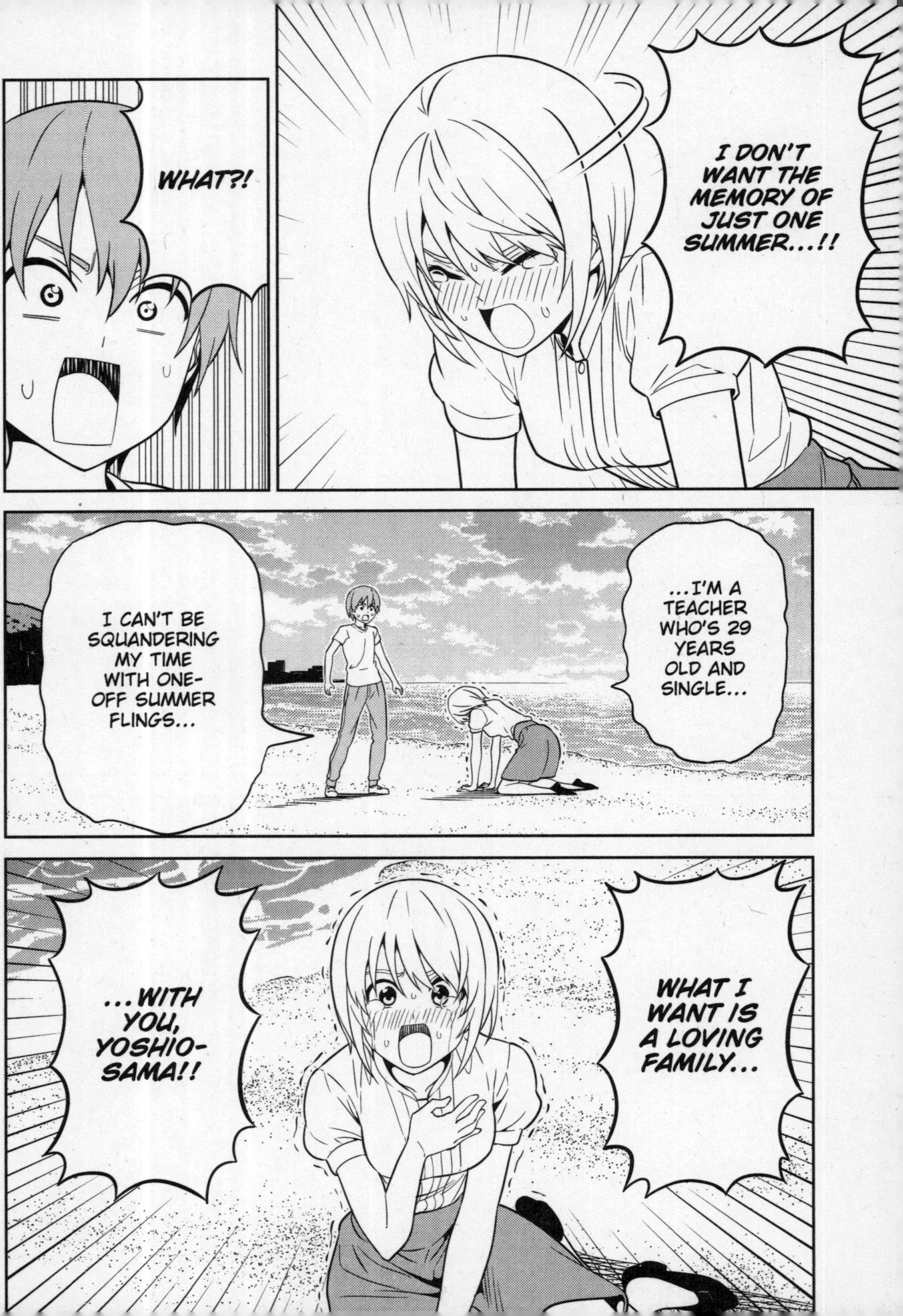
I DON'T WANT THE MEMORY OF JUST ONE SUMMER...!!
WHAT?!
...I'M A TEACHER WHO'S 29 YEARS OLD AND SINGLE...
I CAN'T BE SQUANDERING MY TIME WITH ONE-OFF SUMMER FLINGS...
WHAT I WANT IS A LOVING FAMILY...
...WITH YOU, YOSHIO-SAMA!!

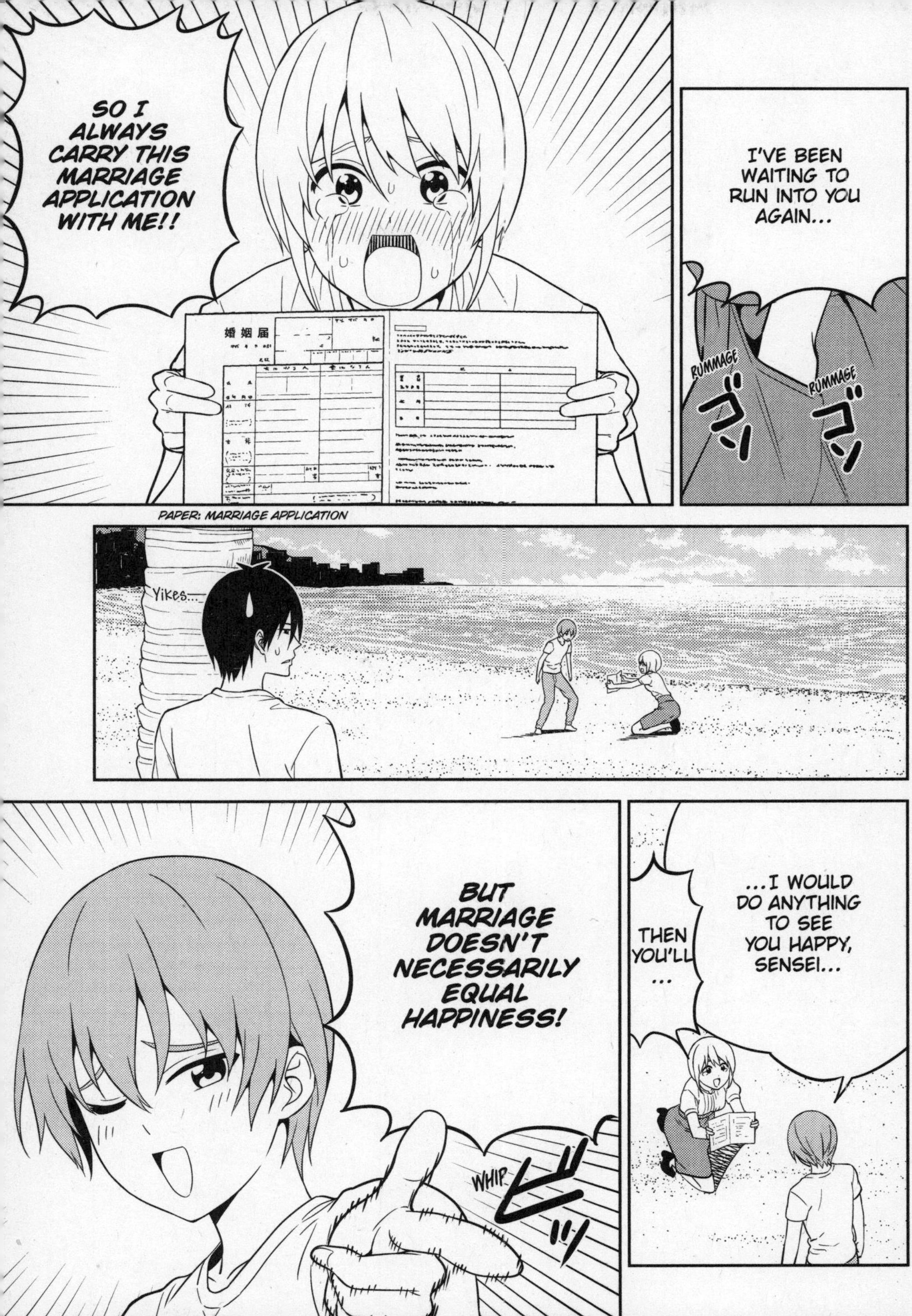
I'VE BEEN WAITING TO RUN INTO YOU AGAIN...
RUMMAGE
ゴソ
RUMMAGE
ゴソ
SO I ALWAYS CARRY THIS MARRIAGE APPLICATION WITH ME!!
婚姻届
PAPER: MARRIAGE APPLICATION
Yikes...
...I WOULD DO ANYTHING TO SEE YOU HAPPY, SENSEI...
THEN YOU'LL ...
BUT MARRIAGE DOESN'T NECESSARILY EQUAL HAPPINESS!
WHIP
ビッ

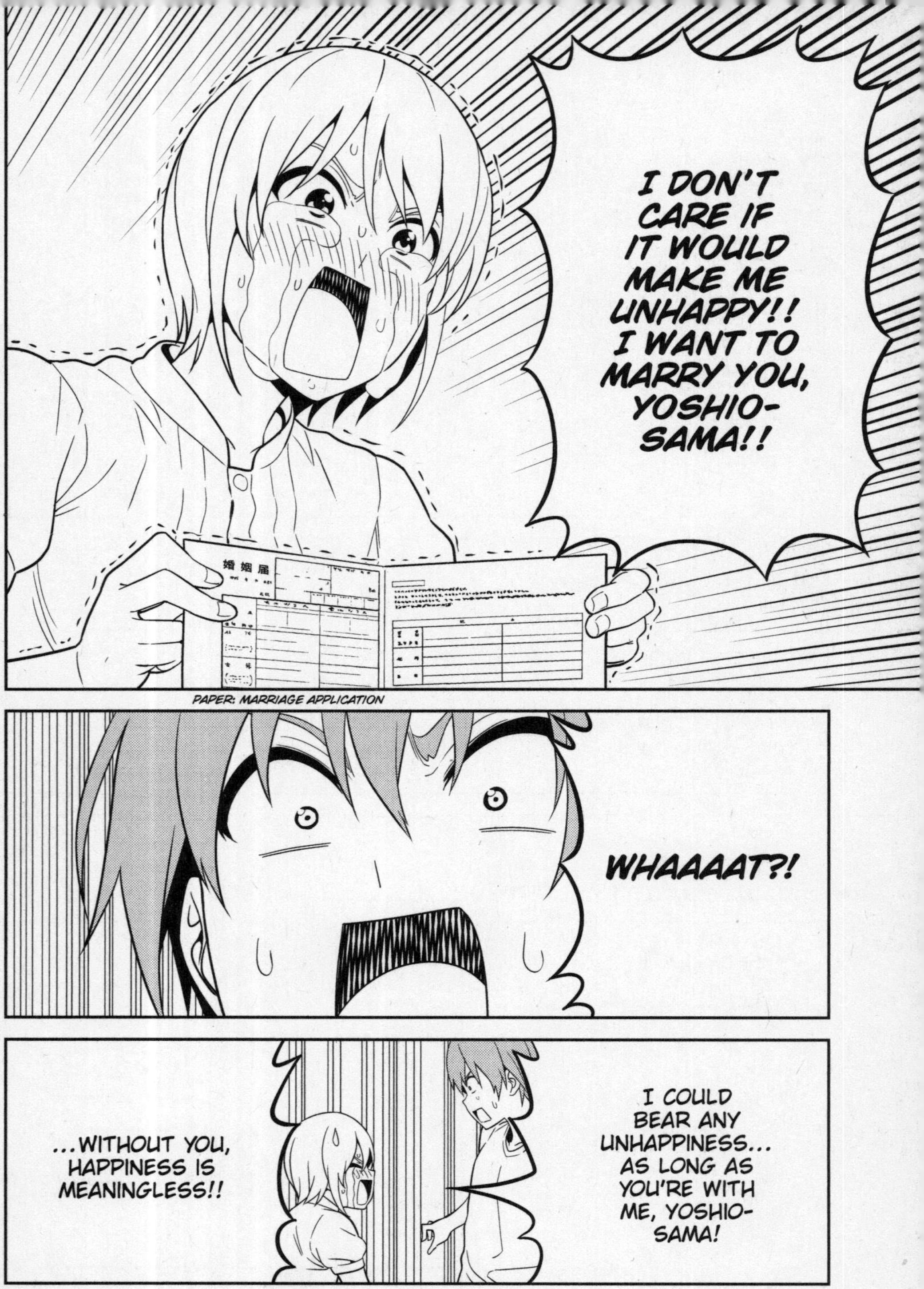
I DON'T CARE IF IT WOULD MAKE ME UNHAPPY!! I WANT TO MARRY YOU, YOSHIO-SAMA!!
婚姻届
PAPER: MARRIAGE APPLICATION
WHAAAAT?!
I COULD BEAR ANY UNHAPPINESS... AS LONG AS YOU'RE WITH ME, YOSHIO-SAMA!
...WITHOUT YOU, HAPPINESS IS MEANINGLESS!!

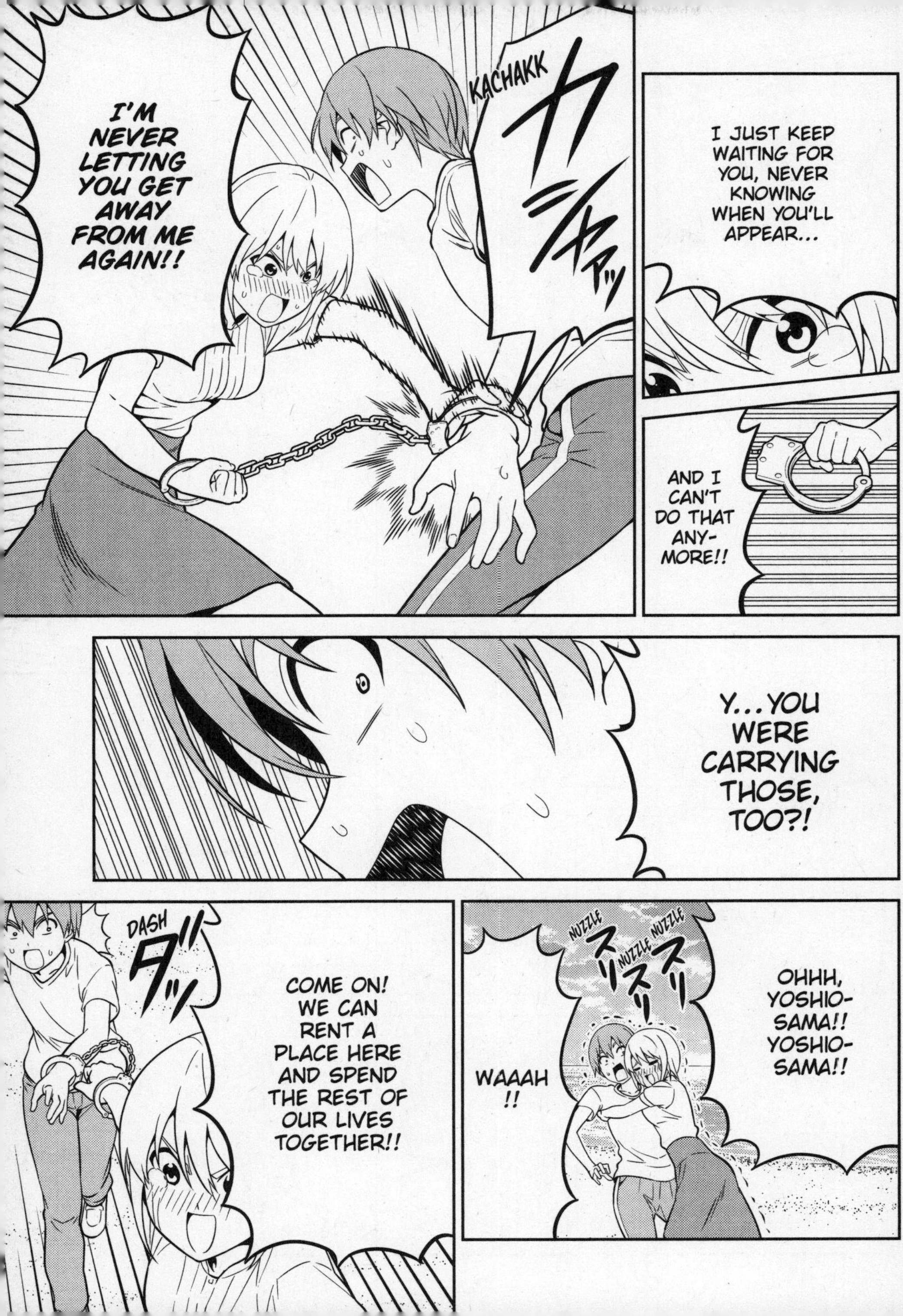
I JUST KEEP WAITING FOR YOU, NEVER KNOWING WHEN YOU'LL APPEAR...
AND I CAN'T DO THAT ANY-MORE!!
KACHAKK
カシャアッ
I'M NEVER LETTING YOU GET AWAY FROM ME AGAIN!!
Y...YOU WERE CARRYING THOSE, TOO?!
NUZZLE
スリ
NUZZLE
スリ
NUZZLE
スリ
OHHH, YOSHIO-SAMA!! YOSHIO-SAMA!!
WAAAH!!
DASH
ダッ
COME ON! WE CAN RENT A PLACE HERE AND SPEND THE REST OF OUR LIVES TOGETHER!!

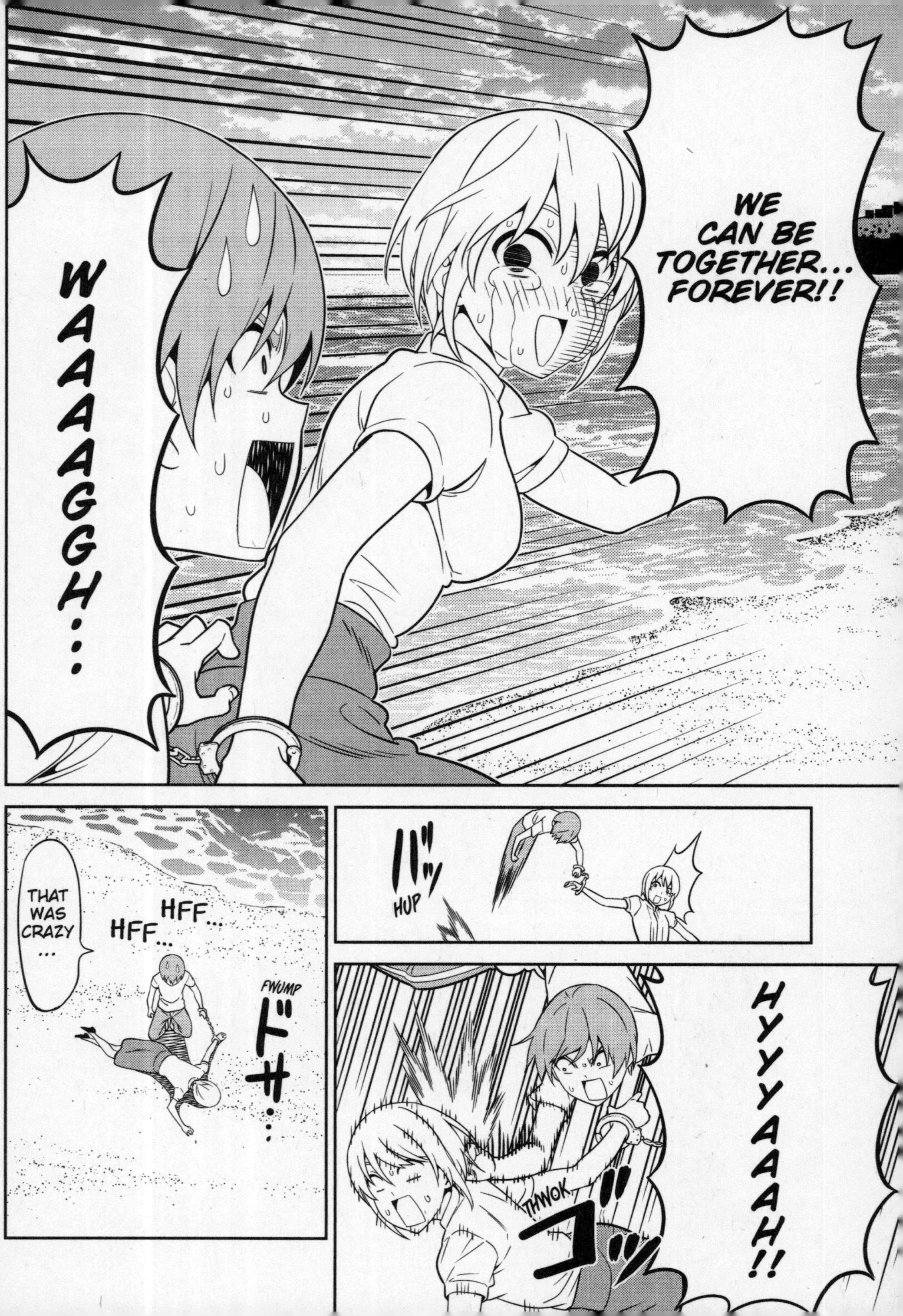
WE CAN BE TOGETHER... FOREVER!!
WAAAAAGGH...
バッ
HUP
HYYAAAAH!!
ゴッ
THWOK
HFF... HFF...
THAT WAS CRAZY...
ドサ...
FWUMP

Was That a Pun?

...WE GOT THE HANDCUFFS OFF, AT LEAST...

...

THIS HAS BEEN ONE INTENSE SUMMER...

(The high pressure drew me in, my)

Aho-Girl

\\'ahôˌgərl\\ *Japanese, noun.*

A clueless girl.

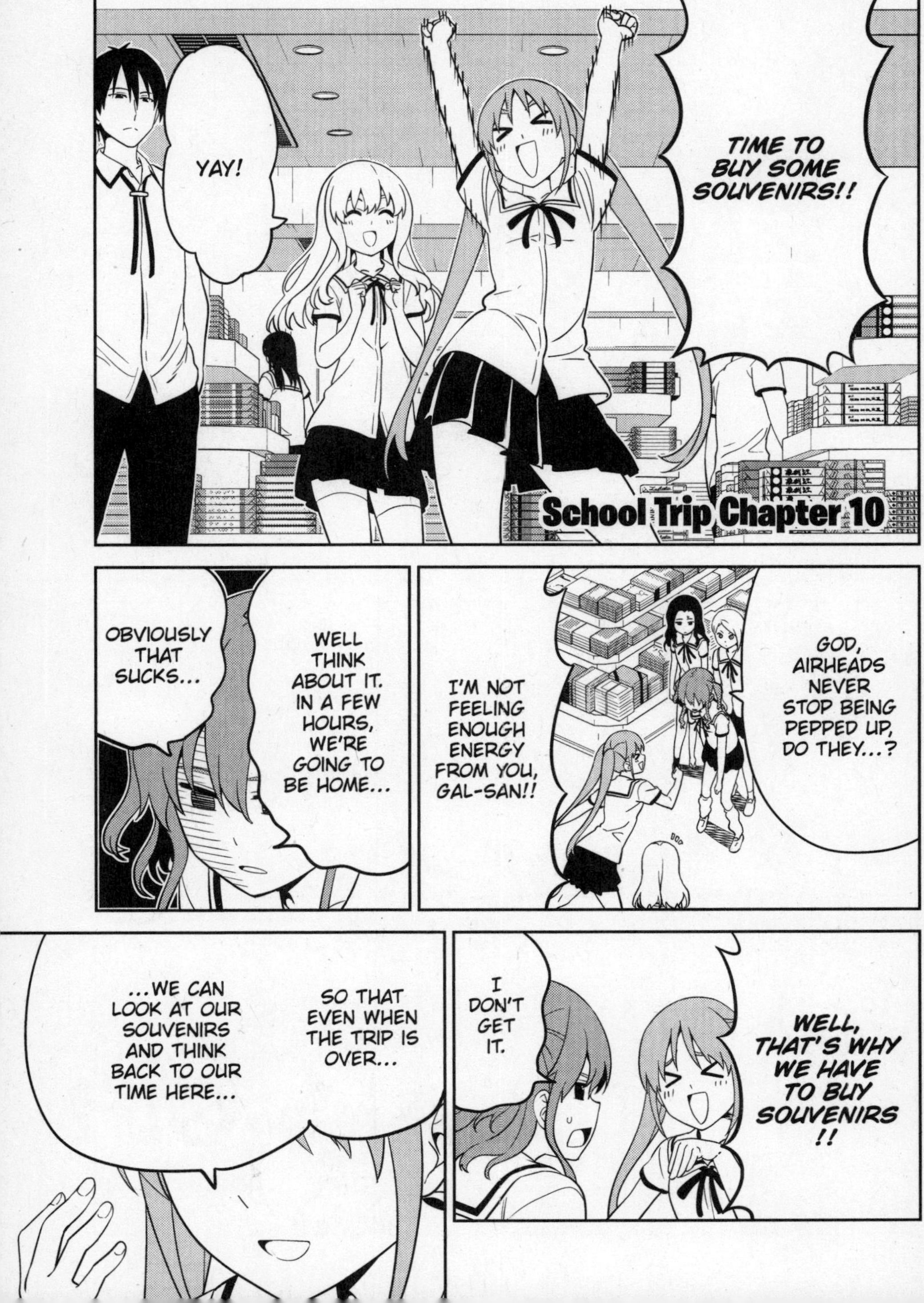
TIME TO BUY SOME SOUVENIRS!!
YAY!
School Trip Chapter 10
GOD, AIRHEADS NEVER STOP BEING PEPPED UP, DO THEY...?
I'M NOT FEELING ENOUGH ENERGY FROM YOU, GAL-SAN!!
WELL THINK ABOUT IT. IN A FEW HOURS, WE'RE GOING TO BE HOME...
OBVIOUSLY THAT SUCKS...
WELL, THAT'S WHY WE HAVE TO BUY SOUVENIRS!!
I DON'T GET IT.
SO THAT EVEN WHEN THE TRIP IS OVER...
...WE CAN LOOK AT OUR SOUVENIRS AND THINK BACK TO OUR TIME HERE...

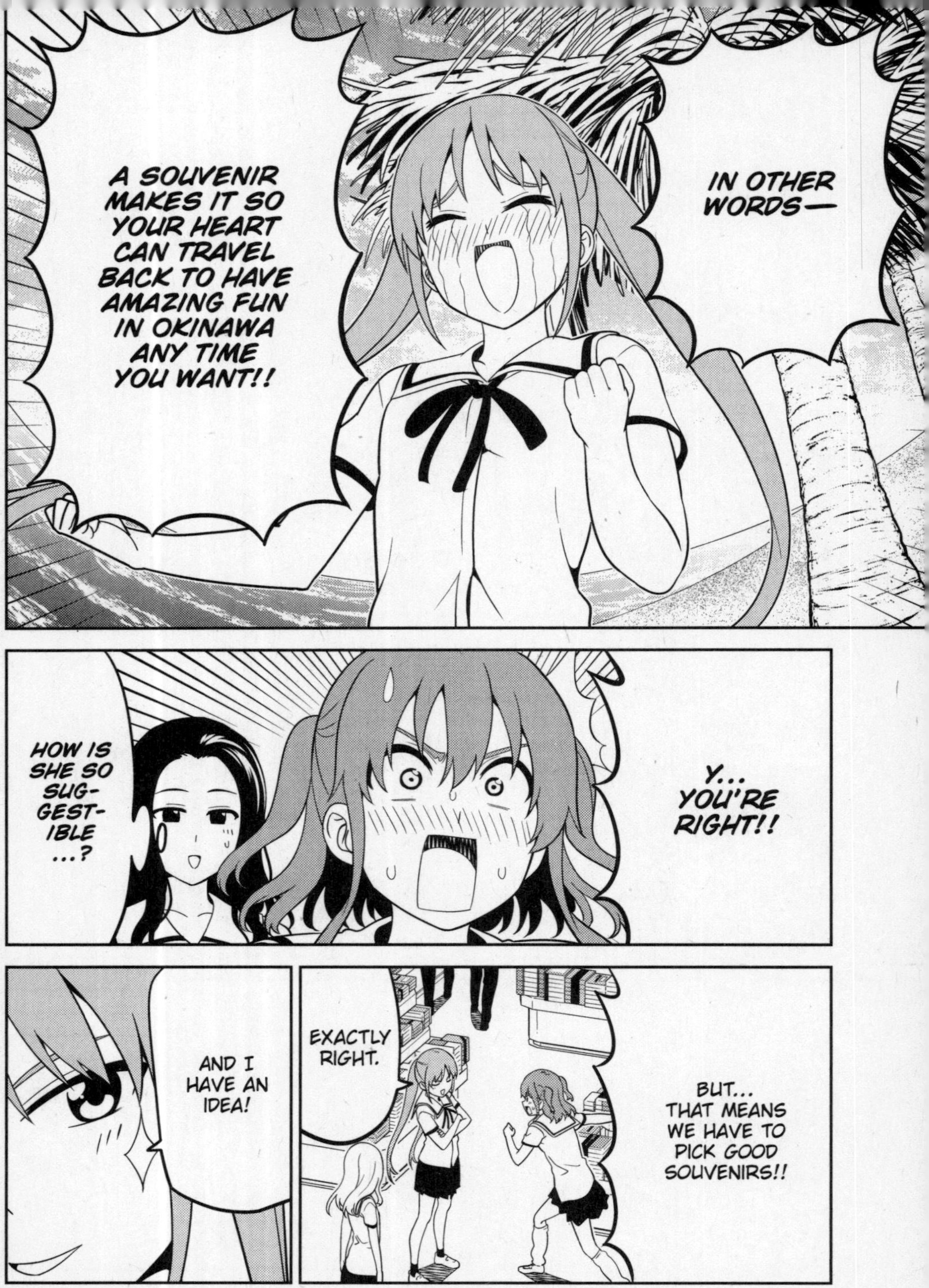
IN OTHER WORDS—
A SOUVENIR MAKES IT SO YOUR HEART CAN TRAVEL BACK TO HAVE AMAZING FUN IN OKINAWA ANY TIME YOU WANT!!
Y... YOU'RE RIGHT!!
HOW IS SHE SO SUG-GEST-IBLE ...?
BUT... THAT MEANS WE HAVE TO PICK GOOD SOUVENIRS!!
EXACTLY RIGHT.
AND I HAVE AN IDEA!

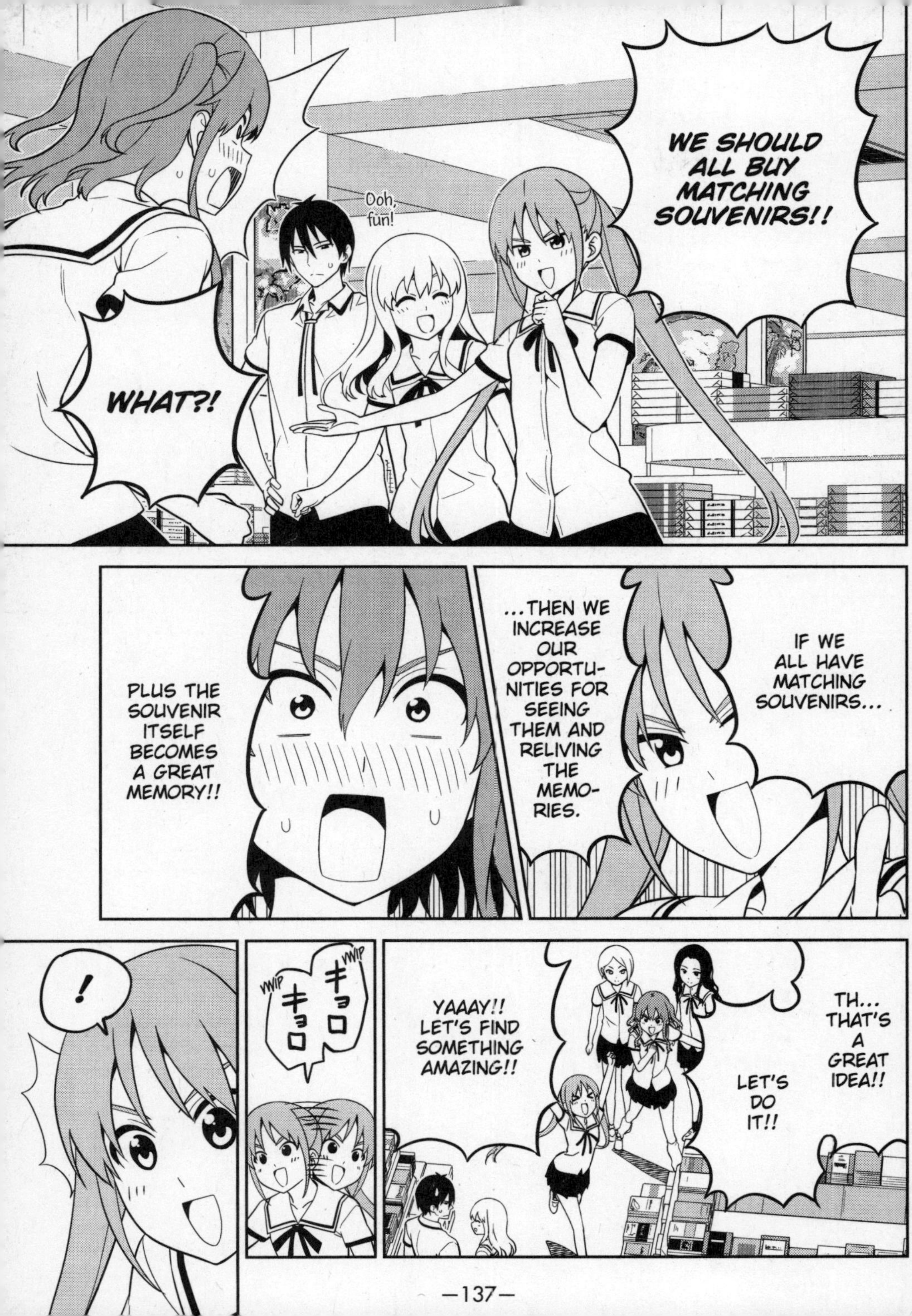
WE SHOULD ALL BUY MATCHING SOUVENIRS!!
Ooh, fun!
WHAT?!
IF WE ALL HAVE MATCHING SOUVENIRS...
...THEN WE INCREASE OUR OPPORTU-NITIES FOR SEEING THEM AND RELIVING THE MEMO-RIES.
PLUS THE SOUVENIR ITSELF BECOMES A GREAT MEMORY!!
TH... THAT'S A GREAT IDEA!!
LET'S DO IT!!
YAAAY!! LET'S FIND SOMETHING AMAZING!!
キョロ
VWIP
キョロ
VWIP
!

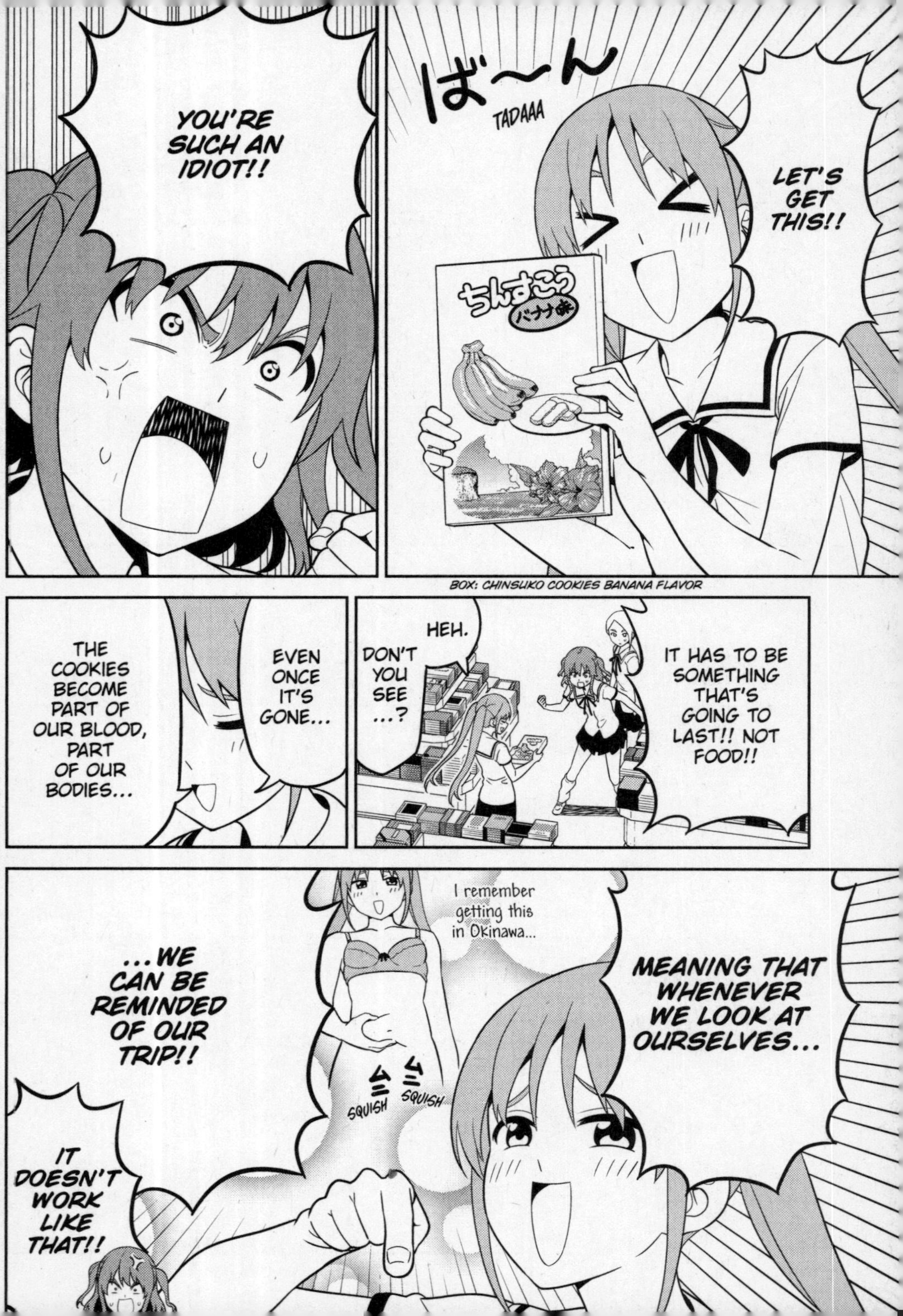
ば〜ん
TADAAA
LET'S GET THIS!!
ちんすこう
バナナ味
YOU'RE SUCH AN IDIOT!!
BOX: CHINSUKO COOKIES BANANA FLAVOR
IT HAS TO BE SOMETHING THAT'S GOING TO LAST!! NOT FOOD!!
HEH.
DON'T YOU SEE ...?
EVEN ONCE IT'S GONE...
THE COOKIES BECOME PART OF OUR BLOOD, PART OF OUR BODIES...
MEANING THAT WHENEVER WE LOOK AT OURSELVES...
I remember getting this in Okinawa...
...WE CAN BE REMINDED OF OUR TRIP!!
ムニ
SQUISH
ムニ
SQUISH
IT DOESN'T WORK LIKE THAT!!

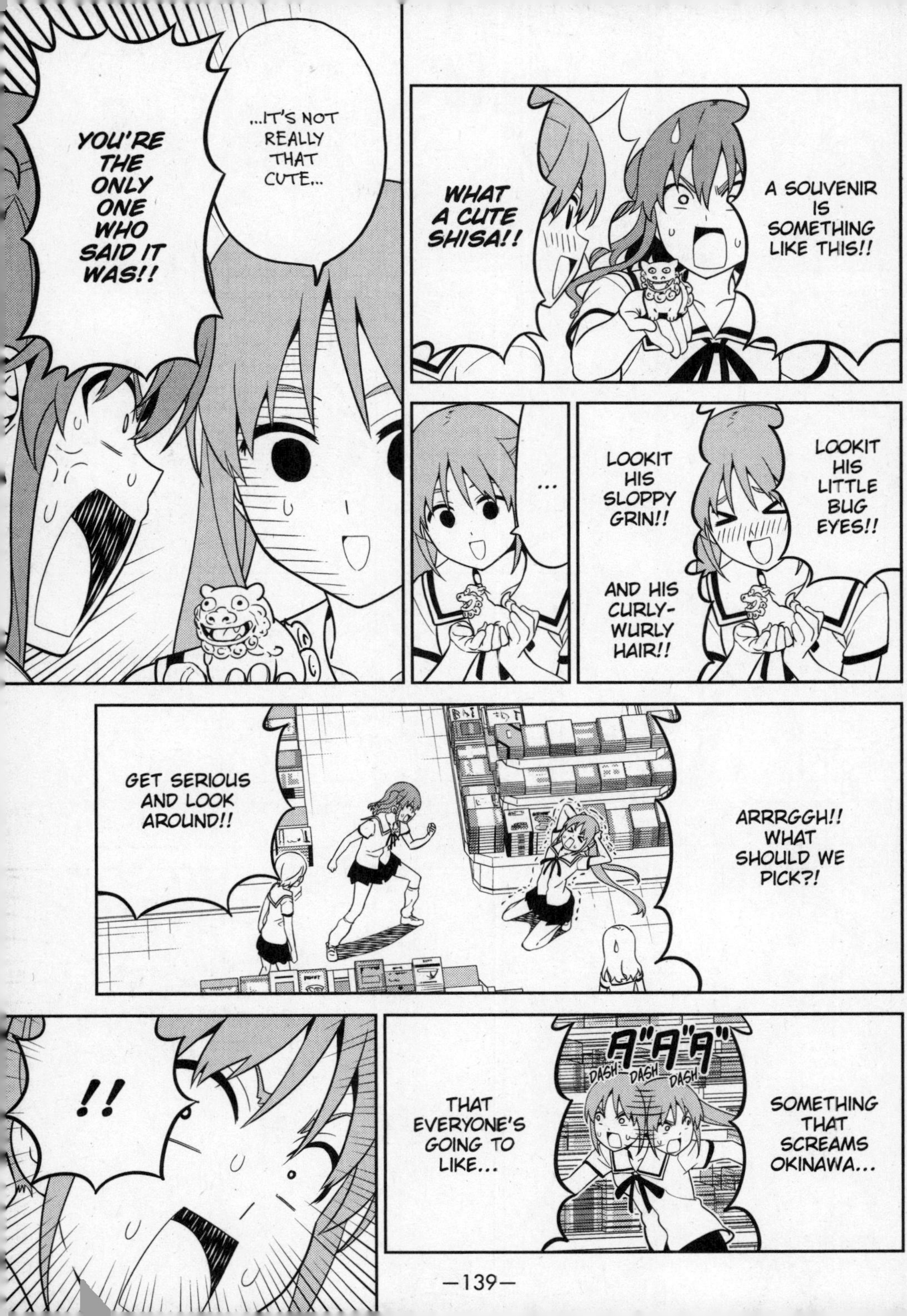
A SOUVENIR IS SOMETHING LIKE THIS!!
WHAT A CUTE SHISA!!
LOOKIT HIS LITTLE BUG EYES!!
LOOKIT HIS SLOPPY GRIN!!
AND HIS CURLY-WURLY HAIR!!
...
...IT'S NOT REALLY THAT CUTE...
YOU'RE THE ONLY ONE WHO SAID IT WAS!!
ARRRGGH!! WHAT SHOULD WE PICK?!
GET SERIOUS AND LOOK AROUND!!
ダダダ
DASH DASH DASH
SOMETHING THAT SCREAMS OKINAWA...
THAT EVERYONE'S GOING TO LIKE...
!!

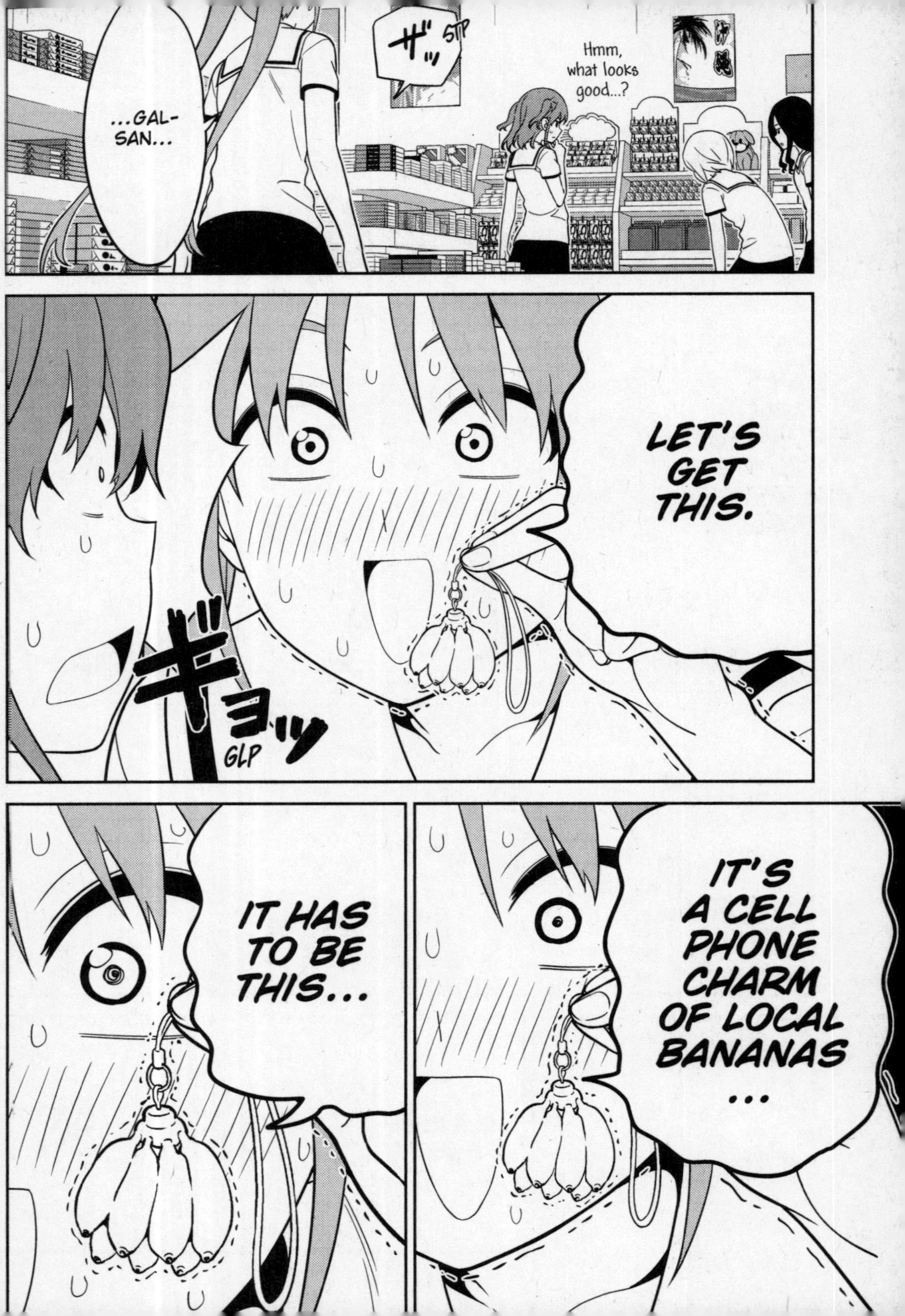
Hmm, what looks good...?
ザッ
STP
...GAL-SAN...
LET'S GET THIS.
ギョッ
GLP
IT'S A CELL PHONE CHARM OF LOCAL BANANAS ...
IT HAS TO BE THIS...

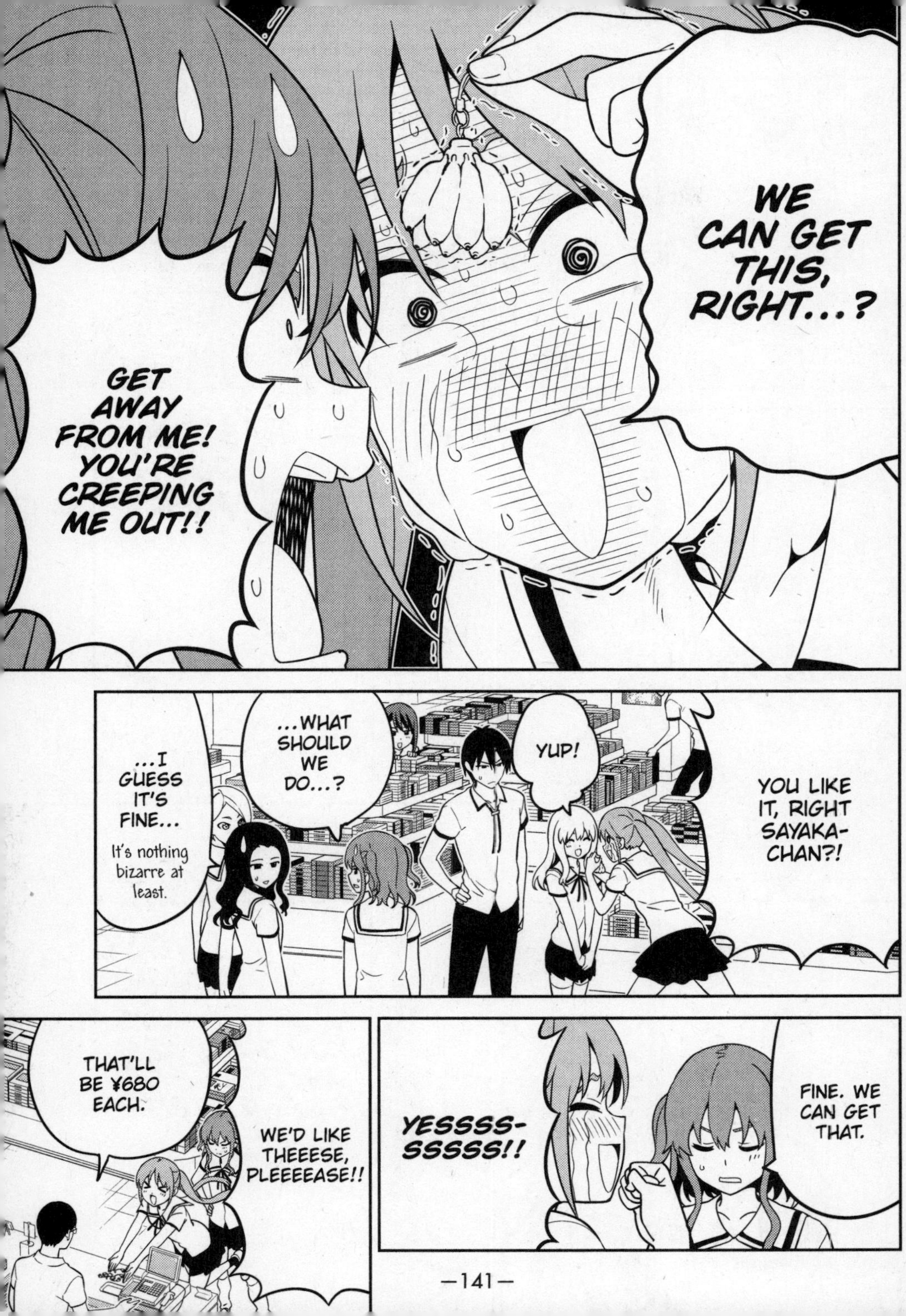
WE CAN GET THIS, RIGHT...?
GET AWAY FROM ME! YOU'RE CREEPING ME OUT!!
YOU LIKE IT, RIGHT SAYAKA-CHAN?!
YUP!
...WHAT SHOULD WE DO...?
...I GUESS IT'S FINE...
It's nothing bizarre at least.
FINE. WE CAN GET THAT.
YESSSS-SSSSS!!
WE'D LIKE THEEESE, PLEEEEASE!!
THAT'LL BE ¥680 EACH.

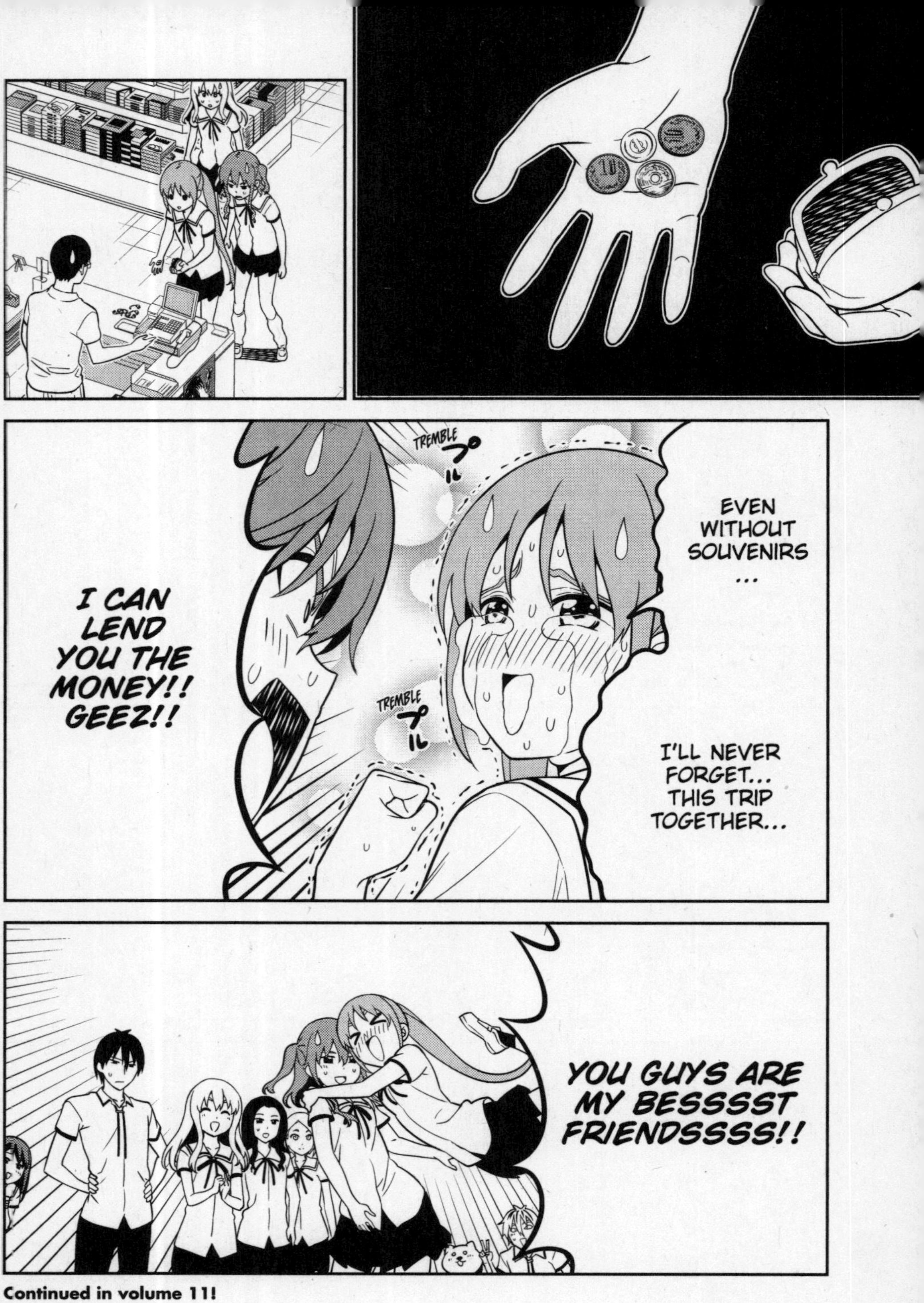
TREMBLE プル
EVEN WITHOUT SOUVENIRS ...
I'LL NEVER FORGET... THIS TRIP TOGETHER...
TREMBLE プル
I CAN LEND YOU THE MONEY!! GEEZ!!
YOU GUYS ARE MY BESSSST FRIENDSSSS!!

Continued in volume 11!

You Look Like You Had Fun

I'LL SEE YOU AT SCHOOL, OKAY! BYE!!
YEAH, BYE.

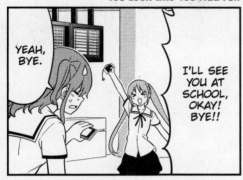

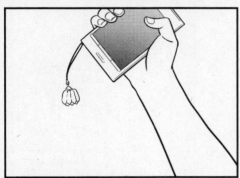

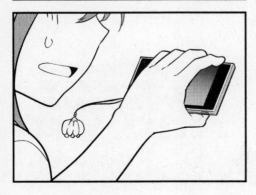

(Summer memories—hand-in-hand, we walk along)

Aho-Girl

\ˈahôˌɡərl\ *Japanese, noun.*
A clueless girl.

SPECIAL EDITION: THE ATTACK ON AOI YUKI-SAN!

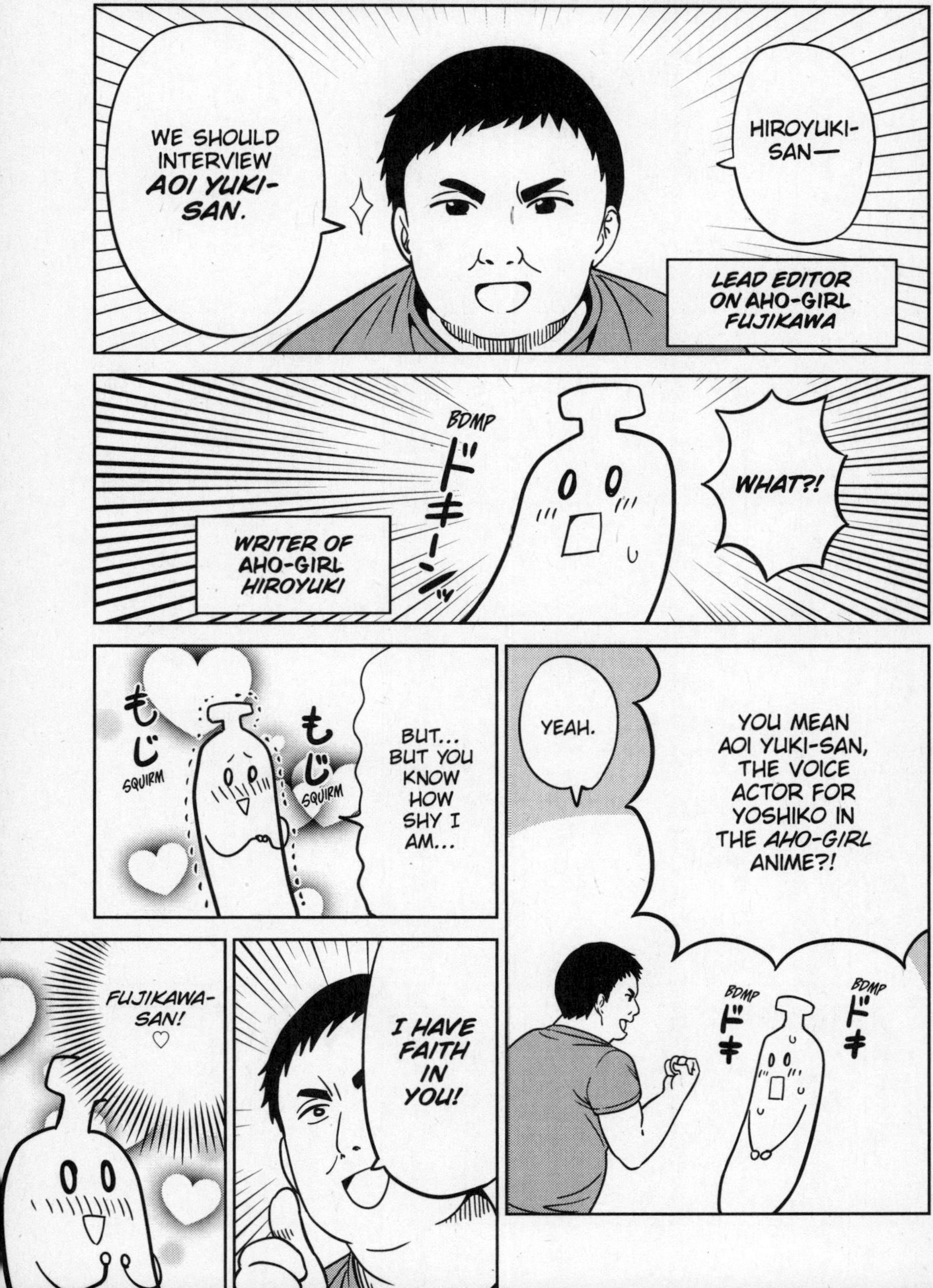
HIROYUKI-SAN—
LEAD EDITOR ON AHO-GIRL FUJIKAWA
WE SHOULD INTERVIEW AOI YUKI-SAN.
WHAT?!
BDMP
ドキーン
WRITER OF AHO-GIRL HIROYUKI
YOU MEAN AOI YUKI-SAN, THE VOICE ACTOR FOR YOSHIKO IN THE AHO-GIRL ANIME?!
YEAH.
BDMP
ドキ
BDMP
ドキ
BUT... BUT YOU KNOW HOW SHY I AM...
もじ
SQUIRM
もじ
SQUIRM
I HAVE FAITH IN YOU!
FUJIKAWA-SAN! ♡

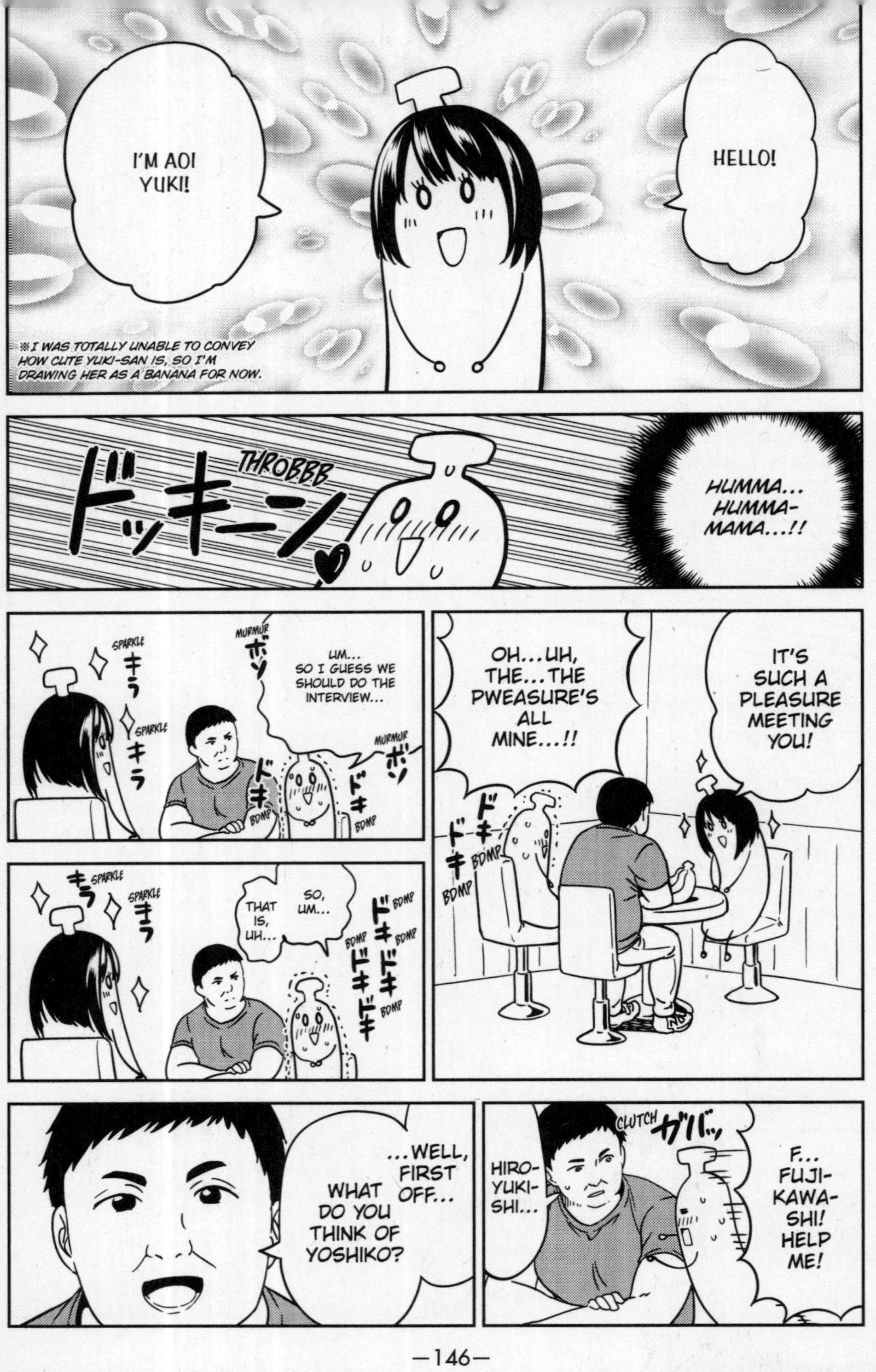
HELLO!
I'M AOI YUKI!
※I WAS TOTALLY UNABLE TO CONVEY HOW CUTE YUKI-SAN IS, SO I'M DRAWING HER AS A BANANA FOR NOW.
HUMMA... HUMMA-MAMA...!!
THROBBB
ドッキーン
IT'S SUCH A PLEASURE MEETING YOU!
OH...UH, THE...THE PWEASURE'S ALL MINE...!!
ドキ BDMP
ドキ BDMP
MURMUR ボソ
UM... SO I GUESS WE SHOULD DO THE INTERVIEW...
MURMUR ボソ
ドキ BDMP
ドキ BDMP
SPARKLE キラ
SPARKLE キラ
SO, UM...
THAT IS, UH...
ドキ BDMP
ドキ BDMP
ドキ BDMP
ドキ BDMP
SPARKLE キラ
SPARKLE キラ
F... FUJI-KAWA-SHI! HELP ME!
CLUTCH ガバッ
HIRO-YUKI-SHI...
...WELL, FIRST OFF...
WHAT DO YOU THINK OF YOSHIKO?

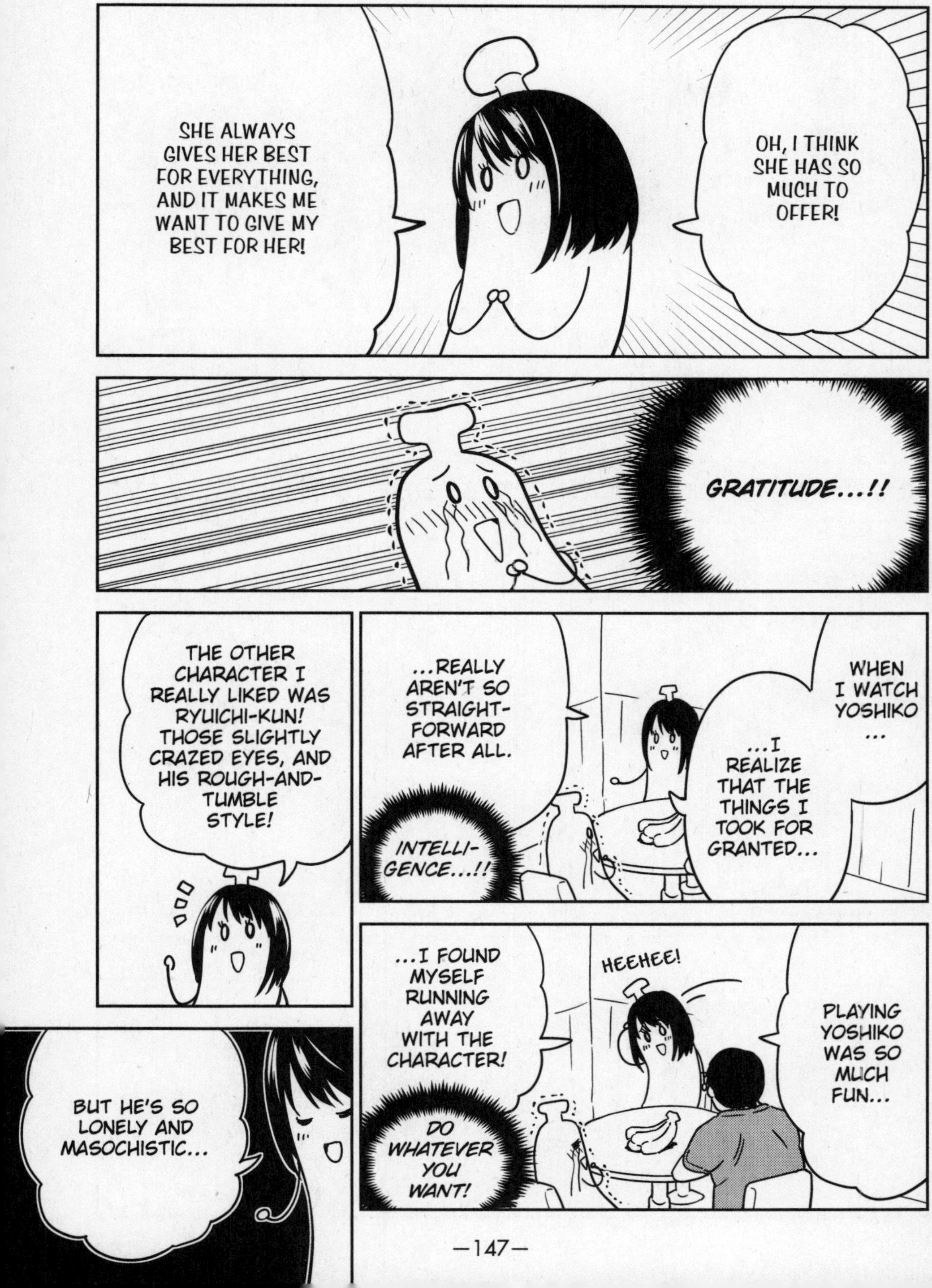
OH, I THINK SHE HAS SO MUCH TO OFFER!
SHE ALWAYS GIVES HER BEST FOR EVERYTHING, AND IT MAKES ME WANT TO GIVE MY BEST FOR HER!
GRATITUDE...!!
WHEN I WATCH YOSHIKO...
...I REALIZE THAT THE THINGS I TOOK FOR GRANTED...
...REALLY AREN'T SO STRAIGHTFORWARD AFTER ALL.
INTELLIGENCE...!!
PLAYING YOSHIKO WAS SO MUCH FUN...
HEEHEE!
...I FOUND MYSELF RUNNING AWAY WITH THE CHARACTER!
DO WHATEVER YOU WANT!
THE OTHER CHARACTER I REALLY LIKED WAS RYUICHI-KUN! THOSE SLIGHTLY CRAZED EYES, AND HIS ROUGH-AND-TUMBLE STYLE!
BUT HE'S SO LONELY AND MASOCHISTIC...

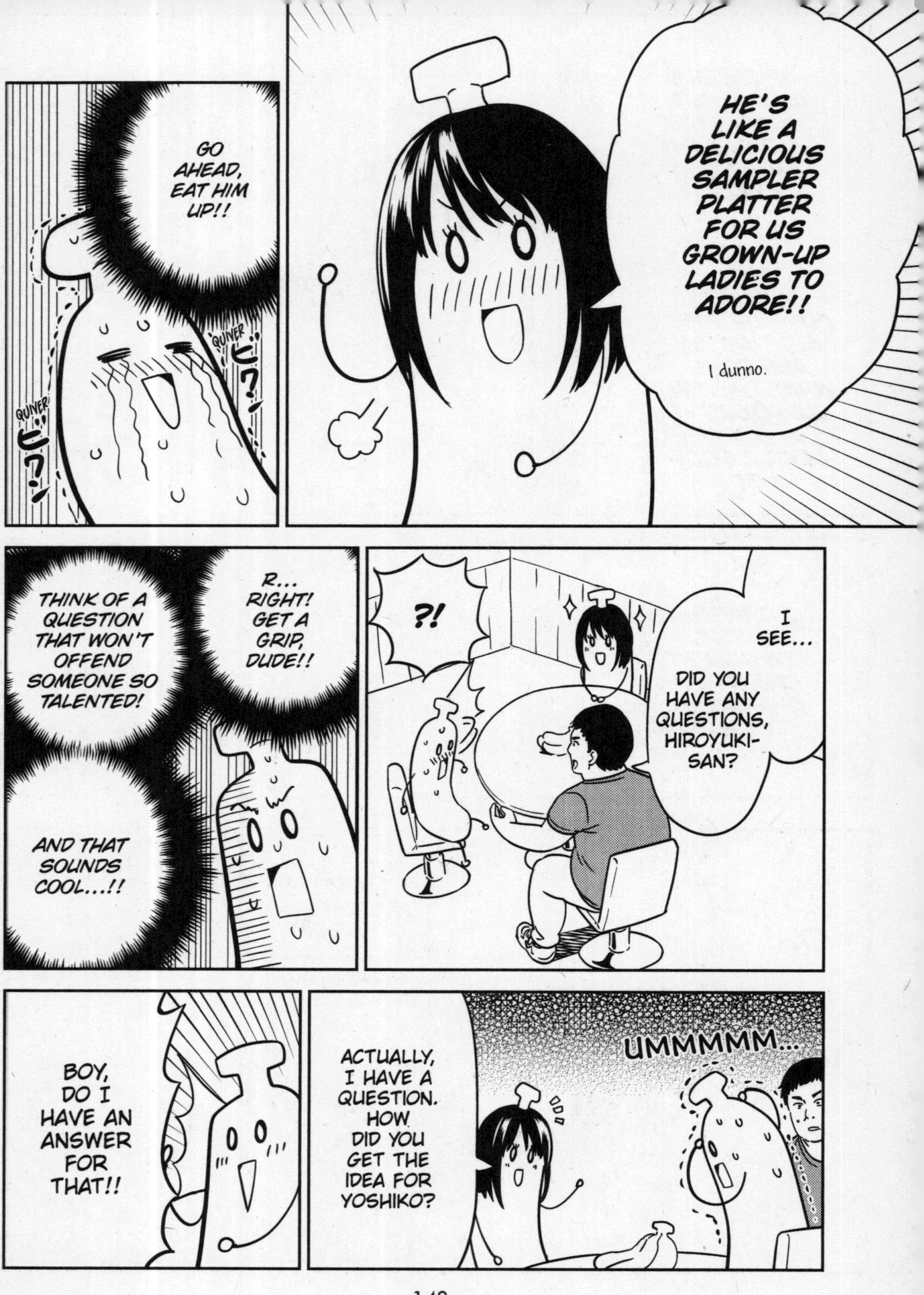
HE'S LIKE A DELICIOUS SAMPLER PLATTER FOR US GROWN-UP LADIES TO ADORE!!
I dunno.
GO AHEAD, EAT HIM UP!!
QUIVER
QUIVER
?!
I SEE...
DID YOU HAVE ANY QUESTIONS, HIROYUKI-SAN?
R... RIGHT! GET A GRIP, DUDE!!
THINK OF A QUESTION THAT WON'T OFFEND SOMEONE SO TALENTED!
AND THAT SOUNDS COOL...!!
UMMMMM...
ACTUALLY, I HAVE A QUESTION. HOW DID YOU GET THE IDEA FOR YOSHIKO?
BOY, DO I HAVE AN ANSWER FOR THAT!!

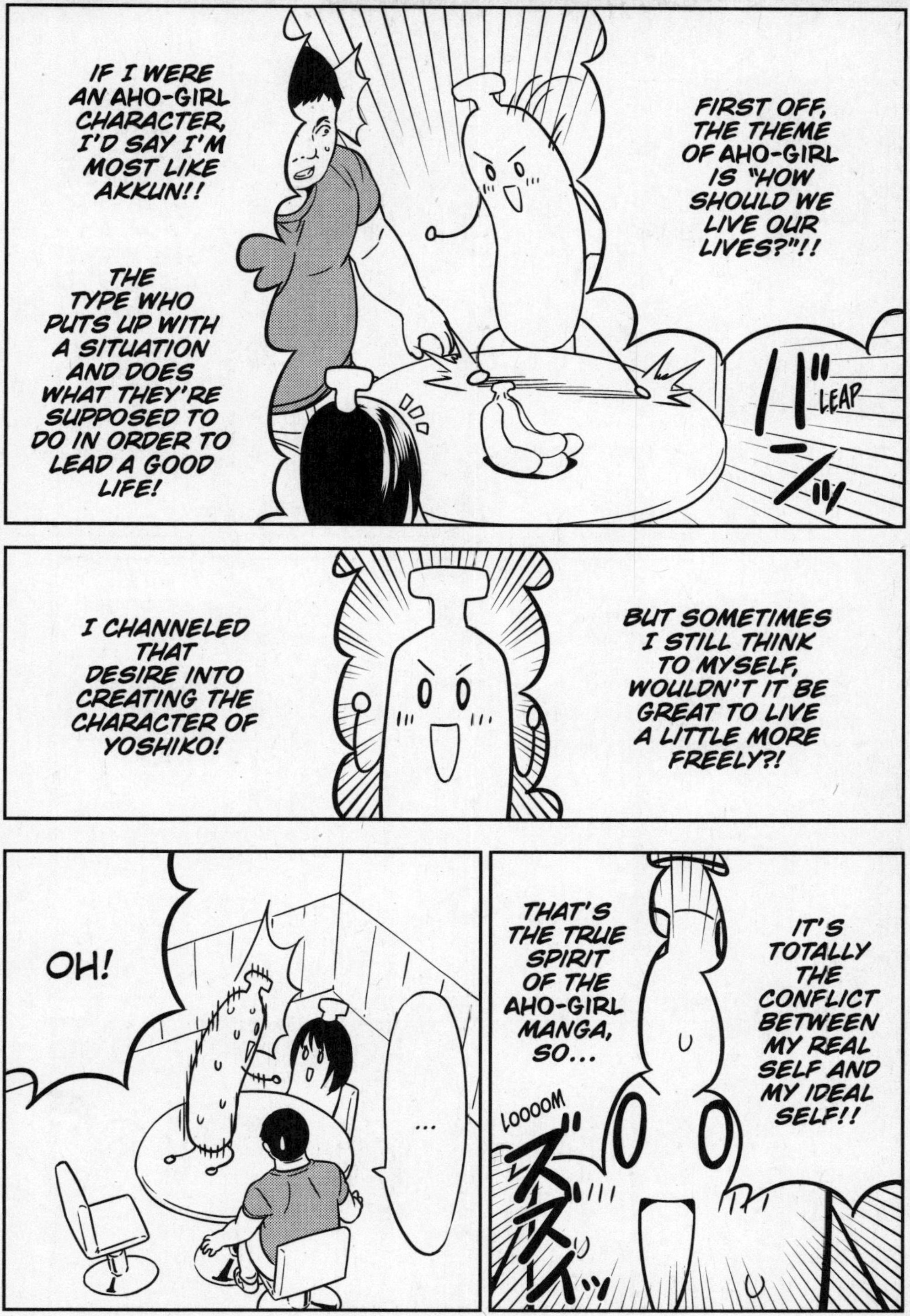
FIRST OFF, THE THEME OF AHO-GIRL IS "HOW SHOULD WE LIVE OUR LIVES?"!!
LEAP
IF I WERE AN AHO-GIRL CHARACTER, I'D SAY I'M MOST LIKE AKKUN!!
THE TYPE WHO PUTS UP WITH A SITUATION AND DOES WHAT THEY'RE SUPPOSED TO DO IN ORDER TO LEAD A GOOD LIFE!
BUT SOMETIMES I STILL THINK TO MYSELF, WOULDN'T IT BE GREAT TO LIVE A LITTLE MORE FREELY?!
I CHANNELED THAT DESIRE INTO CREATING THE CHARACTER OF YOSHIKO!
IT'S TOTALLY THE CONFLICT BETWEEN MY REAL SELF AND MY IDEAL SELF!!
THAT'S THE TRUE SPIRIT OF THE AHO-GIRL MANGA, SO...
LOOOOM
OH!
...

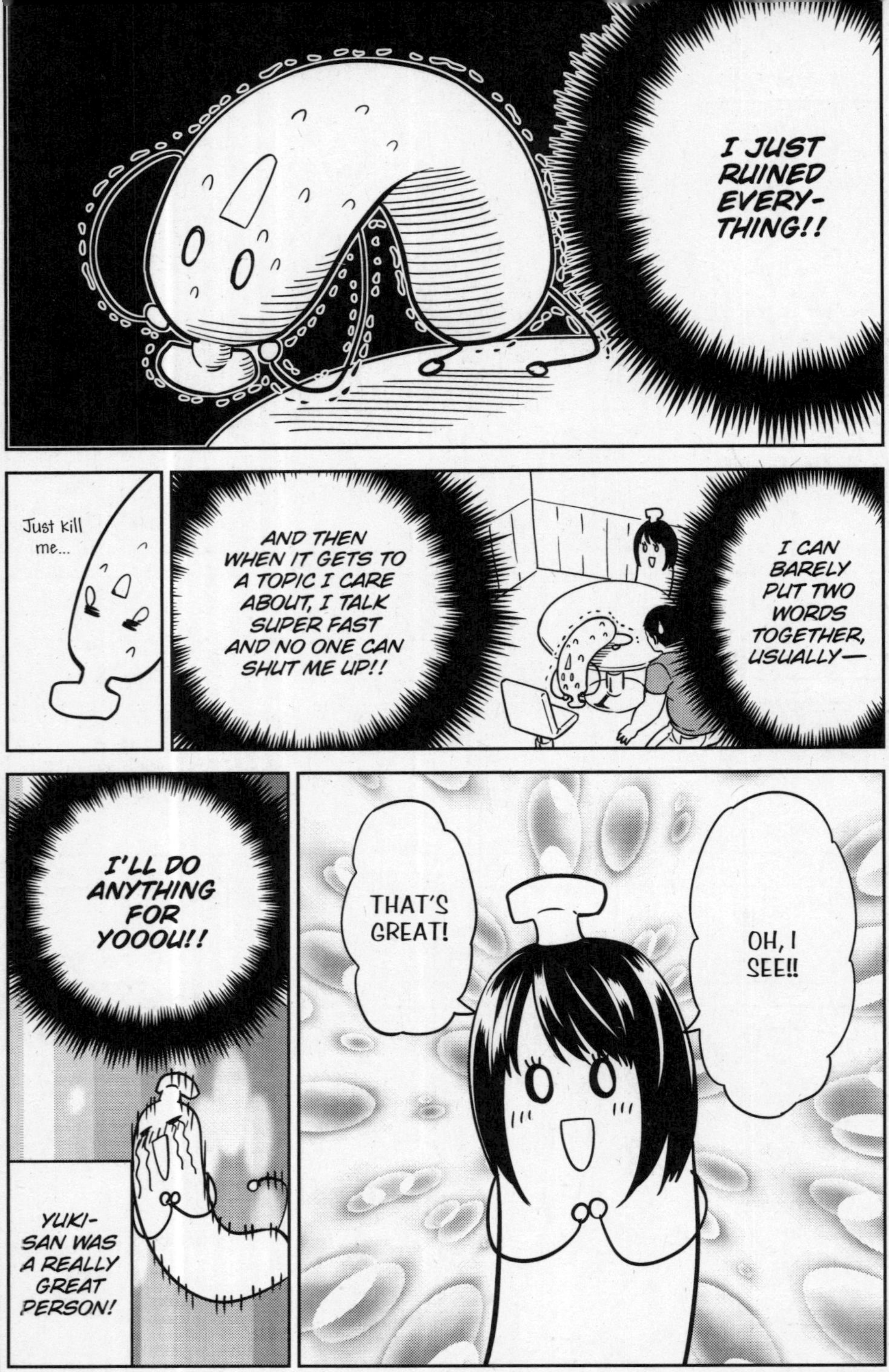
I JUST RUINED EVERY-THING!!
I CAN BARELY PUT TWO WORDS TOGETHER, USUALLY—
AND THEN WHEN IT GETS TO A TOPIC I CARE ABOUT, I TALK SUPER FAST AND NO ONE CAN SHUT ME UP!!
Just kill me...
OH, I SEE!!
THAT'S GREAT!
I'LL DO ANYTHING FOR YOOOU!!
YUKI-SAN WAS A REALLY GREAT PERSON!

The Specter of the All-new Comic

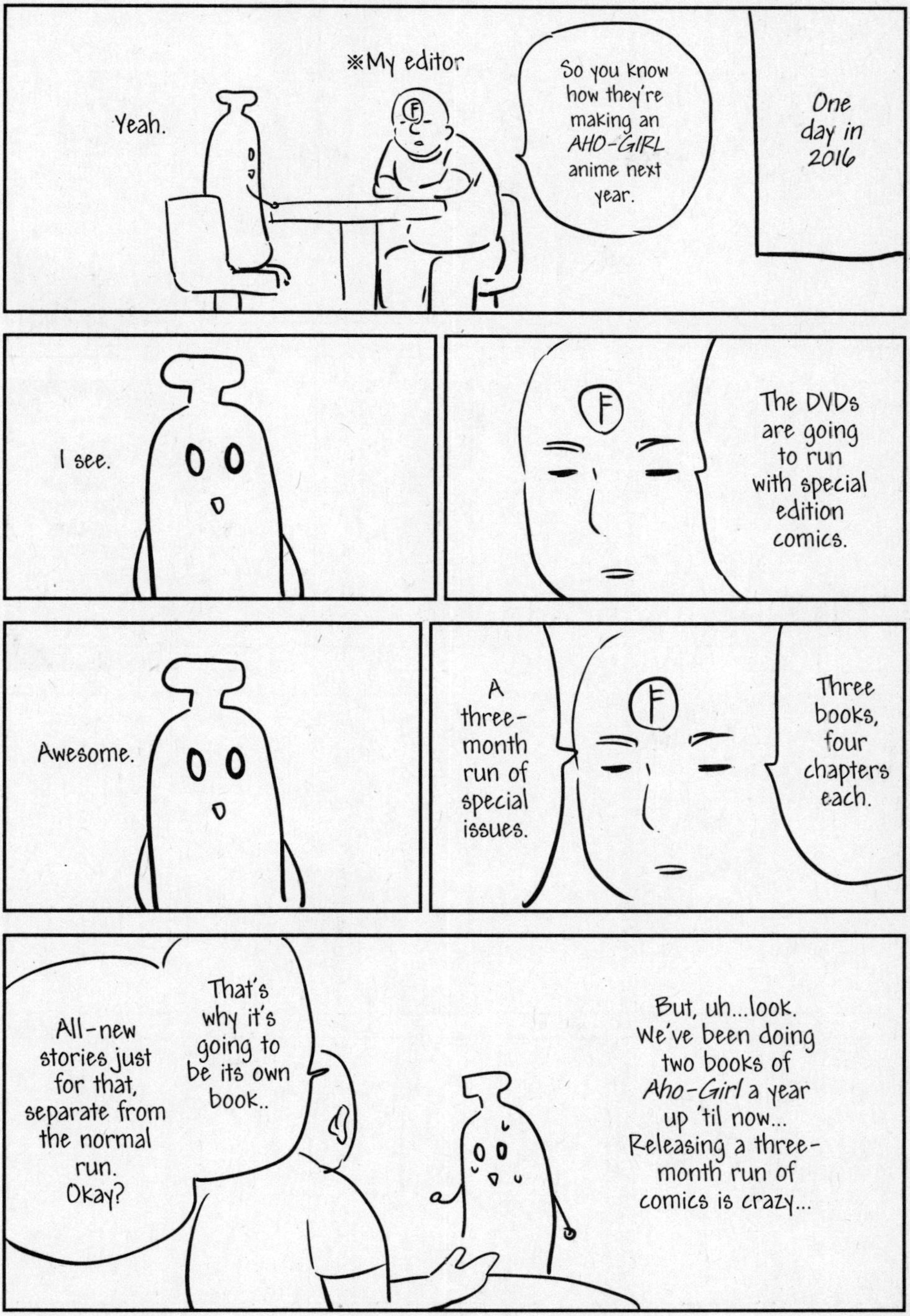

One day in 2016
So you know how they're making an *AHO-GIRL* anime next year.
※My editor
Yeah.
The DVDs are going to run with special edition comics.
I see.
Three books, four chapters each.
A three-month run of special issues.
Awesome.
But, uh...look. We've been doing two books of *Aho-Girl* a year up 'til now... Releasing a three-month run of comics is crazy...
That's why it's going to be its own book..
All-new stories just for that, separate from the normal run. Okay?

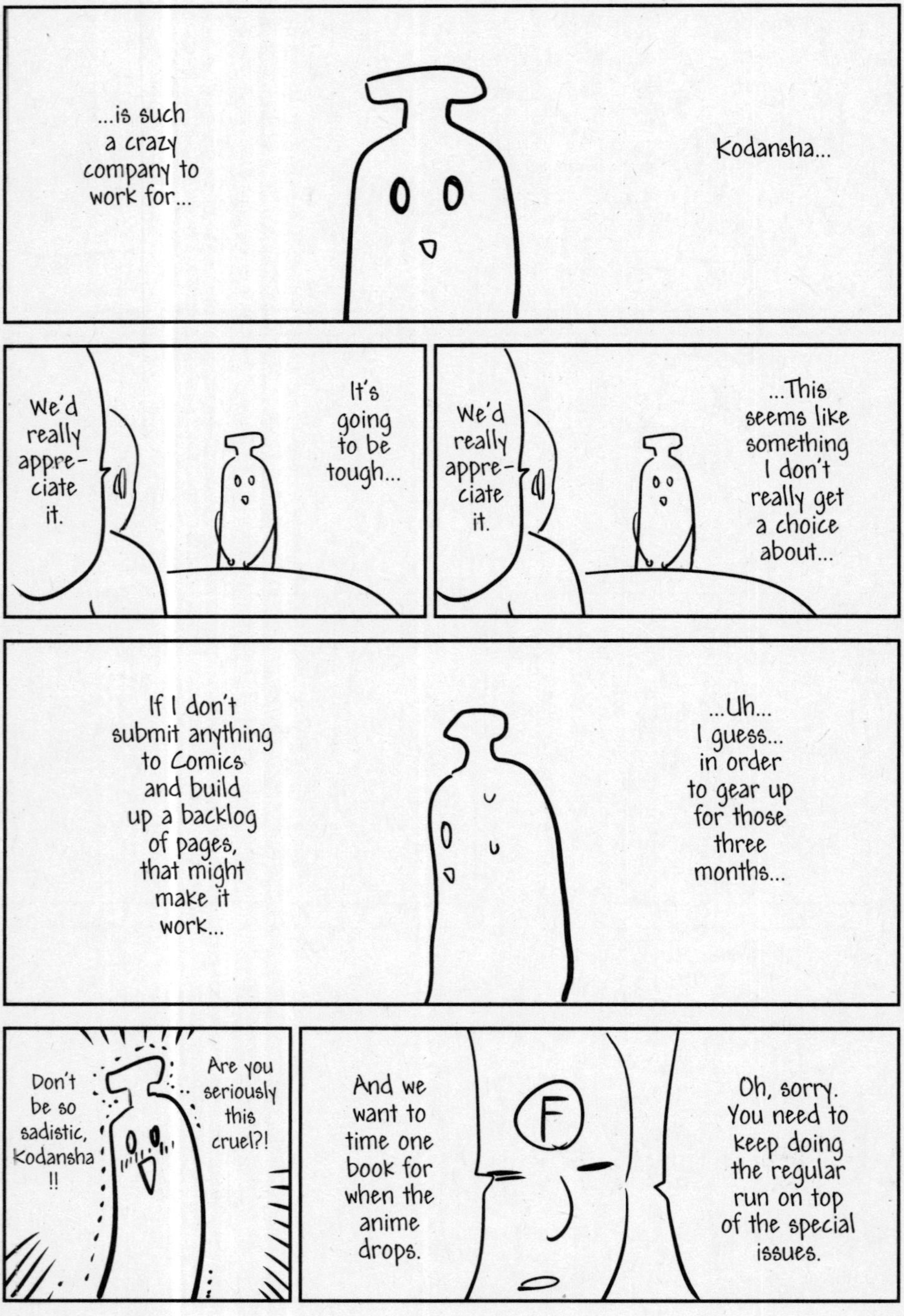
Kodansha...
...is such a crazy company to work for...
...This seems like something I don't really get a choice about...
We'd really appre-ciate it.
It's going to be tough...
We'd really appre-ciate it.
...Uh... I guess... in order to gear up for those three months...
If I don't submit anything to Comics and build up a backlog of pages, that might make it work...
Oh, sorry. You need to keep doing the regular run on top of the special issues.
And we want to time one book for when the anime drops.
Are you seriously this cruel?!
Don't be so sadistic, Kodansha!!

Aho-Girl

\\'ahô͵gərl\\ *Japanese, noun.*
A clueless girl.

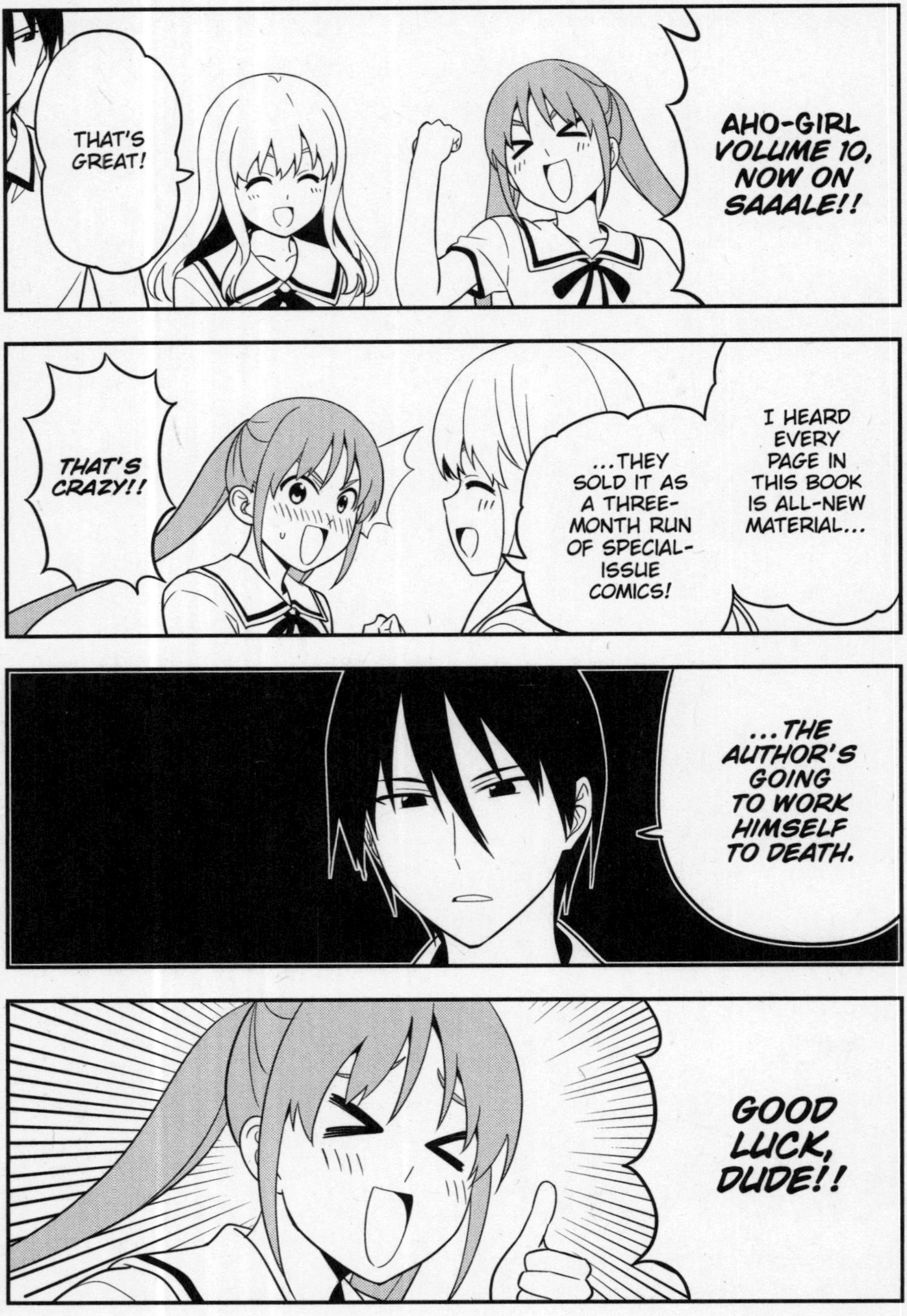
AHO-GIRL VOLUME 10, NOW ON SAAALE!!
THAT'S GREAT!
I HEARD EVERY PAGE IN THIS BOOK IS ALL-NEW MATERIAL...
...THEY SOLD IT AS A THREE-MONTH RUN OF SPECIAL-ISSUE COMICS!
THAT'S CRAZY!!
...THE AUTHOR'S GOING TO WORK HIMSELF TO DEATH.
GOOD LUCK, DUDE!!

TREMBLE
プル
TREMBLE
プル

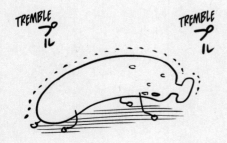

Aho-Girl

\\'ahô͵gərl\\ *Japanese, noun*.
A clueless girl.

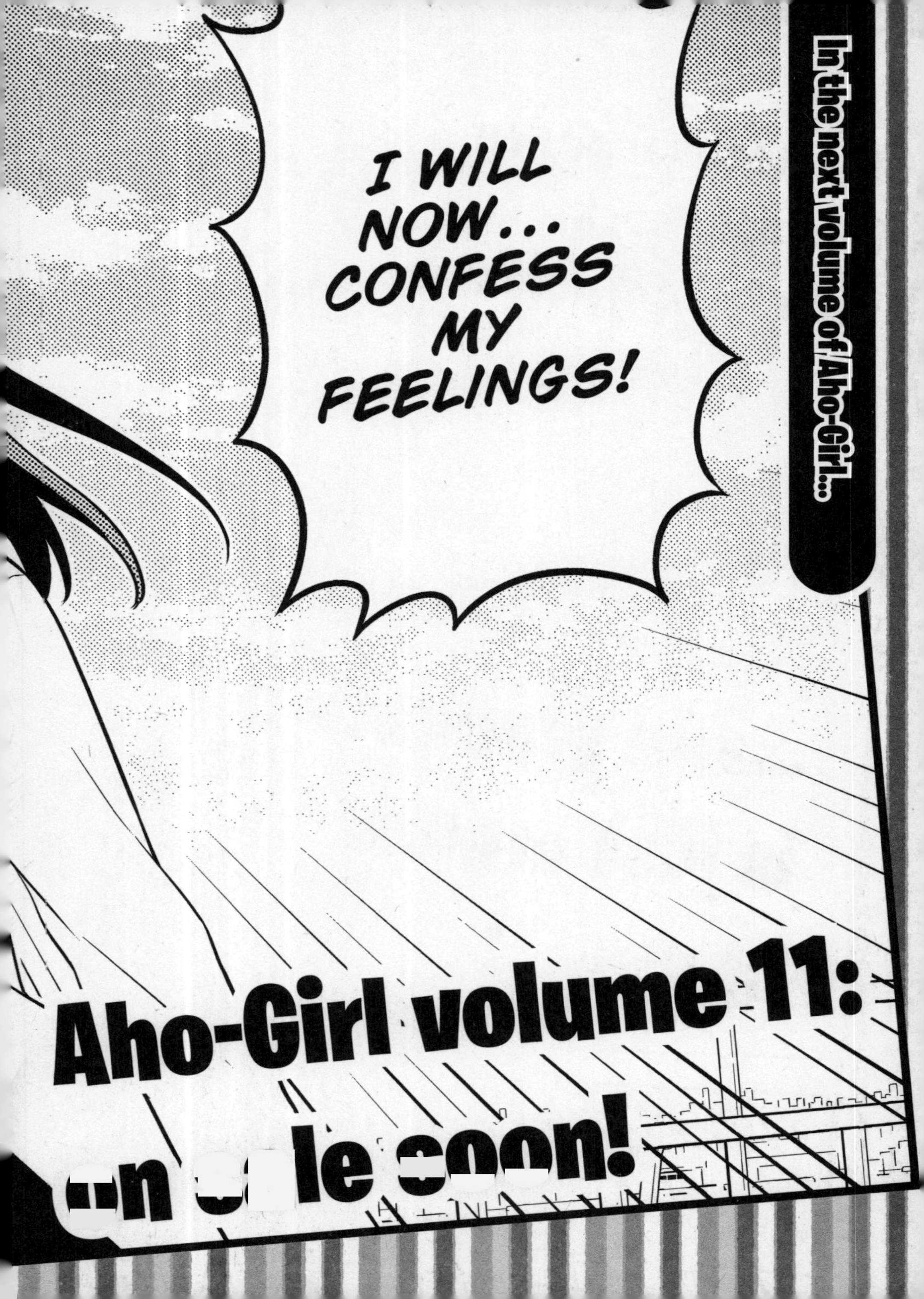
In the next volume of Aho-Girl...
I WILL NOW... CONFESS MY FEELINGS!
Aho-Girl volume 11:
On sale soon!

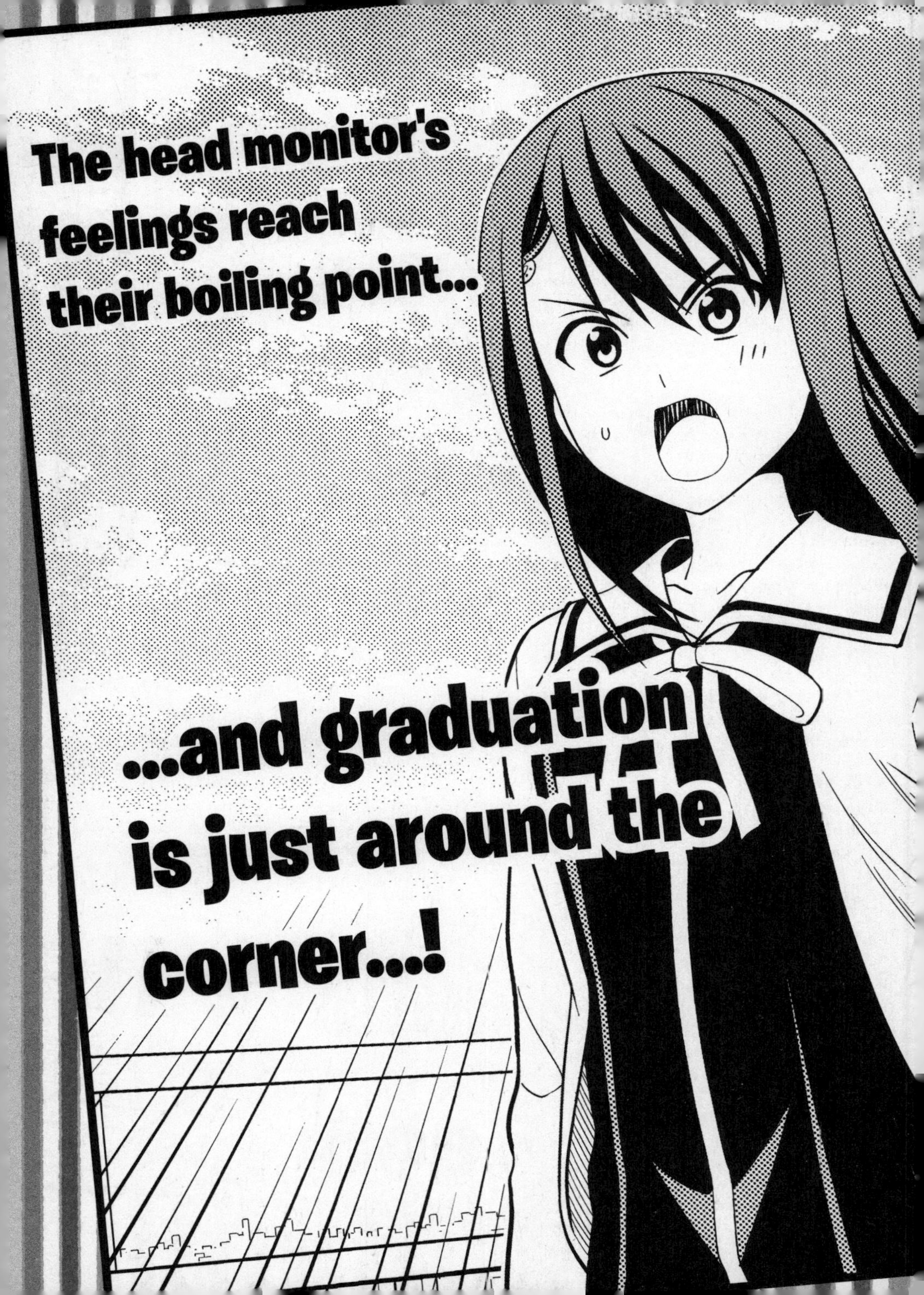
The head monitor's feelings reach their boiling point...
...and graduation is just around the corner...!

Translation Notes

Page 2

"Aggravated straight man"

This is an explanatory gloss of the Japanese term "tsukkomi." The *tsukkomi* and *boke* duo are a common trope in *manzai*-style stand-up comedy routines. The boke, like Yoshiko, draws over-the-top and just plain stupid conclusions to the *tsukkomi*'s set-ups. The *tsukkomi* tries to remain calm and reasonable during the act, but is invariably pushed into extreme and sometimes violent reactions out of his frustration.

Page 3

"Gals"

The term "gal" (Japanese *gyaru*) refers to a broad segment of popular youth culture in Japan that began in the mid-1990s. The term encompasses many distinct subcultures with different stereotyped behaviors (such as extreme tanning, bleached-white hair, or casual dating in exchange for spending money) that are considered contrary to prevailing Japanese morality. In general, though, most people who are labeled by the term "gal" merely subscribe to a particular fashion aesthetic characterized by loose socks (the familiar slouchy socks that hang loose around the ankles), lightly bleached hair, extensive nail art or cell phone bangles, and school uniform skirts that are rolled up at the waist to be scandalously short.

"Head Monitor"

The head monitor's title in Japanese includes the word *fuuki*, which roughly translates to "moral order" or "discipline." She would not be merely checking for hall passes the way a hall monitor in a Western school might, and would be more broadly responsible for reporting anything in violation of the moral standards of the institution.

"G Cup"

Going by Japanese bra sizing conventions, the head monitor's "G cup" would be roughly equivalent to an American DDD.

Page 18

"Come on in"

The original Japanese is *menso-re*, which is the Okinawan dialect form of "welcome (to our establishment)."

Page 21

"International Street"

A bustling two-mile-long street in Naha (the capital of Okinawa) lined with souvenir and novelty stores, shopping arcades, restaurants, bars, and night clubs.

"Soki soba"

This is an iconic Okinawan dish of thick soba noodles in a ramen-like soup, topped with boneless pork ribs.

Page 23

"Choraumi Aquarium"

The actual aquarium is called "Churaumi," meaning "beautiful ocean" in the Okinawan dialect. It is considered one of the best aquariums in all of Japan, and is part of the sprawling Ocean Expo Park. If you imagine Okinawa as a nearly-straightened, elongated "S," the aquarium complex is located on a peninsula off the northwest curve, whereas Naha (where the students will be staying) is located at the base of the "S," approximately 55 miles away.

Page 25

"Blue Cave"

This is a naturally eroded cave on the seashore, where sunlight is refracted by the seawater inside to illuminate the cave with pale blue light. It is a popular destination for snorkeling and scuba diving.

Manzamo

Cape Manzamo is a distinctive seaside rock formation popular with tourists for the picturesque sunset views it offers.

Page 32

"Reggae > sandy beaches >>"

This is part of the refrain for the 2006 song "Suirenka" (Water Lily Flower) by Shonan no Kaze. The song is a summer anthem in a reggae-hip-hop style.

Page 40

"So hot, my heart's burning up"

This is a lyric from the song "E.G. summer RIDER" by the E-girls, released in 2016.

Page 60

"Falling like rain in the night, watch, the Perseid"

This is a lyric from the 2015 song "R.Y.U.S.E.I." ("shooting star" rendered as an acronym) by the third incarnation of the pop group J Soul Brothers, which is a sub-group of a supergroup called Exile Tribe. The song was part of a year-long series of singles taking their themes from the seasons, with "R.Y.U.S.E.I." representing the summer installment.

Page 69

"Happy New Year"

Children (and even some young adults in college) receive money, called *otoshidama*, as part of Japanese New Year's celebrations. Money is placed in an envelope decorated with New Year's motifs or popular characters and is the past. However, here she is dreamily reminiscing about Yoshio, the boy who stole her heart. Contrary to her usual pattern for addressing students, she uses his first name and the reverential -*sama* suffix. Such a form of address is typical of swooning tween girls admiring an unattainable heartthrob, and shows that Oshieda-sensei has abandoned any thought of her superior, authoritative role as teacher when it comes to this particular student.

Page 134
"The high pressure drew me in, my"
This is a lyric from a 2016 single by KEYTALK called "Summer Venus." The lyric refers to high atmospheric pressure, as in weather, and reads in full: "The cobalt blue sea, the sky stretching overhead, the high pressure drew me in, my heart pulsing for you."

Page 138
"Chinsuko cookies"
Chinsuko are a traditional type of Okinawan cookie with a texture somewhat like shortbread.

Page 139
"Shisa"
Shisa are extremely common in Okinawa as a type of guardian talisman. Something of a cross between a lion and a dog, pairs of shisa are often placed outside the entrances to homes or on roofs to ward off evil spirits and protect good spirits within.

Page 141
"¥680"
Roughly equivalent to $6.50 each. The coins Yoshiko has in her palm on the next page total ¥71.

Page 144
"Summer memories—hand-in-hand, we walk along"
This is a lyric from a 2003 song called "Summer Memories" by Ketsumeishi. The full lyric reads "Summer memories—hand-in-hand, we walk along the shore."

Page 146
"Fujikawa-shi"
The honorific suffix "shi" is typically used in writing, and is only used in spoken Japanese in very formal situations with an unfamiliar person, where another suffix or title might be inappropriate. For example, here, Hiroyuki and Fujikawa are taking a hierarchically neutral, but still formal and polite, stance toward each other in mixed company while carrying out the official business of the interview.

given to children by their parents, grandparents, and aunts and uncles, somewhat like Christmas presents in the West. Traditionally, children are expected to save some portion of the money they receive as a way of learning responsible financial habits. How long they retain those habits is another question…

Page 74
"We're messing around too much; we're children of summer"
This is a refrain in the song "Summer Nude" by the rock group the Magokoro Brothers, released in 1995.

Page 81
"But you eat fish all the time"
Yoshiko refers specifically to *saba* and *aji*, two types of fish that are both translated as "mackerel" in English.

Page 88
"You ever notice all those June"
This is a lyric in a 2002 song by RIP SLYME called "Paradise Baby," where the full lyric asks "You ever notice all those June babies?"

Page 102
"Barefoot, bewitching"
This is a refrain in a 2006 song by T.M. Revolution called "HOT LIMIT." The full line refers to a "barefoot, bewitching mermaid."

Page 123
"I'll Never Surrender This Desire"
This is the title of a 1995 song by Naomi Tamura. The opening line can be translated as "Aiming for a future that won't be stopped, holding tight to this desire that I won't ever surrender." Yoshiko vaguely evokes this song in her excuse.

Page 124
"Your sexy pheromones got me"
This is a lyric from the 2008 song "Ikenai Taiyo" (roughly, "I'm Losing It in the Sun") by Orange Range.

Page 125
"Yoshio-sama"
As in most cultures, teachers in Japan are considered socially superior to their students and deserving of respect. Therefore, within the Japanese framework of honorific suffixes, teachers have a wide latitude to use any of the suffixes denoting equality or social superiority when addressing their students, or to omit any suffix at all (this is most common with male teachers). This would mean that Oshieda-sensei would, in a typical student-teacher relationship, refer to her students by their last names as "Akutsu-kun" or "Hanabatake-san," as she has done in

"He's like a delicious sampler platter for us grown-up ladies to adore!!"
In the original Japanese, Yuki-san compares Ryuichi to a *kaisendon*, literally a rice bowl topped with seafood sashimi. Although *kaisendon* includes dishes with only one type of seafood, they are most often something like a seafood sampler platter, featuring a variety of raw or broiled seafood served atop rice.

Aho-Girl

\\ˈahô͵gərl \\ *Japanese, noun.*
A clueless girl.

Again!!

Kinichiro Imamura isn't a bad guy, really, but on the first day of high school his narrow eyes and bleached blonde hair made him look so shifty that his classmates assumed the worst. Three years later, without any friends or fond memories, he isn't exactly feeling bittersweet about graduation. But after an accidental fall down a flight of stairs, Kinichiro wakes up three years in the past... on the first day of high school! School's starting again—but it's gonna be different this time around!

Vol. 1-3 now available in **PRINT** and **DIGITAL**!
Vol. 4 coming August 2018!
Find out **MORE** by visiting:
kodanshacomics.com/MitsurouKubo

ABOUT **MITSUROU KUBO**

Mitsurou Kubo is a manga artist born in Nagasaki prefecture. Her series *3.3.7 Byoshi!!* (2001-2003), *Tokkyu!!* (2004-2008), and *Again!!* (2011-2014) were published in *Weekly Shonen Magazine*, and *Moteki* (2008-2010) was published in the seinen comics magazine *Evening*. After the publication of *Again!!* concluded, she met Sayo Yamamoto, director of the global smash-hit anime *Yuri!!! on ICE*. Working with Yamamoto, Kubo contributed the original concept, original character designs, and initial script for *Yuri!!! on ICE*. *Again!!* is her first manga to be published in English.

Again!! © Mitsurou Kubo /Kodansha Ltd.

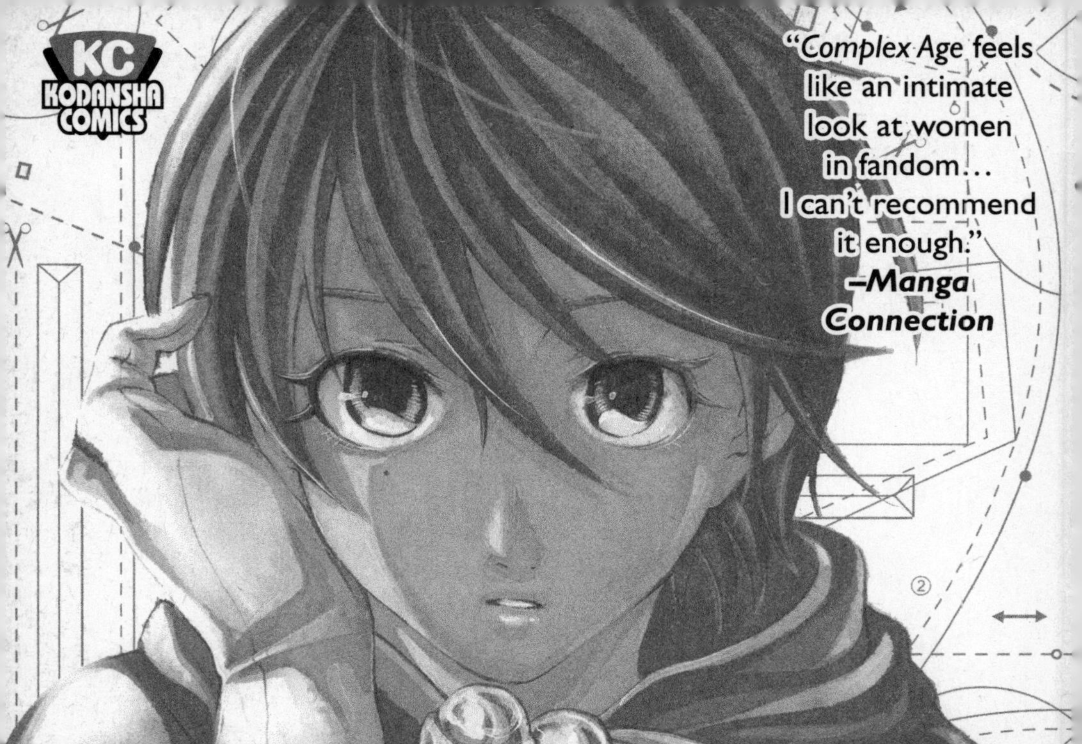
KC
KODANSHA COMICS
"*Complex Age* feels like an intimate look at women in fandom… I can't recommend it enough."
–Manga Connection
complex age
yui sakuma

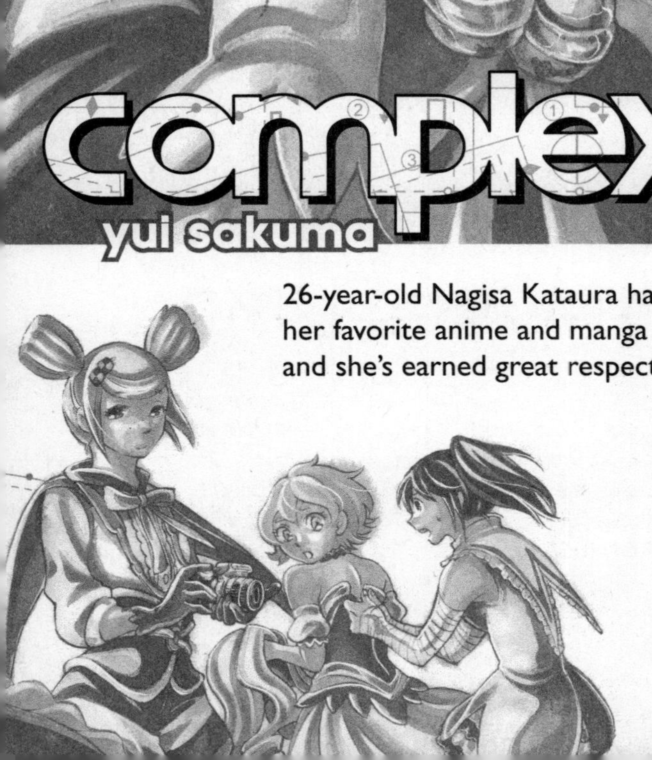

26-year-old Nagisa Kataura has a secret. Transforming into her favorite anime and manga characters is her passion in life, and she's earned great respect amongst her fellow cospayers. But to the rest of society, her hobby is a silly fantasy. As demands from both her office job and cosplaying begin to increase, she may one day have to make a tough choice—what's more important to her, cosplay or being "normal"?

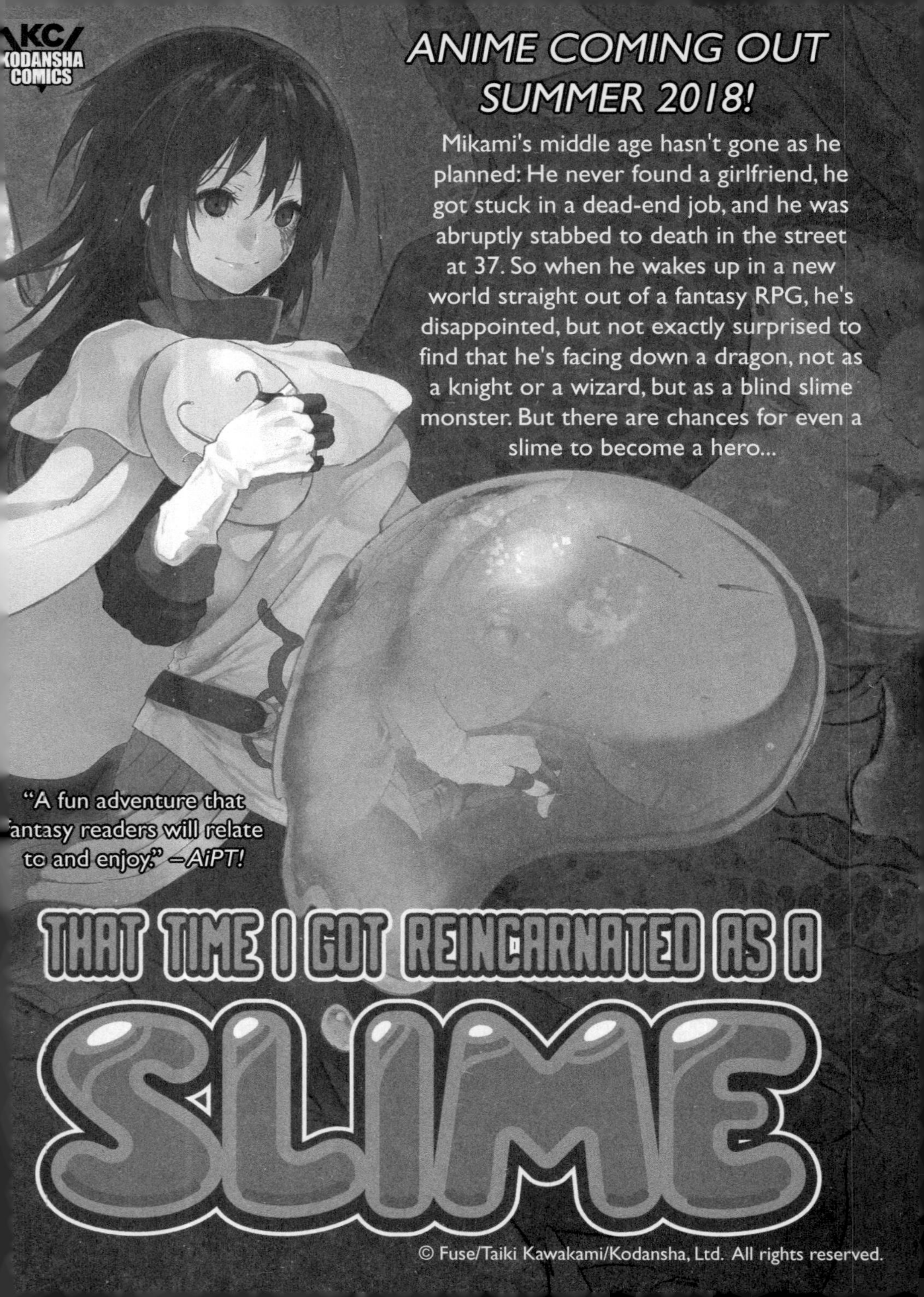
KC KODANSHA COMICS
ANIME COMING OUT SUMMER 2018!
Mikami's middle age hasn't gone as he planned: He never found a girlfriend, he got stuck in a dead-end job, and he was abruptly stabbed to death in the street at 37. So when he wakes up in a new world straight out of a fantasy RPG, he's disappointed, but not exactly surprised to find that he's facing down a dragon, not as a knight or a wizard, but as a blind slime monster. But there are chances for even a slime to become a hero...
"A fun adventure that fantasy readers will relate to and enjoy." —AiPT!
THAT TIME I GOT REINCARNATED AS A
SLIME
© Fuse/Taiki Kawakami/Kodansha, Ltd. All rights reserved.

KC KODANSHA COMICS

In love, there are no save points.

NOW AN ANIME!

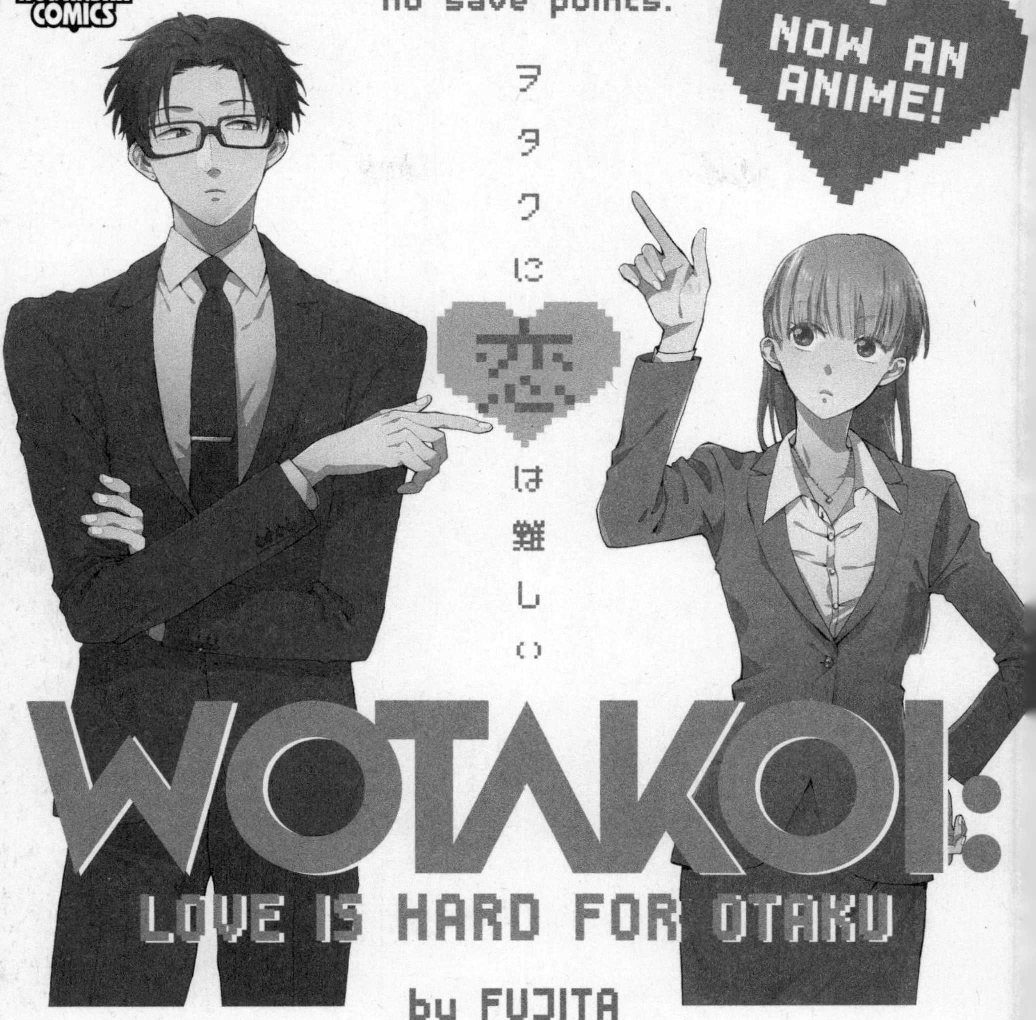
ヲタクに恋は難しい

WOTAKOI: LOVE IS HARD FOR OTAKU

by FUJITA

Narumi has had it rough: Every boyfriend she's had dumped her once they found out she was an otaku, so she's gone to great lengths to hide it. At her new job, she bumps into Hirotaka, her childhood friend and fellow otaku. When Hirotaka almost gets her secret outed at work, she comes up with a plan to keep him quiet. But he comes up with a counter-proposal: Why doesn't she just date him instead?

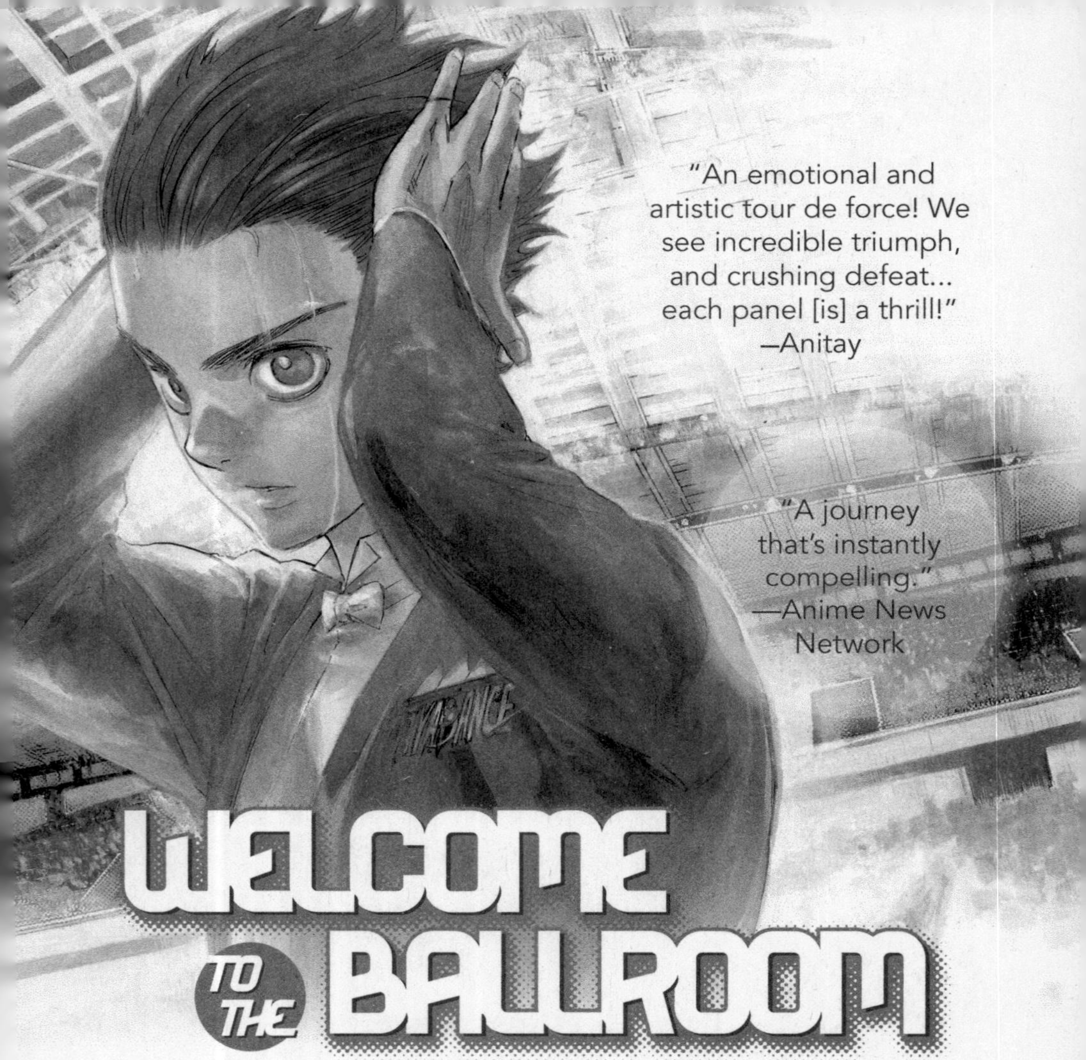

"An emotional and artistic tour de force! We see incredible triumph, and crushing defeat... each panel [is] a thrill!"
–Anitay

"A journey that's instantly compelling."
—Anime News Network

WELCOME TO THE BALLROOM

By Tomo Takeuchi

Feckless high school student Tatara Fujita wants to be good at something—anything. Unfortunately, he's about as average as a slouchy teen can be. The local bullies know this, and make it a habit to hit him up for cash, but all that changes when the debonair Kaname Sengoku sends them packing. Sengoku's not the neighborhood watch, though. He's a professional ballroom dancer. And once Tatara Fujita gets pulled into the world of ballroom, his life will never be the same.

KC KODANSHA COMICS

KC
KODANSHA
COMICS

The award-winning manga about what happens inside you!

"Far more entertaining than it ought to be... what kid doesn't want to think that every time they sneeze a torpedo shoots out their nose?"
—Anime News Network

Strep throat! Hay fever! Influenza! The world is a dangerous place for a red blood cell just trying to get her deliveries finished. Fortunately, she's not alone…she's got a whole human body's worth of cells ready to help out! The mysterious white blood cells, the buff and brash killer T cells, even the cute little platelets— everyone's got to come together if they want to keep you healthy!

Cells at Work!
はたらく細胞

By Akane Shimizu

© Akane Shimizu/Kodansha Ltd. All rights reserved.

KC
KODANSHA
COMICS

A new
series
from the
creator
of *Soul
Eater*, the
megahit
manga and
anime seen
on Toonami!

"Fun and lively...
a great start!"
-Adventures in
Poor Taste

FIRE FORCE

By Atsushi Ohkubo

The city of Tokyo is plagued by a deadly phenomenon: spontaneous human combustion! Luckily, a special team is there to quench the inferno: The Fire Force! The fire soldiers at Special Fire Cathedral 8 are about to get a unique addition. Enter Shinra, a boy who possesses the power to run at the speed of a rocket, leaving behind the famous "devil's footprints" (and destroying his shoes in the process). Can Shinra and his colleagues discover the source of this strange epidemic before the city burns to ashes?

© Atsushi Ohkubo/Kodansha Ltd. All rights reserved.

KODANSHA COMICS

The Black Museum The Ghost and the Lady

By Kazuhiro Fujita

Deep in Scotland Yard in London sits an evidence room dedicated to the greatest mysteries of British history. In this "Black Museum" sits a misshapen hunk of lead—two bullets fused together—the key to a wartime encounter between Florence Nightingale, the mother of modern nursing, and a supernatural Man in Grey. This story is unknown to most scholars of history, but a special guest of the museum will tell the tale of The Ghost and the Lady...

Praise for Kazuhiro Fujita's *Ushio and Tora*

"A charming revival that combines a classic look with modern depth and pacing... **Essential viewing both for curmudgeons and new fans alike.**" — Anime News Network

"**GREAT!** The first episode of Ushio and Tora captures the essence of '90s anime." — IGN

© Kazuhiro Fujita/Kodansha Ltd. All rights reserved.

KC
KODANSHA
COMICS

Japan's most powerful spirit medium delves into the ghost world's greatest mysteries!

Story by Kyo Shirodaira, famed author of mystery fiction and creator of *Spiral*, *Blast of Tempest*, and *The Record of a Fallen Vampire*.

Both touched by spirits called yôkai, Kotoko and Kurô have gained unique superhuman powers. But to gain her powers Kotoko has given up an eye and a leg, and Kurô's personal life is in shambles. So when Kotoko suggests they team up to deal with renegades from the spirit world, Kurô doesn't have many other choices, but Kotoko might just have a few ulterior motives...

IN/SPECTRE

STORY BY KYO SHIRODAIRA
ART BY CHASHIBA KATASE

© Kyo Shirodaira/Kodansha Ltd. All rights reserved.

H A P P I N E S S

——ハピネス——

By Shuzo Oshimi

From the creator of *The Flowers of Evil*

Nothing interesting is happening in Makoto Ozaki's first year of high school. His life is a series of quiet humiliations: low-grade bullies, unreliable friends, and the constant frustration of his adolescent lust. But one night, a pale, thin girl knocks him to the ground in an alley and offers him a choice. Now everything is different. Daylight is searingly bright. Food tastes awful. And worse than anything is the terrible, consuming thirst...

Praise for Shuzo Oshimi's *The Flowers of Evil*

"A shockingly readable story that vividly—one might even say queasily—evokes the fear and confusion of discovering one's own sexuality. Recommended." —The Manga Critic

"A page-turning tale of sordid middle school blackmail." —Otaku USA Magazine

"A stunning new horror manga." —Third Eye Comics

KC
KODANSHA
COMICS

© Shuzo Oshimi/Kodansha Ltd. All rights reserved.

"Parasyte fans should get a kick out of the chance to revisit Iwaaki's weird, violent, strangely affecting universe. Recommended." -Otaku USA Magazine

"A great anthology containing an excellent variety of genres and styles." -Manga Bookshelf

Based on the critically acclaimed classic horror manga

The first new *Parasyte* manga in over 20 years!

NEO ParaSyte f

BY ASUMIKO NAKAMURA, EMA TOYAMA, MIKI RINNO, LALAKO KOJIMA, KAORI YUKI, BANKO KUZE, YUUKI OBATA, KASHIO, YUI KUROE, ASIA WATANABE, MIKIMAKI, HIKARU SURUGA, HAJIME SHINJO, RENJURO KINDAICHI, AND YURI NARUSHIMA

A collection of chilling new *Parasyte* stories from Japan's top shojo artists!

Parasites: shape-shifting aliens whose only purpose is to assimilate with and consume the human race... but do these monsters have a different side? A parasite becomes a prince to save his romance-obsessed female host from a dangerous stalker. Another hosts a cooking show, in which the real monsters are revealed. These and 13 more stories, from some of the greatest shojo manga artists alive today, together make up a chilling, funny, and entertaining tribute to one of manga's horror classics!

© Hitoshi Iwaaki, Asumiko Nakamura, Ema Toyama, Miki Rinno, Lalako Kojima, Kaori Yuki, Banko Kuze, Yuuki Obata, Kashio, Yui Kuroe, Asia Watanabe, Mikimaki, Hikaru Suruga, Hajime Shinjo, Renjuro Kindaichi, Yuri Narushima/Kodansha Ltd. All rights reserved.

© Hiroyuki Takei/Kodansha Ltd. All rights reserved.

KODANSHA COMICS

New action series from Hiroyuki Takei, creator of the classic shonen franchise Shaman King!

In medieval Japan, a bell hanging on the collar is a sign that a cat has a master. Norachiyo's bell hangs from his katana sheath, but he is nonetheless a stray — a ronin. This one-eyed cat samurai travels across a dishonest world, cutting through pretense and deception with his blade.

NeKoGaHara

STRAY CAT SAMURAI

By
Hiroyuki Takei

hrya

Aho-Girl volume 10 is a work of fiction. Names, characters, places, and incidents are the products of the author's imagination or are used fictitiously. Any resemblance to actual events, locales, or persons, living or dead, is entirely coincidental.

A Kodansha Comics Trade Paperback Original.

Aho-Girl volume 10 copyright © 2017 Hiroyuki
English translation copyright © 2018 Hiroyuki

All rights reserved.

Published in the United States by Kodansha Comics, an imprint of Kodansha USA Publishing, LLC, New York.

Publication rights for this English edition arranged through Kodansha Ltd., Tokyo.

First published in Japan in 2017 by Kodansha Ltd., Tokyo, as *Aho Gaaru* volume 10.

ISBN 978-1-63236-651-1

Printed in the United States of America.

www.kodanshacomics.com

9 8 7 6 5 4 3 2 1

Translator: Karen McGillicuddy
Lettering: S. Lee
Editing: Paul Starr
Kodansha Comics edition cover design by Phil Balsman